PATH TO THE SOUL

What Dr. Bedi has done is unique. He has combined Jungian psychoanalytic insight with his own finely-honed clinial intuition.

This book invites and facilitates the kind of simple but profound clarity of thought that helps us cope. It is the path to an island of peace in the turbulent, chaotic ocean of life, as we know it today.

Dr. Bedi, in a sensitive and compelling manner, provides the reader with a map to explore a journey toward psychological and spiritual individuation and the *Path to the Soul* — "a sacred place where the soul lives."

DINSHAH D. GAGRAT

M.D., Director of Adult Services, Milwaukee Psychiatric Hospital; Assistant Clinical Professor, Medical College of Wisconsin, USA

PATH

to the

SOUL

The Union of Eastern and Western Wisdom to Heal Your Body, Mind, and Soul

ASHOK BEDI

New Age Books

ISBN: 81-7822-221-3

First Indian Edition: Delhi, 2005

(First published by Weiser Books, an imprint of Red Wheel/Weiser LLC,
York Beach, Maine, USA as *Path to the Soul*)

Disclaimer

The suggestions in this book are meant to support, not substitute, for medical or psychiatric care. Kindly continue treatment with your medical or psychological practitioner. Use the recommendations in this book to enhance your understanding of the problems and illness and to support your treatment plan. All case examples in this book are hypothetical composites from my clinical work. All details have been scrambled and disguised. Any apparent similarity to any person is purely coincidental.

Published by
NEW AGE BOOKS
A-44 Naraina Phase-I
New Delhi-110 028 (INDIA)
Email: nab@vsnl.in
Website: www.newagebooksindia.com

Printed in India
at Shri Jainendra Press
A-45 Naraina Phase-I, New Delhi-110 028

*I dedicate this book to my wife Usha,
my daughter Ami, my son Siddhartha,
and my grandson Signe.*

*They have kept the fragile pieces of my soul
in their sacred safekeeping whenever I have
strayed away from my personal journey on the
Path to the Soul.*

Contents

Acknowledgments

In the process of writing *Path to the Soul*, I have been fortunate to meet many wonderful people who have mentored and guided my journey. They are: Father Valace, Dr. Terrence Lear, Irv Raffe, Diane Martin, Fred Gustafson, and my peers at the C. G. Jung Institute of Chicago. My very special gratitude and thanks to Boris Matthews, who guided me at every step, challenging me to clarify and deepen the concepts discussed in this book. As Arjuna says of Lord Krishna, "He was no ordinary charioteer."

I thank my patients, who shared their stories with all of us to assist on the journey. I hope their healing experience has been just as rewarding as my own learning and healing from the sacred encounter with them.

And thank you to all of you who provided practical assistance: Nancy Ferguson for her invaluable research, to my son, Siddhartha Bedi, for creating and maintaining the website, pathtothesoul.com, and to Paul Akre, Paul de Angeles, Gloria Ehlen, Shay Harris, Astrid Mellenkamp, Marilyn Olson, Lee Rafel, Jody Rein, Chris Roerden, and Jan van Schaik.

Thanks go to John Peters for graphically interpreting my concept of the chakras, and to Brian Malloy for the photographs.

Pursuing the path has involved many sacrifices. The most important was the sacrifice of precious time earmarked for my loving wife, Usha, my daughter, Ami, my son, Siddhartha, and my grandson, Signe. They have generously given of their time, love, and support.

Introduction

There is story about the Parsis' migration to India that captures the spirit of this book. Several hundred years ago, the Parsi sect, followers of Zoroaster who were persecuted by their Persian rulers, took to the seas to find a new home. After a long odyssey, they arrived on the shores of India, seeking political asylum. The Parsi elders dropped anchor in an Indian harbor and sent their emissary to the King of India requesting permission to immigrate. The Indian king sent his messenger to the Parsi flagship with a goblet full to the brim with milk. The message was that India was already overpopulated and had no room for newcomers, just as the goblet had no room for more milk. The Parsi elders sent back their emissary with the same goblet full to the brim, but they mixed honey in the milk. Their message: "We come in peace. We will mingle in your culture like honey in milk. We will enhance and sweeten your culture without intruding or taking up space." The Parsis kept their promise. Over the past several hundred years, they have been a beacon of peace and wisdom in a land divided by cultural, political, and religious differences.

The Eastern wisdom conveyed in the Hindu template that I offer in this book is not meant to intrude or replace the tremendous spiritual, intellectual, medical, or scientific accomplishments of the West. Rather, my intention is to deepen and amplify your journey to the soul using this template in conjunction with your existing framework of choice. I do not seek to convert or proselytize, but rather to show how you may be able to make use of some Hindu ideas in addressing and answering the pressing emotional, psychological, and spiritual issues in your life. Whatever your faith or persuasion, my purpose is to help you toward a richer, more satisfying life, both psychologically and spiritually.

The central claim of the world's great spiritual traditions is that we can grow and develop (or evolve) from where we now are upward in the hierarchy of being toward the ultimate level of spirit or soul. The purpose of this book is to remind us of our ability to do that, and to relate how my integration of Western psychiatry and the Eastern spiritual tenets of my Hindu heritage have helped me, and consequently my patients, rediscover their own religious and spiritual ground and continue on the journey to the soul.

You may ask why I, a Western-trained physician and psychiatrist, would write a book drawing together Eastern spirituality and Western psychiatry. The simple answer is: I had to write it. I had to reconcile the two worlds in which I live.

Whenever I felt lost in complex questions of my life as a child and a young man in India, I visited my grandmother in her kitchen, her informal "consulting room." She always knew when something was on my mind. Usually, I would not spontaneously level with her about my problems. After all, I was a straight-A medical student in my corner of the world, and she just my grandmother, so it was beneath my youthful pride to consult with her. At times like these, she would break the ice and tell me some story, often a mythological tale from ancient India. But I left India for England and, later, America.

Over the past twenty-five years in the Western world, in my encounters with thousands of individuals struggling with a host of medical and psychiatric illnesses, I have found that my Western medical training took me up to a certain point in the treatment of their problems, but that treatment then stalled. Depressed women and men, for example, would feel their symptoms alleviated, but still not feel happy. Something was missing from their healing. Their neurochemistry was restored to normal, but they continued to struggle and search for some deeper meaning to their lives and their suffering.

I tried all the elegant psychoanalytic and psychiatric theories, attempting to untangle their feelings of lack of meaning and an absence of both happiness and deeper purpose in their lives. In my urgent search for an answer to this nagging, residual problem, I found myself turning to my Indian traditions, myths, stories, and spiritual framework. Gradually the jigsaw puzzle started to come together for me and for my patients.

I learned that what my patients were missing was a bridge to the soul, to the essence of Being, and to the meaning of the life into which they had been born. The Eastern way helped me understand the uniqueness of each of my patients and the special significance of their life stories. Suddenly, my patients' problems made sense. Their illnesses and symptoms were no longer only physical pains and neurochemical imbalances, but were now crucial symbols. Their problems were pointing in the direction the soul was trying to take them so that they might make their precious contributions of selfhood to community and to humanity. Once I "got it," amazingly, my patients also "got it," and they too found the path to the soul.

In my own journey as a psychiatrist and an immigrant, symbols from my Hindu soul appeared in my life and dreams to befriend and guide me whenever I felt lost and uncertain in my professional and personal life. For example, several years ago when I was feeling alone, lost, and uncertain about the meaning and the purpose of my "exile" in Milwaukee, my soul gifted me a dream image to reassure and guide me.

I dreamed that *I was back at my alma mater, St. Xavier's College, in India, having supper in the college cafeteria with my mentor, Father Vallace, and two other Jesuit fathers. Later we went to the chapel and prayed together.* The dream had a profoundly peaceful impact on me.

Initially, I rightfully thought that, in my dark hour of distress, my three father-mentors had appeared to reassure me. On deeper reflection, however, the image of my grandmother came to mind. Whatever story she told, it always had a unique answer to my unstated question. For some of the biggest questions about the broader issues of the world at large, she told the story of the Trimurti, the Hindu Trinity composed of Brahma, Vishnu, and Shiva. I again heard her telling me that the gods often presented themselves to us in human form, and then I realized that these three Jesuits fathers were manifestations of the holiest Hindu

Trimurti, the Hindu Trinity

Trinity: Brahma, the god of creation, Vishnu, the god of maintenance of peace and right order, and Shiva, the god of the destruction of evil. The holiest Hindu Trinity, the Trimurti, had appeared in my dream to reassure and guide me.

Their message was that, although I might feel alone in America, I was not abandoned. This dream and its message reaffirmed me in my work and spurred me on the path to the soul. I realized that part of my spiritual task was to take up a project that had long preoccupied me: creatively integrating Eastern and Western healing philosophies. I decided to write this book, which is my humble beginning in the mammoth task of integrating my Eastern and Western experiences and knowledge. I want you to benefit from my struggles and my discoveries.

In an attempt to creatively integrate my Eastern background and my Western psychological and psychiatric training, I present the fundamental concepts of Hindu spiritual thought, illustrate them with case vignettes, and correlate them with Western psychiatric and philosophical concepts wherever possible. I have relied heavily on my background as a Hindu, raised in India, later groomed in the Western philosophical tradition through my Jesuit schooling, and, still later, strengthened by my psychiatric training and practice as a psychiatrist and a psychotherapist in India, England, and the United States. In the present account, I have drawn from Hindu thought to conceptualize and help me understand how spiritual and psychological healing work together.

I invite you to come with me on the path to the soul as I have discovered it. May what you read in these pages further your healing as it has furthered the healing in my patients and myself.

This is my ashram, my spiritual home. Welcome.

chapter one

The Soul and the Path

Know that that by which all this is pervaded,
is indestructible;

Nothing can work the destruction
of this which is imperishable.
—Bhagavad Gita[1]

Michael, a patient of mine, brought a vivid dream to his session with me one day. In the dream, *Michael takes off in a small amphibious plane. He is concerned that he may be flying too close to some treetops. But then he realizes he has no control over his plane! As he looks out the cockpit window to scan his surroundings for a safe place to crash, he sees a much larger plane ahead of him. Each time the larger plane maneuvers, his little plane makes the same maneuver. Then he realizes there must be an invisible cable linking his plane with the larger plane ahead of him, and that his plane is actually not a plane at all, but a glider. At best, he can follow the movements of the large plane, and at worst, he can fight them.*

Michael had come to me for therapy under pressure from his employer. Although he was technically proficient, he did his job joylessly. Nobody wanted to work with him. His employer said he could not get along with anybody on the job. Michael had been

---

1. *Bhagavad Gita*, Antonio de Nicolás, trans. (York Beach, ME: Nicolas-Hays, 1990), chapter 2, verse 17, p. 33.

a military pilot and had wanted to fly commercial aircraft following his discharge. After his discharge, however, his parents had pressured him to enter a technical field. For many years, he continued to fly his private plane, but, as he became more and more depressed, hopeless, and isolated, he flew less and less. Finally, he sold his plane. Michael's difficulties at work mirrored his unhappy personal life. Although he and his ex-wife had shared a few interests, they had not been happy. Michael had remained in the marriage "for the sake of the children." When they left home, he felt his situation was no longer bearable, and he and his wife divorced.

When we are caught in a limited view of life, the soul often sends us a dream to give us a deeper view—the soul's view—of our situation. Dreams make a precious contribution to living out of the Soul. Throughout this book, I have quoted my own and my patients' dreams to illustrate the whispers of the soul that nudge and guide us to live a spiritually informed life.

Michael's dream came at a critically low point in our work. Michael believed he had to do everything by sheer effort of will, yet he felt he couldn't muster the energy necessary to continue, let alone undertake new tasks and responsibilities. He felt empty inside, as if he had lost his soul and couldn't go on. Michael was afraid he was going to crash. However, his dream showed him that there was another source of energy that could keep him airborne if he stayed connected and let it guide him.

Michael's dream told him—and me—that something greater than he, something beyond his control, was leading him on an invisible path toward a destination he could not foresee. The great Swiss psychiatrist C. G. Jung had similar dreams that shed light on Michael's dream and on the relationship between his glider and the large plane.

THE INDIVIDUAL AND THE HIGHER POWER

Throughout his life, C. G. Jung was gifted with powerful dreams and parapsychological experiences. Jung devoted his life to understanding the meaning of dream imagery. In October 1958, Jung had a dream that he understood as depicting the relationship between him and some higher power. In the dream, several

UFOs fly over Jung's house. One of them ". . . came speeding through the air: a lens with a metallic extension which led to a box—a magic lantern. At a distance of sixty or seventy yards it stood still in the air, pointing straight at me. I awoke with a feeling of astonishment. Still half in the dream, the thought passed through my head: 'We always think that the UFOs are projections of ours. Now it turns out that we are their projections. I am projected by the magic lantern as C. G. Jung. But who manipulates the apparatus?'"[2]

Jung had a similar dream in 1944. In that dream, he was on a hiking trip. As he walked along a little road through a hilly landscape, he came to a small wayside chapel:

> *The door was ajar, and I went in. To my surprise there was no image of the Virgin on the altar, and no crucifix either, but only a wonderful flower arrangement. But then I saw that on the floor in front of the altar, facing me, sat a yogi—in lotus posture, in deep meditation. When I looked at him more closely, I realized that he had my face. I started in profound fright, and awoke with the thought: "Aha, so he is the one who is meditating me. He has a dream, and I am it." I knew that when he awakened, I would no longer be.*[3]

Jung's two dreams, and Michael's dream, vividly depict a relationship between the individual and something else that is perceived as superior.

In psychological language, we say that, in our waking state, we are unconscious of this "something else" that we cannot define more precisely than to say that an image of it exists from our dreams. Nevertheless, the dreams reveal that it is there and is depicted as crucial to our existence. Spiritual traditions would not hesitate to call the UFO, the yogi, and the large plane images of a higher power.

---

2. C. G. Jung, *Memories, Dreams, Reflections* (New York: Pantheon Books, 1961), p. 323.
3. C. G. Jung, *Memories, Dreams, Reflections*, p. 323.

THE PARABLE OF THE RING

In Gotthold Ephriam Lessing's dramatic poem, "Nathan the Wise" (1779),[4] Sultan Saladin of Jerusalem summons Nathan, a rich Jew known as "the Wise." In a private audience, the Sultan poses a question to Nathan: "Since you are so wise, tell me: What belief, what law makes the most sense to you?" Then the Sultan leaves Nathan alone for a few minutes to reflect on his answer.

"I have to proceed carefully," Nathan says to himself. "And how am I going to do that? I can't come across as a dyed-in-the-wool Jew. And even less as no Jew at all. Because then he'll ask me why I'm not a Moslem. . . . I've got it! It's not only children you can satisfy with a story.

"Many, many years ago," Nathan begins, "there lived a man in the East who had a priceless ring. The stone was an opal that sparkled with a hundred colors. It had the mysterious power to make the wearer who believed in its power beloved before God and man. The man of the East always wore the ring, never taking it from his finger, and devised a means to keep it always in his family line: he would pass it on to his most beloved son, regardless of birth order, and that son would become the head of the house by the power of the ring.

"This went on for generations," Nathan continued, "till it came to a man who had three sons, each of whom he loved equally. From time to time one or the other would seem to be more dear, and in a weakness of love the father secretly promised the ring first to one, then to another, then to the third. All went well until the old man knew that he was approaching death. What was he to do?

"Secretly he sent for an artist, and bid him spare no expense or time to make two rings indistinguishable from the original. And in the course of time the artist returned with three rings. When he examined them, the old father could not tell which were new,

4. I am paraphrasing and retelling the ring parable. A good English translation is that of Bayard Quincy Morgan, *Nathan the Wise: A dramatic poem in five acts* (New York: Ungar, 1955).

which was the original. Relieved and at peace, he summoned each of his sons to him individually, blessed each, gave each a ring, and died in peace.

"After their father was buried, the sons came together, each proclaiming that their father had blessed him, which was true, and had give him a precious ring, which was also true. Each said he was the head of the house. They argued. They fought. But they could not identify the one genuine ring."

"Rings?" the Sultan exclaims. "Don't play games with me. I asked you about beliefs, laws!"

"Let us return to the rings," Nathan continues. "The three sons go to the judge. Each swears that his father had blessed him—which was true—and had given him a ring—which was also true. 'Well,' the judge says, 'I'm not here to solve riddles. Are you waiting for the true ring to open its mouth and speak? Unless you can produce your father and he can identify the true ring, then quit wasting my time. But wait!' the judge continued. 'I understand that the ring has a magical power to make its wearer beloved before God and man. That will be the way to decide, because the false rings don't have that power. Which of you loves the others the best?' And the sons were silent. 'Speak,' the judge commanded, 'why don't you speak? Surely the true ring works in the present and not only in the past? Each of you loves himself best of all? Then you are all deceived deceivers! Apparently the true ring got lost, and to conceal and replace the loss your father had two more rings made.'"

"Magnificent!" the Sultan exclaimed.

Nathan continued. "So the judge said, 'If you want my advice rather than my judgment, listen. Accept the situation as it is. Each of you has a ring and a blessing from your father. Perhaps he wanted to put an end to the tyranny of the one and only true ring that dominated his house. Surely, he did love each of you equally, and did not want to hurt any one of you. So be it! And here is my advice.'" Nathan paused.

"The judge," he said, "looked at each of the sons. And then he spoke: 'Let each of you strive to live the power the true ring is supposed to have. Let this power manifest in gentleness, heartfelt tolerance, compassion, and submission to God. And then when the powers of the stone shine through your children's children, I invite you to come before this bench again. Then a wiser man than I will sit upon it, and pass judgment. Go now!'"

• • •

Each person has or seeks a path to the soul, to the higher power, to God. Ultimately, all paths lead to the same destination, although, from outside, each path looks unique and is distinct in its external particulars. Each path has something to offer. As you will see in the following pages, I take from the Hindu, Christian, medical, psychiatric, and analytical paths what I have found to work for me and for my patients. As the distance between individuals and peoples on this planet grows ever shorter and we come into ever closer contact with one another, we must learn to honor each others' paths. More: we must discover and integrate what another path offers that our own path lacks. Then we will discover that, fundamentally, we all want the same things.

WHAT PEOPLE REALLY WANT

What do people really want? What is it that we all reach for, pursue, dream of? Hindu ethics recognizes four pursuits that embrace everything a person could desire: pleasure, wealth, freedom, and a life in harmony with the higher power and the order of the universe. This is called the "fourfold good," *chaturvarga*. A life in harmony with the higher power, *dharma*, is the sure guide for the other three: pleasure, which is known as *kama;* wealth, known as *artha;* and freedom or liberation, known as *moksha*. (I discuss these four concepts in greater detail in chapter 10.) The first three seem obvious—who doesn't want to experience pleasure, to have wealth, and to feel free? However, we can satisfactorily achieve kama, artha, and moksha only when dharma—the "indestructible presence"—is our guide. In other words, only a life informed by an adequate spirituality leads to lasting pleasures, to the wealth that neither moth nor rust nor thief can attack, and the freedom from mundane entanglements that sees them from the perspective of a higher power. In this endeavor, spirituality and psychology can and should work together.

Spirituality and Psychology

It is an unfortunate accident of history that spirituality and psychology got further and further separated. Beginning in the 18th century, with the Age of Enlightenment, and accelerating in the 19th, the methodology of the physical sciences was applied to the study of the human mind and soul. This led to a soulless psychology in the late 19th and much of the 20th centuries. Fortunately, more and more people are realizing that a psychology that ignores spirituality is just as impoverished as a spirituality ignorant of psychology. Part of the task I have set myself in this book is to contribute to building a bridge between the two.

Michael's dream shows a relationship between the individual human being and something greater. Christianity teaches that we are created in the image of God; Hinduism holds that the *atman*, individual soul or self, is the emanational creation of Brahman, the Transcendent Absolute, the all-pervading energy and Supreme Lord, or Primal soul. In the language of Jungian psychology, we say that the large plane, the apparatus behind the UFO, and the yogi correspond to the archetype of the God-image.

Archetypes themselves are unrepresentable, like the field of a magnet. Only when we place a piece of paper or glass over a magnet and sprinkle iron filings on it does the shape of the magnetic field emerge. Likewise, we experience the various archetypes when they appear in consciousness as images and ideas, or when they shape our emotions and behavior in typically human ways. Archetypes are universal patterns or motifs. They are the basic content of religious imagery and ritual, of mythologies, legends, fairy tales. They shape our dreams and visions, and, as mentioned, they structure our typically human life situations and experiences. Hence, to speak or dream of being at a crossroad is to employ an archetypal image referring to a time and place of momentous life choice, just as falling in love or reflecting on the meaning of one's life in old age are experiences patterned by the corresponding archetypes.

It is very important to understand the term "God-image." When I say that the large plane, the UFO, and the yogi correspond to the archetype of the God-image, I am definitely not saying that any one of them is God. Many followers of religious traditions, and often the traditions themselves, typically—and unfortunately—do not distinguish between the image and what it represents. St. Paul made the clear distinction between God and God-image when he wrote: "Now we are seeing a dim reflection in a mirror; but then we shall be seeing face to face" (1 Corinthians 13:12).[5]

Hindu thought likewise clearly differentiates the deity from various images of the deity. Earlier, I said that the *atman*, the individual soul or self, is the emanational creation of Brahman. Brahman is described as the Transcendent Absolute, the all-pervading energy and Supreme Lord or Primal Soul. As such, Brahman is without qualities, formless, unrepresentable, totally transcending manifest existence. However, many Hindu God-images have been formed to represent various aspects of Brahman. Likewise, in Islam and Judaism, God as God is immaterial and therefore invisible, but by no means unreal. In the dreams cited, therefore, the archetype of the God-image appears in various guises.

There is another important parallel between Christian belief, Hindu belief, and depth psychology. In the Christian gospel, Matthew admonishes us to seek a new standard, higher than the old, to grow beyond convention and tradition: "You must therefore be perfect just as your heavenly father is perfect" (Matthew 5, 48). Hinduism teaches that the individual soul (the atman) must unfold and grow to full maturity and the realization of its innate oneness with God. Both the Christian and the Hindu points of view recognize that the essence of the individual is divine. Both also point out that, through growth and maturation, we must transform our merely natural condition into a "higher" condition if we are to realize our innate oneness with the divine.

Jungian psychology speaks a different language here, using the term "individuation," but the message is similar. "We could

5. This and all subsequent biblical references come from The Jerusalem Bible.

. . . translate individuation," Jung writes, "as 'coming into selfhood' or 'self-realization.'"[6]

Individuation is powered by a driving force in each of us that propels us to consciously actualize our unique psychological reality, including our strengths and our weaknesses. Ultimately, individuation leads to the experience of a transpersonal regulating force or authority as the center of our individual psyches. "It is," Jung writes, "as if the guidance of life had passed over to an invisible centre."[7]

The Individual soul and the Primal soul

For hundreds, perhaps thousands, of years, women and men have written about the soul. In speaking of the individual soul (the atman) and the Primal Soul (Brahman), I like to use the ancient image of the droplet and the ocean: the individual soul is like a droplet of water in the ocean of the Primal Soul. Metaphors are our attempt at expressing experiences that we cannot otherwise put into words or images; they are attempts to comprehend the otherwise incomprehensible. To continue the metaphor, the essence of both the ocean and each individual droplet is water. The ocean—the Primal Soul, Brahman, God, or cosmic order—is boundless. The droplet—the individual soul—is limited. The three dreams mentioned above depict the individual soul's relationship of dependence on the Primal Soul.

The individual soul depends ultimately on the Primal Soul for its very existence; but the Primal Soul also depends on the individual soul. How can this be? Over the ages, many mystics have realized that the individual soul is the medium through which the Primal Soul incarnates in the created human world. In other words, the Primal Soul works through us in the world, whether we know it or not.

---

6. C. G. Jung, *Two Essays in Analytical Psychology*. The Collected Works, vol. 7. (Princeton: Princeton University Press, 1966), ¶266. (Subsequent references to the Collected Works will be indicated as CW.)

7. C. G. Jung, "Commentary on 'The Secret of the Golden Flower,'" CW13, ¶77.

Mystics and seers of all ages have proclaimed the intimate relationship between the Primal Soul, the higher power, God, and human beings. For example, the 17th-century German doctor and mystic, Angelus Silesius (Johann Scheffler, 1624–77), expressed the same idea of the relationship between God and oneself:

I know that without me
God can no moment live;
Were I to die, then He
No longer could survive.

. . . .

In me is God a fire
And I in Him its glow;
In common is our life,
Apart we cannot grow.

. . . .

I am not outside God,
Nor leave I Him afar;
I am His grace and light,
And He my guiding star.[8]

In these aphorisms, Angelus Silesius voices the interdependence of God and humankind. Neither can exist without the other. Humankind and God are inseparable.

The 20th-century German poet, Rainer Maria Rilke, expressed the same idea even more strikingly when he worried about what God would do without him, comparing himself to God's pitcher, His drink, His garment.[9]

An old Chinese story beautifully illustrates the interrelationship between the individual soul and the Primal Soul or natural order.

---

8. From the "Cherubinisher Wandersmann" in Scheffler's *Sämtliche Poetische Werke,* I. Rosenthal, ed. (Regensburg, 1862), pp. 5ff. (Cited from Jung, CW6, p. 256f.)

9. R. M. Rilke, *Rilke's Book of Hours,* A. Barrows and J. Macy, trans. (New York: Riverhead Books, 1996), p. 74.

The Rainmaker of Kiochau

Once there was a great drought in a certain part of China. For months there had been no rain, and the situation became desperate. The Catholics made processions; the Protestants prayed; and the Chinese shot off guns to frighten away the evil spirits. Nothing helped. Finally, they said, "We'll fetch the rainmaker." A wizened old man, the rainmaker, came from another province. When he appeared, all he asked for was a quiet little hut somewhere, and he locked himself in for three days.

On the first, and the second, and the third day, nothing happened. The sky remained clear, the sun fierce. But on the fourth day, clouds began to form on the horizon, and soon there was a great snowstorm at a time when no snow was expected. The town was full of rumors about the wonderful rainmaker. A European living there went to the rainmaker, curious as to how he had made it rain.

"What did you do?" he asked. "Do?" the rainmaker replied. "I didn't do anything." "But look at all the snow!" the European objected. "How did you make it snow? They do call you the rainmaker." "I did not make it snow," the little old man said, "I am not responsible." "Then what have you been doing these three days?" "Oh, I can explain that," the rainmaker said. "I come from another country where things are in order. Here they are out of order. Therefore, when I got here, I was not in the natural order of things either. So I had to wait three days until I was back in the natural order, and then naturally the rain came."[10]

In Michael's dream, the Primal Soul moves Michael's glider along an invisible path he cannot foresee. In the story of the rainmaker, the rainmaker has to realign himself with the natural order of things, at which point the snow falls. The relationship between the individual soul and the Primal Soul, the natural order, is

10. Retold after C. G. Jung, *Mysterium Coniunctionis*, CW14, p. 419, note 211.

reciprocal: each needs the other. The natural order, the Primal Soul, can guide and lead, but the individual has to cooperate and follow for the natural order to prevail. When we get in tune with the natural order of things, the Primal Soul, we are the instruments used by the Primal Soul so it can manifest in the created world.

INDIVIDUATION AND SPIRITUAL EVOLUTION

Whenever we cannot affirm the fullness of our being and have to suppress a part of it, we fall into disharmony with ourselves. Having to suppress a talent, an interest, a facet of our personality, or believing we cannot safely affirm all that we sense and feel moving in us, twists us into a caricature of who we really are. Similarly, when we are unable to face our aggressive and destructive urges and deny their existence, we fail to take psychological responsibility. Again, we fall into disharmony with ourselves.

Individuation means that we work at coming to terms with everything that moves in us, whether those urges and impulses appeal to us or appall us. When we can say of ourselves, "As I am, so I act," we can be at one with ourselves, even though it may be difficult, and we can accept responsibility for ourselves, even though we may struggle against it.

Individuation means more than self-awareness. As C. G. Jung says, "The meaning and purpose of the process is the realization, in all its aspects, of the personality originally hidden away in the embryonic germ-plasm; the production and unfolding of the original, potential wholeness."[11]

When we individuate, we make the most of our strengths, which usually is not so very difficult. We also have to face our inferiorities and weaknesses, and take responsibility for them. This means making amends for hurtful acts we have committed, suffering with our failings that humiliate us again and again, and civilizing our shadow as far as we can. Wholeness is not perfection.

11. C. G. Jung, "Two Essays on Analytical Psychology," CW7, ¶186.

The Hindu spiritual position is akin to the notion of individuation, but expresses similar ideas in different terms, some of which go beyond the psychological position. As noted above, the atman is the "soul body" and its essence, not the physical body, emotions, external mind, or personality.[12] (The external mind or personality comes closer to the idea of ego and our repertoire of skills in meeting the world, the persona.) Where individuation speaks of wholeness rather than perfection, the Hindu idea of the evolution of the individual soul (atman) is of a progressive unfoldment, growth, and maturation toward the inherent divine destiny, which is the return of the individual soul (the droplet, in the earlier metaphor) to the Primal Soul (the ocean, Brahman). Hence, to use a different metaphor, each individual soul is like a seed that must unfold out of all that binds or limits it and keeps it (for a time) from manifesting its full potential, which is its essential oneness with the Primal Soul.

Three tethers keep the individual soul bound and limited. These three are fundamental concepts that I will discuss in detail in the next chapter, and to which I will refer time and again in the course of this book.

The first tether is the belief that the created, manifest world is the whole of reality. This is called *maya*. It is misleading to translate maya as "illusion." There is nothing illusory about the brick wall we run into time and again, whether it be masonry or a metaphorical brick wall. The created world, maya, is "illusion" only in the sense that it is a limited reality, a manifestation of invisible but real force, the creative aspect of God.

Our actions and their consequences constitute the second tether, which Hindus call karma. Many people know the word karma. Usually we hear it in the phrase, "creating bad karma." In fact, the term *karma* embraces both actions and the consequences (good as well as bad) that necessarily follow. To put it

---

12. Actually, the exact meaning of *atman* has to be determined according to context. I am using *atman* to refer to the essence, the innate pattern, the self-god within, that spark of divinity in each of us.

differently, all actions create consequences that in some way bind us. For example, when we do something "bad," our conscience may bother us; those who have suffered the effects of our actions may be angry with us or seek revenge; we may even fall afoul of the law and be penalized. Likewise our "good" actions can also tether us. For example, our self-satisfaction at having done something "good" can puff us up with (spiritual) pride. But, even if we do not get inflated with how good we are, the gratitude and praise of the beneficiaries of our actions can limit us by encouraging us to hide or deny our shadow qualities, potentially seducing us into pretending (even to ourselves!) that we are better than we know we really are. Like maya, karma is a fundamental concept I will refer to many times in the following pages.

The third, and perhaps fundamental, tether is ignorance of dharma. Ignorance of dharma obscures the natural wisdom, light, unity, and humility of the soul and allows spiritual ignorance, egotism, and pride to manifest. If you recall Michael's airplane dream, you will recognize that he suffered from ignorance of dharma in the sense that he did not know his aircraft was actually a glider being pulled by the large plane. He thought his aircraft was fully under his control. Ignorance of dharma, of course, has many forms.

In the chapters that follow, I will be discussing numerous examples that illustrate dharma, and how my patients and I have worked with their ignorance of dharma, their karma, and their maya to reveal the spark of divine light that glowed within them.

Individuation and spiritual evolution, you see, view the same process from different vantage points. They are complementary: one attends to what the other overlooks. Both Hindu thought and Jungian psychology recognize that the fullest possible realization of our innate being is necessary. Clinical experience shows that, ultimately, each individual has to recognize that his or her consciousness is, at best, the agent of a superior force, and that cooperation with that force leads to a sense of fulfillment and satisfaction—to being in harmony with oneself.

Hinduism speaks of *svadharma*, the law of one's own being. Jungian psychology recognizes that, when we cannot follow the law of our own being and make real what is potential, we become twisted, split, and fall into a civil war within ourselves. Hindu thought speaks of the atman—the individual soul—returning to Brahman—the Primal Soul.

The spiritual significance of evolution is that the incarnated world provides the medium through which the Primal Soul becomes manifest. Spiritual evolution and individuation demand that we adapt to the world around us and to the world within us. Let us now consider the concept of adaptation.

Adaptation: Outer and Inner

Militarily, it is never a good idea to fight on two fronts at the same time, but human beings have little choice. We must adapt to the "outer" and "inner" worlds. When we adapt, we find the "fit" between ourselves and our circumstances.

Michael, my patient, was ill-adapted to both worlds. He was far from being in harmony with himself and, consequently, was poorly adapted to his work-world and to his marriage. He had relinquished his passion for flying and lost his soul-connection.

In life, our first task, of course, is to adapt well enough to the world we perceive to enable us to survive. We make choices, take actions, and experience outcomes. Sometimes our actions satisfy us, because they lead to the ends we envisioned. At other times, however, we are surprised and disappointed by the results. Our actions appear to satisfy "outer" circumstances, but leave us dissatisfied "inside." We have not found the balance, the "fit," between inner and outer adaptation.

The "outer world" usually lets us know in no uncertain terms when our outer adaptation is faulty. As with Michael, the boss may tell us we are not doing the job; the bill collector calls; people we have wronged retaliate or avoid us; we drive too fast and get a speeding ticket; our lover or spouse or child gets angry at us. The inner world, likewise, protests when we are not adapted to it. People in our society, however, have a harder time recognizing these messages.

Hindu thought speaks of adaptation in terms of *dharma*, which is often translated as "law." But the concept of "law" is far too narrow. When we actualize our inherent "law" or nature, we fulfill our dharma.[13]

This definition places dharma very close to the psychological concept of the archetype, which, as I said earlier, refers to inherent or innate patterns that shape our thoughts, images, emotions, and behavior, including our individual development, stages of life, interactions with others, and relationship to transpersonal forces.

The four main areas or aspects of dharma include *svadharma* (the law of one's own nature), *ashrama dharma* (the patterns of the stages of life), *varna dharma* (the law of one's own kind), and *reta dharma* (cosmic or divine law). Of course, as in all historical belief systems, these Hindu concepts have been translated and retranslated into specific rules and codes over the centuries that tend to obscure the underlying archetypal facts to which they actually refer. But, since the four Hindu terms pretty well cover the life span and all human concerns, I will use them throughout this book (along with their psychological equivalents).

When we are consumed with the outer—earning our living, trying to get ahead—how does the inner speak? What are the whispers of the soul? How does the soul try to alert us to our faulty inner adaptation? What is the language of the soul? How do its footprints manifest in our consciousness? When we are lost in our maya, and karma is in the service of adaptation to outer life, how does the soul beckon us onto a path of dharma?

Western psychology and Eastern spirituality have gifted us with some important frameworks to decipher the code of the soul's whispers. The soul speaks gently at first, via our dreams and fantasies, to direct us onto our dharmic path. If we ignore this gentle nudge, it speaks louder, through our relationships, fascinations, and problems. Important relationships, be they precious or problematic, embody reflections of our soul that psychol-

13. Subramuniyaswami, *Dancing with Siva* (Kappa, HI: Himalayan Academy, 1993), p. 710.

ogy calls projections. If we choose not to see the reflections of our soul in the enchantment or disappointment of our relationships, the soul has to amplify its message. These are our hang-ups—that is, our complexes.

Our hang-ups are a source of tremendous problems for us. They also can be a bridge to the soul if we decode their deeper meaning and intention. They disrupt our business-as-usual and get us into deeper water, and it is only in the murky waters of our depths that we find the treasures of our soul. If we somehow fit a square peg in a round hole and ignore our complexes, the soul amplifies its messages through synchronistic events and accidents. Accidents stop us in our tracks, forcing us to discover new and creative ways to deal with the challenge they pose. This new and creative detour often has the result of getting us into our dharmic and spiritual life. But if we still do not pay attention, the soul further intensifies its call and uses its last resort, sending us an emergency message through medical or psychiatric illness.

Embedded in an illness is a message from the soul to get us into the spiritual groove of our existence. Hindus believe that, if we miss this last call, we must go through another cycle as a lower life-form until we earn another opportunity to reincarnate as human and undertake the necessary karma to reach our potential. Our present human existence is a precious gift and a window in an endless cycle of reincarnations, an opportunity to break loose from the vicious round of maya, karma, and dharma. Freedom from these cycles is called moksha by Hindus and *nirvana* by Buddhists. Christians might call this *salvation* (without the idea, of course, of reincarnation). A soul in moksha is like a purified raindrop that reunites with the soul of the Primal Ocean. Atman and Brahman become one. Then we no longer see darkly in the mirror, but face to face.

Whispers of the Soul

The soul speaks to us in many idioms. If only we could or would listen, our lives would be much more meaningful. Earlier I mentioned a few of the ways the soul tries to communicate with us: through our dreams and fantasies; our relationships, fascinations, and problems; and our complexes. Let's look at these and some other paths to the soul more closely.

DREAMS

The soul is whispering all the time, if only we knew how to listen. Each night, we dream approximately every 90 minutes, but a great many people do not attend to their dreams. As a general rule, dreams offer a view of our life situation that compensates or balances our one-sided conscious view. Michael's dream showed him not only that he was not going to crash, but that a higher power was actually leading him onward.

Another patient of mine, Phil, dreamed that he fell in love with a sea turtle. To understand this message from his soul, you need to know that he is a caustic, controlling, fast-moving, hard-driving man. The obvious link between Phil and his dream is the fable of the tortoise and the hare. Phil is a hare, always sprinting. Falling in love with the sea turtle imaged the necessary compromise. The dream did not mean that Phil should become a sea turtle, only that the blend—hare plus sea turtle—would average out to the proper pace, and better adapt Phil to his own nature and to the world around him. (There is, of course, more meaning in the dream and more to Phil than my thumbnail sketch; but this illustrates how dreams function to compensate the conscious attitude.)

RELATIONSHIPS

Relationships are another lens through which the soul tries to show us something important. Typically, when we enter a relationship, we experience the other as fulfilling and completing us in some important way—at least at first, in the "honeymoon" phase. In the course of time, the honeymoon passes. We begin to be disappointed in the other. "You aren't the person I fell in love with." Of course not! The person you fell in love with was partly a reflection of some unknown but attractive facet of your own potential, but you couldn't see it without the other person to mirror it! The disappointment—"disillusionment," as we call it—alerts us that it is time for the relationship to transform into something more mature. "More mature" means that we now have the opportunity to begin to actualize that part of ourselves that previously has been undeveloped or underdeveloped, but reflected to us in the other person. All relationships enter this phase. Alas, too few people realize that the difficult time when projections collapse is not necessarily the death of the relationship, but a chance to deepen both the relationship and our own personalities.

PROJECTIONS

Projections, it is important to note, happen to us. We do not consciously and deliberately "project" onto others. As the above example illustrates, we see in others what we cannot see in ourselves. One important clue to recognizing projections is a strong emotional charge—attraction or repulsion—especially when the emotion tends to endure. In other words, the longer the emotional charge lasts, the more certain we can be that we are experiencing something about ourselves reflected in the other person. Lest you think projections are "bad," I want to add that projection is often the first and most powerful way in which our soul alerts us to a part of ourselves we hadn't discovered, but are now ready to develop and include in our conscious personality. Unfortunately, many people miss the golden opportunity to discover more about themselves than the collapse of a projection offers and move on, only to project and be disappointed again and again. In other words, we fall in love (or in hate) with our unknown self via other people.

COMPLEXES

The technical name for our emotional hot spots, our hang-ups, is the "feeling-toned complex." When we have a hang-up—or one has us—our normal personality is taken over. Typically, we attempt to disown what just came through us. We say, "I wasn't myself; I don't know what got into me." These hang-ups get us into difficulties in our relationships and compromise our inner and outer adaptation. Over time, our complexes tend to persist if we do not attend to them. For example, the compulsive tendency to compete, to become easily angered, behave seductively, or compulsively overwork, to feel overly responsible and easily victimized—are personality patterns that can become repetitive behaviors, even when such responses are not called for. When a complex seizes us, we become overly emotional, we blame others for what we are feeling, we act more primitively, it takes us a long time to cool down. At these times, the complex overwhelms the normal strengths and attributes of our personality. All of us have complexes, or rather, complexes have us! None of us is immune.

While complexes that "get us" can create difficulties, they are also an important bridge to our soul. If the sand-grit of our hang-ups is incubated long enough in the oyster of spiritual life, then the pearl of our soul emerges. In my life experience and clinical practice, I have been deeply moved by witnessing the wondrous phenomenon of how women and men courageously use the raw material of their hang-ups as stepping-stones to the soul. Truly, they make gold out of lead.

Sara struggles with what we call depression and codependency. She tends to get overly involved in a caretaker role in all her relationships, to the relative exclusion of her emotional need for nurturance. She has a caretaker complex (or, more precisely, it often has her). This attitude became extremely burdensome to her and she became clinically depressed. In therapy, Sara learned to differentiate caring for others from detachment, when appropriate. Her hang-up, however, was the seed for her calling as a community leader, a task she commendably fulfilled. (I discuss Sara in greater detail in chapter 2.)

SYNCHRONISTIC EVENTS

The soul often whispers to us through synchronistic events. A synchronistic event occurs when we recognize that two or more causally unrelated events resemble each other and catch our attention. For example, you're trying to remember the name of a childhood classmate. In the course of conversation, somebody mentions the very name you had been searching for. Synchronistic events can be a powerful "heads-up," calling us to pay attention. Another example that many have experienced is the thunder clap that resounds just as we are making some very important statement. Of course, not all synchronistic events are so transparent, and sometimes we do not recognize a synchronistic series until we look back and see all the clues.

For example, one patient kept noticing advertisements for exercise cycles. Time and again, he opened the newspaper and there was a store advertising exercise equipment, including cycles. Then, he reported that his neighbor had an exercise cycle in his garage sale, but my patient did not buy it. For six months, he noticed no exercise cycle ads. Then he had a mild heart attack. As part of his rehabilitation program, his doctor prescribed exercise, specifically on an exercise cycle!

ACCIDENTS

When we don't pay attention, the message has to be more powerful, perhaps in the form of an accident. Once, when I was on a radio talk show discussing dreams, a listener called in to report that, for several years, he had a recurring dream of falling off a roof, but never hitting the ground. Then he no longer had the dream. He asked me what I thought. To answer his question, I had to find out more about him—how he lived, what sort of work he did. He told me that he worked as a roofer. He liked to live it up—no challenge was too outrageous, no risk too great. "Doc, there's nothing I wouldn't try at least once!" he boasted. "Well," I said, "sounds as if, for you, the sky's the limit." "Oh, yeah! Try anything at least once." "So," I continued, "what was going on about the time you no longer had the falling dream?" "Well," he said, "I don't know. I was out of work for a while there. Seems as if I didn't have that dream after that." "Oh, you were out of work? How did that come about?" I asked.

"You see," he said, "I was up on this roof one day and just stepped off the edge. Dumbest thing I ever did! Hit the ground and broke my pelvis. Laid me up for months. Hurt, too."

"I think I understand," I replied. "Seems as if you took lots of risks without considering the consequences; always pushing the envelope. Dreams try to show us an image that balances and corrects our conscious view of things. Repeatedly, you had the falling dream. Then, when you fell, or stepped, off the roof, you no longer had the falling dream. It looks as if the dream were trying to show you how risky your lifestyle was. When you didn't get the message from the dream, the next step was the accident."

"Well, Doc," he said, now more thoughtfully, "I guess you're right. That fall sure did knock some sense into me."

SYMPTOMS AND ILLNESSES

What happens if we don't pay attention to dreams, collapsed projections, synchronistic events, or accidents? Often, we develop symptoms and fall ill (as did my patient who suffered the mild heart attack). Illnesses often develop over time, heralded by symptoms. We don't feel well, aren't as energetic as we are accustomed to be. Symptoms alert us that our body is not functioning properly, that we are not taking care of ourselves adequately, or that we have contracted something noxious. Of course, medical conditions call for medical diagnosis and appropriate medical treatment. But we also do well to consider that medical and psychiatric symptoms may be encoded messages from the soul. In other words, symptoms may also be symbols.

Although I will discuss symptoms as symbols more fully in chapter 3, it is important to clarify here what is and is not a symbol, and why a symptom may mean more than the medical condition to which it refers. As I use the term, a symbol is the best possible expression for something otherwise unknown to us. Something whose meaning or reference is fully known—like the red octagon bearing the word "STOP"—is not a symbol in my usage. An image becomes a symbol for us only when we still find the image fascinating and meaningful, even though we are at a loss to say what its unexpressed meaning is. In this sense, a person to whom we have a powerful emotional response or reaction that we cannot account for becomes a symbol. In other words, the carrier of our projection (of a part of ourselves we don't recognize) is, for us, the best possible representation of that unknown aspect of ourselves.

Likewise, a medical symptom can be symbolic. We have all heard someone say, "It's all in your head!" when the doctor has been unable to identify a medical condition even though we feel miserable. The term often applied to these sorts of complaints is "psychosomatic." Fortunately, medical practitioners are becoming more sensitive to the reality of "psychosomatic" complaints, although many people fear being labeled as crazy when no organic problem can be identified. While we should exhaust all the possibilities of medical diagnosis, we should also seriously consider these sorts of conditions as messages from our soul encoded in the body. The hard-driving executive (or middle-manager trying to survive) who has a heart attack at 40 or 45 is a classic example in our society.

Working sixty to eighty hours a week leaves very little time for anything but eating, showering, commuting, and a little sleep. Usually, the overworked person in our society neglects personal health and "matters of the heart"—meaningful relationships, compassion, empathy. Eventually, the heart protests against such mistreatment in the form of cardiac problems, sometimes preceded by noticeable symptoms. When people see their doctors about symptoms, we hope that they find one who knows that lifestyle has an effect on physical conditions, and who will listen to the symbols.

THE SOUL SPEAKS THROUGH THE SMALL

The Primal Soul often presents itself to us in seemingly insignificant events and experiences. It is the "still small voice," something we can easily overlook in the rush of modern life. It may speak to us in a dream, a chance encounter, a meaningful coincidence, or even an accident or illness. Yet if the Primal Soul is to help us, we must help it by listening carefully, by nurturing its message, and building a place for it in our conscious lives.[14]

Hindu tradition also reflects this concept of the soul speaking through the apparently small and insignificant. (In chapter 2 I will relate the Hindu story of Vamana, a dwarf reincarnation of Lord Vishnu, which illustrates how the "small" is actually the

14. C. G. Jung, *Aion*, CW9, ii, ¶257.

manifestation of the infinite.) In Christianity, Jesus was born in a manger in Bethlehem, and the question was later asked, "Can anything good come out of Nazareth?" (John 1, 46).

We do not travel the path to the soul by leaps and bounds. The path to the soul is a life's work made up mostly of seemingly trivial acts and events. The devil, as people say, is in the details. So also is the higher power. C. G. Jung tells the story of the person who asked the rabbi why it was that, although people used to hear the voice of God, now nobody does. The rabbi responded that perhaps they did not stoop low enough.

People usually manage the "big" events of life pretty well. It's the daily challenges that get many people down. The big events—births, deaths, catastrophes, all of which are ancient experiences of the human race and are therefore appropriately called archetypal—lift us out of the daily round. Big events, archetypal events, cut through our personal idiosyncrasies to our human core where archetypal responses to archetypal challenges take over. The seemingly "small stuff" of life challenges us because we have to learn to respond from our essence, from our soul. We all know how to manage "big" events in life, but how we spend time listening to a friend in need when we are preoccupied, or help a child with homework when we are tired, or play with a dog when we would rather watch the ball game are the times when our soul can speak the loudest.

When we look back over our life history, or when someone writes our brief obituary, the big stuff is often glossed over. What is recognized as important are the "small" encounters of life through which our soul spoke. A spiritual life honors the small, the seemingly insignificant, the undervalued, the marginal. As Jesus said, "I tell you solemnly, in so far as you neglected to do this to one of the least of these, you neglected to do it to me" (Matthew 25:45).

For most of us who are seeking the Primal Soul in the "big" events, in momentous enterprise or magnificent insights, it is worthwhile to remember that, often, the soul speaks through those aspects of our experiences and relationships that may be considered marginal, devalued, and insignificant. Many of us look for clues to the soul in the joys or tribulations of the past or seek a reflection of our individual soul in glorious events, experiences, and endeavors in the future. Yet, clinical experience and spiritual wisdom reiterates time and again that we discover the soul only here and now, or not at all.

BEING IN THE PRESENT

The great meditation traditions remind the practitioner that the human mind is unruly, a wayward animal that we must gently but firmly bring back to the path time and again. This ancient image aptly depicts the difficulty we all have in focusing our attention on what is immediately before us. The past seduces us by its lure of a ready explanation for our present difficulties. It insulates us from the challenge of living in the present with integrity and reverence for the sacred moment in which our individual soul is in communion with the divine in all things. Who among us does not know of someone who is lost in the past, bemoaning his or her lot, or feeding on stale and fading memories of glory?

Just as seductive as the past is the maya of the future—the unlived, the possible. Living in our fantasies of the future excludes living up to the challenge of the sacred present moment. To live in the future is to abdicate our responsibility to honor the opportunity to care for our individual soul and encounter the Primal Soul, because that meeting can only take place now. To live in the fantasies of the future is not to live at all.

Living here and now, however, can be both a bed of roses and a bed of nails. When we live in the present, we have to deal with whatever *is*. When we live in the moment and maintain our awareness of dharma, we have an opportunity to create the transformative moment. By holding this dual focus, we see the eternal in the temporal. We have the possibility of aligning our actions and their consequences (karma) with the meaning and mystery of our individual existence in the larger picture, our dharma.

But this means that, before we act in the present, we must reflect on the meaning of our choices and actions in the context of our own dharma and of our place in the tapestry of the Primal

Soul. This calls us to move from acting reflexively to reflecting actively.

ACTIVE AND REFLECTIVE LIVING

Adaptation to the inner and outer worlds requires that we act and reflect. Often, we do not reflect adequately until something doesn't turn out the way we intended. When things turn out differently than we expected, we often begin to realize one of the great laws of life: our actions bear necessary consequences. With this realization, we discover what the Hindu calls *karma*. Karma (which I will discuss in much greater detail in the next chapter) means actions and their necessary, anticipated consequences. As our awareness of karma deepens, we "look before we leap"; we consider the possible and probable outcome before we act; we budget before we spend. As our karma consciousness develops, we learn how not to trip ourselves up, how not to make problems for ourselves.

Reflection and action then form a feedback loop: our actions and their outcomes provide the data for our reflection; and our reflection guides our actions more and more wisely. Before we become conscious of our karma, we act reflexively. As our karmic consciousness deepens, we act after reflecting on the deeper meaning of our behavior. When we mature into our soul-consciousness, or what Hindus call our dharmic life, we become more respectful of our inner life, and more actively reflective on the inner life. The vessel of our life then becomes a sacred container for our soul. It becomes a medium through which the Primal Soul incarnates in our personal life. This transformation, from acting reflexively to reflecting actively, is a crucial prerequisite for a spiritually informed life. Through it, we learn how to better discern the circular path to the soul.

FOLLOWING THE CIRCULAR PATH

The image of circling round a core of meaning—circumambulation[15]—helps us visualize and understand how we discover our

---

15. C. G. Jung, *Aion*, CW9, ii, ¶257.

individual soul's right relationship to the Primal Soul. Often when we look back over our lives, they appear to have followed tortuous, serpentine, zigzagging, obstacle-ridden courses full of false starts, blind alleys, and pointless detours. Often, we see that we have had to perform tasks that we would have preferred not to undertake. Nevertheless, we gradually may begin to discern a pattern in these apparently meandering lives. We may discover that we play a part of a larger pattern that embraces us as well as many others. Then we notice that the events of our lives have been circling around some central, organizing theme, goal, or destination.

Literal or figurative circular motions—circumambulations—express the impulse or intention to define, relate to, approach, or protect the center of the circle and what is enclosed in it. This practice of encircling is an "archetypal idea," that is, an idea that is ancient, that occurs in many cultures and times, and that has a powerful emotional effect on people. When we draw a magic circle around us, we prevent something valuable from escaping, or we protect ourselves against hostile forces or influences.[16]

Once a young boy just on the threshold of puberty was referred to me for therapy. He told me he felt as though he were being blown to pieces. When I suggested he draw how that felt to him, he sketched a fragmenting male face. I said, "Just so we will be able to find his pieces, I'm going to draw a circle around him to keep his fragments from drifting away," and I drew the magic circle on his paper. The magic circle I had drawn deeply affected the boy's psyche, telling him that I would not let him fall apart. Subsequent therapy sessions felt shallow by comparison. Soon, he was able to continue without seeing me; the crisis had passed; the circle had contained him; he had not been blown to bits.

An example of circular movement in Christian ritual comes from the Mass. The priest makes the sign of the cross three times over the substances in the thurible, twice from right to left, and once from left to right. The counterclockwise movement (from

16. C. G. Jung, "The Tavistock Lectures," CW18, ¶409.

right to left) corresponds psychologically to a circumambulation downward, in the direction of the unconscious, while the clockwise (left to right) movement goes in the direction of consciousness. In other words, both what we are aware of (consciousness) and what we are not (the unconscious) must be included in the magic circle.[17]

The psychological implication is obvious. In our life's journey, we have to integrate our detours through both realms, the conscious and the unconscious, to attain that wholeness we experience when our individual soul is in communion with the Primal Soul. The route to fulfilling our soul's potential is circuitous. We must follow the tortuous, meandering, roundabout, labyrinthine path that we mark with substantial accomplishments but litter with our false starts, wrong turnings, and failed efforts.

Looked at in the context of circumambulating the center along a labyrinthine path, our life's journey may be construed as balancing inner and outer as we discover the center, the meaning of our individual existence in the bigger picture of the Primal Soul. At the personal level, we each create a self: an identifiable, stable personality, part of our sense of who we are, our identity. At the spiritual level, we each discover our own relationship to the greater reality, the higher power, the Primal Soul. The link between the Primal Soul and our outer life is our individual soul, that spark of divinity in each of us that wants to manifest in the world.

One of the most beautiful examples of circumambulation in a spiritual context is the pilgrims' walk in the temple of Borobudur in Java. The plan for the Borobudur stupa is a schematized representation of the cosmos. Borobudur, built in three concentric and ascending circles, was conceived as an initiatory mountain to be ascended by people seeking enlightenment. The lowest circle is strictly an account of life experiences—our manifest world of

17. C. G. Jung, "Transformation Symbolism and the Mass," CW11, ¶318.

maya, full of hopes and joys, but also disappointments, passions, war, sex, disease—so to speak, the realm of our lives as human animals. The middle circle is the domain of learning through which we distinguish ourselves from other animals and awaken to the possibility of enlightenment and the soul—where we develop our awareness of karma, our actions, and their consequences. The third, highest circle is the sphere of revelation, the region of the spirit, dharma, the Primal Soul. As we ascend through each of the circles of the stupa toward the top, we symbolically pass through all life's experiences, describing a spiral that circles around the central axis of meaning. At the very top of the stupa there is an invisible Buddha, the Buddha yet to come. This we understand to mean our full realization of the Primal Soul within us.

The ground plan of the temple is a circle within a square. Psychologically, this structure is a means of protecting the center of the personality from being drawn out and influenced by the lure of maya, the created world with its temptations and deceptions. Such centered deliberation is essential for maintaining the connection between our individual soul and the Primal Soul.

As we circle around some invisible center and reflect on our journey, we gradually discern the reference point, the meaningful core lying at the heart of our existence. We come to see that our efforts to become our authentic selves is more than personal. We see that, in our limited way, we have been serving something much greater than ourselves.

We must realize that most of the "great" accomplishments we may claim are the culmination of many seemingly insignificant acts and insights. The path to the soul is neither straight and narrow nor always smooth and free from obstruction. To follow the path, we need the courage to look at ourselves, as well as the knowledge to understand what we see. Lived in this way, life becomes sacred, lived fully in the temporal and the eternal present, caringly detached from preoccupation with the past or the future. The circular path to the soul is both a personal psychological and spiritual journey and a contribution to the actualization of the Primal Soul on this planet.

A WINDOW TO THE SACRED

No life is insignificant when we see deeply into it; and some lives, though modest in outward appearance and worldly accomplishment, are spiritually great. I want to conclude my thoughts on the path and the soul by sharing with you my experience of a spiritually profound life, and the effect it has had on me.

My friend and I meet infrequently, and then for only twenty minutes or so at a time. His presence affects me deeply. I always experience a sense of relief from whatever is bothering me when I am with him. My life seems more manageable as he and I talk. We seldom discuss "deep" subjects—life and death issues—but rather everyday concerns, like the "new" refrigerator he bought from a scratch-and-dent store that turned out to be defective, or his or my current problematic home project. There's nothing special about the topics of our conversations. What is special is my friend's objective, philosophical, cheerful view of himself and of others. And what makes that very special are the circumstances of my friend's life that were the crucible in which he forged his attitude.

My friend earns a modest living, running his own shop. Some years before I met him, my friend's wife suffered a stroke that severely impaired her intellectual abilities, reducing her to the level of a retarded young child. They have several children who are now grown and off on their own. My friend has never told me the details, but I have pieced together that he assumed the rearing of the children, as well as many, if not all, the household chores and duties. My friend brings his wife to work with him, and she sits and watches television or looks at the pictures in magazines in a back room. A few times, I have seen them interact—or, more precisely—I have observed the way he treats her: gently, respectfully, caringly. He calls her his princess.

My friend could have dealt with his wife's stroke differently. Some men might have become bitter, reviling their lot and turning to alcohol. Others might have taken up with another woman. Not my friend. Somehow, he was able to make the soulful choice of accepting his situation with dignity, and to achieve, not only equanimity, but a genuinely cheerful outlook. I sense a deep spirituality in him. He lives, not only the outer life everybody can see, but the inner life of the soul. My friend, Sam, is a sage, minding his modest shop, but incarnating the divine. He is a living symbol of that greater dimension in each of us, waiting for us to remove the obstacles that hinder it from shining forth through us. As Sam faithfully lives his "local" life, his influence radiates "globally."

The Welfare of Our Planet

A life lived in the soul—like Sam's—constellates life's essence. When we live out the essence of our individual souls, we become quintessential. The life of my friend Sam is an example of such precious, quintessential existence. When we lead such lives, we cleanse the droplet of the divine with which we have been entrusted of all personal contaminants: we retire the consequences of our past actions, and act in such a way that we accumulate no new burdens. In other words, we retire old karma, and the new karma we create bears us closer to the soul, to fulfilling our calling, our dharma. When we live a soulful life, we enhance the lives of those around us; we contribute to the quality of life of our communities; we do our small part in creating a culture informed by soul. In this way, we return our droplet of soul to the ocean of Primal Soul. We have the choice of making the spiritual ocean more toxic or more pristine by our actions.

When we encounter another being, human or animal, plant or stone, friend or foe, we have a choice to make. We can either see our darkest shadow or our deepest soul reflected in the mirror of the other across from us. When we live out of the soul, we cannot help but see its reflection in the other. To honor such a sacred encounter, the Hindus have a tradition of folding their hands in a ritual of greeting, "Namaste!"—"I bow to the divine in thee." Namaste—consciousness sanctifies the present moment.

Dear Reader, "Namaste!" I greet you as together we explore the mystery of our individual souls and our connection to the Primal Soul.

LOOKING AHEAD

In the following chapters, I present several fundamental ideas that have helped people fathom the messages in their suffering and resume their journey on the path to the soul. The two most important ideas to keep in mind as you read this book are simple but profound. First, what we do as individuals helps or hinders "the increasing manifestation of the glory of the spirit in the realm of matter," as Haridas Chaudhuri wrote.[18] Second, the obstacles we encounter, the illnesses we suffer, the emotional and psychological difficulties we experience can be see as stumbling blocks or stepping-stones. If we see them only as stumbling blocks, we will fall again and again. If we see them as stepping-stones, we can learn, heal and restore our souls and our connection with the Primal Soul, and contribute to the evolution of our planet.

As we all struggle to coexist in this fast-shrinking global village, our destinies are ever more intricately intertwined. Our individual karmic choices have a profound impact, not only on the lives of those around us, but on the rest of humanity. This perspective gives each one of us tremendous authority and awesome responsibility to enhance or annihilate our collective existence.

It's up to us. I hope you will join me on the path to the soul.

POINTS TO PONDER

NOTE: The preceding chapter does not cover the material to answer all the questions in the following list. However, make an effort to answer them as well as you can before reading the rest of the book. Answer these questions again after reading the rest of the book and compare your pre- and post-reading responses. Compare the two sets of responses and see how the book might have impacted your perspective on these issues.

1. Do you feel that you live your life primarily as a conscious enterprise, or do you have a sense of some

18. Haridas Chadhuri, *The Essence of Spiritual Philosophy* (New Delhi: HarperCollins, 1990), p. 24.

deeper source, some unconscious dimension that has some impact on your life and its direction?

2. Do you have any method or system for making a connection to your inner life?
3. Are you able to use your dreams as a method of maintaining dialogue with your inner life?
4. Are you able to perceive obstacles and disappointments in your life, not only as setbacks, but potentially as whispers of your inner life trying to point you in directions you may not have thought of consciously?
5. When you are confronted with medical or psychiatric problems, relationship difficulties, your own hang-ups or shortcomings, family problems, failures and adversity, do you see these as difficulties to be overcome as soon as possible, or do you feel that these hold important clues from which you can learn and thereby live a more spiritually informed and meaningful life?
6. As you review your life journey so far, do you feel that all your successes, failures, and detours have revolved around some central theme, as if some invisible force or trajectory were guiding you?
7. Do you have some dawning awareness of a deeper sense of purpose in your life guided by an inner wisdom?
8. As you look back on your life so far, do you have an awareness that, as you were busy pursuing your goals, some unintended life pattern has been emerging? Does this unplanned life pattern have some central theme, meaning, or purpose? How is this pattern at variance with your consciously established life goals?
9. How much of your life is based on demands of outer realities? How much do you reflect on some aspect of your deeper, inner, unconscious life and factor it in your deliberations?

10. When dealing with difficult people, problems, or decisions, do you react to the situation or reflect upon it and its meaning in terms of your outer and inner life before acting?
11. Do you make active efforts to reflect daily or regularly upon the connection between your outer life and your inner life, and how your two worlds interface and impact each other?
12. Looking back upon your life, what small and seemingly insignificant event or encounter has had a significant impact on the course and direction of your life?
13. Do you tend to focus on past problems, past glory, future problems and possibilities, or live in the present moment?
14. As you assess your life to date, what contribution do you feel you have made to the community and humanity? Do you feel that, in some way, you have made this world a better place in which to live?

chapter two

Maya, Karma, and Dharma: The School, the Teacher, and the Lesson

Make your doing, eating, sacrificing, giving, and understanding austerity an offering to me, O Son of Kunti.

Thus you will be freed from good and evil fruits. Released from the bondage of action, and with your self disciplined by the yoga of renunciation, released, you will come to me.

—Bhagavad Gita[1]

Maya, *karma*, and *dharma* have often been called the school, the teacher, and the lesson. The school *(maya)*, of course, is life: our individual nature, the fact that we progress through several developmental stages in the course of life, the reality of being interdependent social creatures, and the ultimate necessity of having some sense of where we fit in the grand scheme of things.

Essentially, this book presents a simple, four-step program to make a journey from your present life to realizing the intentions of your soul. There are four basic human pursuits. The first two are *artha* and *kama*. At the most basic level, artha is the pursuit of wealth, and kama is the pursuit of pleasure. The naïve pursuit of artha and kama is called our maya. When maya no longer feels blissful, something calls us from the depths of the soul. This is the call of our dharma, the intentions of our souls. Once we fulfill our dharma—the calling of the soul—we achieve freedom from the tangles and miseries of the human condition, and are deeply connected to our spiritual moorings. This is the state of

---

1. *Bhagavad Gita*, Antonio de Nicolás, trans. (York Beach, ME: Nicolas-Hays, 1990), chapter 9, verses 27–28, p. 74.

freedom, called *moksha*. Our human lives meander through repeated cycles of maya *and* karma as we fulfill more and more aspects of dharma, until we get as close to the center of the soul as is possible in this lifetime. The journey, though simple in theory, is the opus of a lifetime.

As Benjamin Franklin trenchantly remarked, "Experience keeps a dear school, but fools will learn in no other."[2] We are all fools to some extent. But we take a major step toward becoming wise when we recognize that our experience is our most faithful teacher—a teacher that unrelentingly shows us the effects and consequences of our actions. From the living school of our experience, we have an opportunity to learn the lessons that life holds for each of us: that inborn in each of us is a potential that wants to be realized; that each stage of life calls us to change and grow in specific dimensions; that our interdependence as human beings requires us to find ways of living with one another that accord with our nature and the needs of others; and that our little lives are expressions of the Great Life of the soul working through our individual souls.

Living examples make the notions of school, teacher, and lesson—maya, karma, and dharma—easier to grasp. To illustrate the concepts I present throughout this book, I will recount the stories of real people. All the vignettes I offer are based on my clinical experience, but I have protected the identities of the people on whom I model the examples by creating composite figures. Bob (and Terry, and Sara, whom I will present later) vividly illustrate the workings of maya, karma, and dharma—the school, the teacher, and the lesson.

Bob

For the first few sessions with Bob, it felt to me as if a tornado had swept through my office. He came late, his cell phone rang

---

2. Benjamin Franklin, *Maxim's Prefixed to Poor Richard's Almanac*, 1757 (www.bartleby.com/99/245.html).

even in his psychotherapy session, and he constantly tried to catch up with his multiple projects. Sometimes he called me from his car phone to conduct his session as he dashed from one appointment to another. Yet, behind this mask of enterprise, I could see a frightened little boy trying to please me and, unconsciously, his father and other authority figures in his life.

Bob, an energetic and talented man in his 40s in his second marriage, managed a thriving company he created. But Bob was driven, as he had been since childhood. When he was an adolescent, his father demanded that he be engaged in useful work at all times. Weekends were not opportunities for recreation and relaxation, but two more days of tightly scheduled tasks and chores. As an adult, Bob believed he had to take responsibility for everything that went on in his firm. He found it almost impossible to delegate, and it was difficult to demand prompt payment from customers. He worked twelve-and fourteen-hour days, returning home exhausted and short-tempered. Although he had considerable ability as a sculptor and derived a lot of satisfaction from sculpting, he seldom took time to cultivate this talent. His work, he believed, was really for his family, yet, when he was with them, he was often unable to enjoy their companionship. He frequently resented what he perceived as their ingratitude for his labors. His wife got the worst of it. In Bob's eyes, she was to blame for his bad moods, for not supporting him emotionally, for demanding even more emotional connection with him.

As a child, Bob absorbed both his father's expectations for incessant hard work and his sense of unmitigated responsibility. Those expectations became both an unquestioned emotional reality for Bob and his "real world." As a consequence of his way of working, Bob was exhausted and irritable. By not taking care of his needs for relaxation and recreation, he had become incapable of enjoying his wife and children. In his loneliness, he indulged in binge drinking and, when under stress, he smoked heavily. Moreover, neglecting his natural talent for sculpting probably contributed to his bad moods. "He who desires but acts not, breeds pestilence," as William Blake pointed out in his

"Proverbs of Hell."[3] Bob's early conditioning led to emotional assumptions that constitute the world as he now perceives and experiences it.

Recently, Bob had a serious car accident that took him to the edge of life. Throughout his hospitalization and recovery, his wife was at his side, and his employees expressed great concern for him. Looking his mortality in the face has had a sobering effect on Bob.

There are many Bobs in our world, because we all face fundamentally similar challenges and problems in the school of life. Bob used to take the world around him as he perceived it—the world he grew up in—at face value as the only "real world." Now he sees that life holds more possibilities than his father ever led him to believe. Bob is turning his life around.

MAYA, THE SCHOOL, AND THE "REAL WORLD"

Is the world around us the "real world"? The answer to this question is a *qualified* "yes." The world we live in every day is indeed real, but it is not the whole of reality. Rather, it is a limited reality, or a dimension or level of reality. The world in which we go to work, watch out for cars when we cross the street, fall in and out of love, and strive for things that appear to offer satisfaction is the *manifest* aspect of reality. In Hindu thought, it is called maya.

In the introduction I related my dream of the three Jesuit Fathers who, I realized, represented the Trimurti, the Hindu Trinity composed of Brahma/Saraswati, Vishnu/Laxmi, and Shiva/Shakti.[4] The function of Brahma/Saraswati, the name of the universal force in its aspect as creator, is to bring multiplicity into

---

3. William Blake, *The Marriage of Heaven and Hell* (London & Toronto: J. M. Dent and Sons, Ltd., 1932), plate 7.

4. The Hindu *Trimurti* (*tri* = 3, *murti* = idol, image) should be thought of as three god/goddess couples. The female and the male figures represent different aspects of the deity that are inseparable, although in popular depictions they sometimes appear individually.

being in place of the Primal Unity. Thus, it is Brahma who creates maya, the limited or relative realities in which we actually live on Earth, in collaboration with his consort Saraswati, the goddess of knowledge, arts, academic pursuits, and truth. Creative enterprise remains uninformed and ungrounded if Saraswati is not honored.

Although the word *maya* is often translated as "illusion," this is misleading. The Hindu would say that we do need to take the world seriously since as long as it appears real, we must accept it. But the reality of the created world is a limited reality relative to the reality of the soul.

Of the several meanings embraced by the term *maya*, perhaps its fundamental sense is the cosmic creative force that generates concrete worlds, as well as the captivating nature of what is created, which binds souls.[5] In other words, maya refers to the creative force, to what it creates, and to the fascination it exerts on us.

The cosmic creative force finds expression in many ways, including through us. Much of our world has been created by people. Here I am thinking not only of material aspects of the world—the buildings and roads and "things"—but, equally, of the habits of mind and emotion, the attitudes, and the tacit and explicit patterns of expectation and behavior into which we are born that we naively take for granted until our expectations are disappointed. Thus we assume that manifest reality is the *only* reality.

When we understand maya in this way, we also begin to see that Bob unquestioningly took the reality into which he was born and in which he grew up as "the way the world is." Bob believed what his father taught him: that he had to work incessantly; that he had to assume full responsibility; that everything depended on him; that people only wanted what they could get from him.

Usually, this level of awareness—mayic consciousness—is our primary mode in our "first life," when our attention is focused

---

5. Subramuniyaswami, *Dancing with Siva* (Kappa, HI: Himalayan Academy, 1993), p. 759.

primarily on maya—that is, before we realize that our perception of the world is conditioned by many factors over which we have no control. In the first life, we try to establish our mastery on the material plane to ensure our safety, security, and survival, while we attempt to discharge our responsibilities in our daily lives and meet the developmental requirements of the successive stages of life, as child, adult, partner, parent, wage-earner, and so on.

At the level of consciousness where we accept maya as the whole of reality, our ego consciousness and our persona—the "face" we develop and present to the outside world—are in control. Our need for survival and success fuels our efforts. Affirmation from those around us sustains us at this level of existence. We develop an attitude of "tuning in" to the world *around* us, rather than to the world *within* us. Usually the dictates of the people closest to us—parents, siblings, partners, and others—influence our choices and actions more than does our authentic nature. Our primary instruments of survival at this level of consciousness are our acquired and developed ego skills—social conditioning, external adaptation, education, and training.

THE FACE WE TURN TO THE WORLD: THE PERSONA

"Persona" is the term C. G. Jung uses to designate all those skills that constitute our function of adaptation to the outer world, our "outer" face. Our persona usually differs, to a greater or lesser extent, from our real individuality and authentic self, especially in the first life when maya dominates our consciousness. As we develop the persona we have chosen (or that has been chosen for us by our social environment), we neglect substantial aspects of our possibilities. In the process of adapting to the outer world, we often become narrowly focused, just as diverse sources of light, passed through a concave lens, are concentrated into one sharp point.

In the "second life"—after we have been "disillusioned" and life experience has corrected many of our tacit expectations—we broaden our perspective. As light passing through a prism is refracted into the spectrum of colors, our vision and personality become progressively more differentiated as we deliberately reflect on the choices we have made, their outcomes, the many experiences we have had, and their shades of meaning.

Bob's persona, the face he showed to clients and many others outside his home, was one of competence, patience, understanding, and industriousness. Of course, these qualities are valuable. As with any virtue, however, when carried to an extreme they can become a vice. Bob's patience, competence, understanding, and industriousness turned into liabilities when he could no longer choose from a broader range of responses more attuned to the specific situation. Then other people could and did take advantage of Bob by manipulating his virtues for their own benefit. Since he maintained his persona vis-à-vis the world outside his family, that world seldom saw his bad moods, exhaustion, and sense of being exploited that he often let out at home. (Bob has now integrated more into his persona: he is still competent, patient, understanding, and industrious, but he takes better care of himself by not letting other people take advantage of him. As he takes time for his sculpting and his wife and children, he is enjoying life, actually for the first time!)

Since our persona shows the world only a part of who we are, that part we believe the world will accept, what happens to the rest of who we are? There are two possibilities. First, we may *consciously* refrain from expressing or revealing aspects of who we are when we expect or know those sides of our self will be misperceived, condemned, or rejected. We "keep to ourselves" so that we will not be hurt by the reactions of other people. The second possibility is the face we hide *unconsciously* from the world (and often from ourselves), our "shadow."

The Face We Hide from the World

In the broadest sense, the term "shadow" refers to all of our unlived life, both "good" and "bad." The shadow includes all the relatively inferior parts of our personality, which are often transparent to those who know us well, though we may not be consciously aware of them or may wish not to be so. Moreover, the shadow is a real live force in the psyche with, so to speak, a mind of its own. Perhaps you have noticed that when somebody has made reference to your shadow qualities, traits, habits, and/or attitudes that you do not want to own as part of you, you react with denial, hurt, embarrassment, shame, or anger. Sometimes, our shadows can take over and live through us. When that happens, we typically say, "I wasn't myself," or "I don't know what got into me."

We must not forget, however, that our shadows also hold our unlived lives, perhaps even our greatest gifts, that, for one reason or another, we have not cultivated. These sides of our personality may be hidden because they conflict with who we think we are. This is especially the case when we believe we really are what we present to the world—that is, when we identify with our persona. Other aspects of our personality may have been received with such hostility that we have banished them from our awareness, because letting other people see them has caused us too much pain. There are also potentials in each of us that have not been developed for various reasons: lack of opportunity, fear of what others would think, or early social "programming" that labeled those potentials as somehow unacceptable. Nevertheless, these emotional reactions, attitudes, traits, and potentialities are real and alive in us. This, too, is what is called the "shadow." Sometimes, the shadow slips past our conscious control—for example, when we are dreaming, or when we are very emotional—and lives that "other side" of us.

We saw shadow qualities in Bob's anger and resentment at his wife and children, as well as in his neglected sculpting talent and his difficulty collecting from his clients. Bob, however, did not have command of his anger. Rather, it possessed him, and was directed to the wrong people (his wife and children) much of the time. Bob's anger was in his shadow, that part of his personality that is real, but neither assimilated to his consciousness nor appropriately expressed in the world. In addition to the angry man in him, Bob also had a hurting little boy who felt unloved and unlovable, who believed he always had to earn respect and attention and love. He believed that even crumbs of appreciation never just fell his way. Likewise, his sculpting talent was mostly in his shadow as a latent, uncultivated possibility.

As a consequence of having a shadow, we accumulate a lot of unlived life. This reservoir consists of latent talents that never see the light of consciousness, as well as condemned and rejected aspects of personality. When we identify predominantly with our persona, our function of adaptation to the outer world, the shadow rebels by breaking through our mask at inopportune moments, causing us to say the "wrong thing," to forget the name of the person we are introducing, to stumble over the chair when we are trying to leave the room unnoticed. In facing our shadow, we are forced to recognize that more goes on in us than what we consciously intend or permit. The shadow is not all bad, however. Each of us has many undeveloped talents, traits, and skills that would be of value to us if only we could or would develop them. Recognizing our shadow—both its "good" and its "bad" aspects—is the prerequisite for advancing on the path to the soul.

Persona and shadow develop in tandem as we attempt to form a relationship to the world around us. The manifest world, the maya, into which we are born has been shaped by other people over generations. That is the world in which we have to survive. Whatever our world cannot include, anything that we are not strong or courageous or stubborn enough to insist on expressing, becomes shadow, along with all the possibilities whose developmental time has not yet arrived.

When we take maya as our standard of reference, getting and having often outweighs *being:* getting an education, getting a good job, getting married, getting ahead, having a baby, having a home, having friends. We live much of the first phase of life in a heroic mode of striving. The personal and career work we do is often an expression of pride, competitiveness, and adaptation more than of our authentic nature. Even our important relationships have acquisitive and territorial dimensions to them. Our life is more a reflection of our conquest than of our calling. Our leisure time is riddled with personal or work-related struggles rather than filled with joyful collaboration with people we care for.

When we base our choices and actions more on the allure and temptations of the limited reality of the mayic world, we create consequences or "aftereffects" that we have to deal with sooner or later. In Bob's case, we have already seen some of the consequences of his past actions: bad moods, exhaustion, and an overwhelming sense of responsibility. In these results, we see the effects of emotional decisions and choices that Bob made a long time ago.

Our childhood homes profoundly shape our view of the world. Bob learned his role in life from his father: work incessantly, don't ask for gratitude from anybody, present yourself as a nice guy to the outside world, but at home unload the day's frustrations. Bob unconsciously took what he experienced in his parents' home as a microcosm of the world, as the only reality.

In other words, he took a partial reality—maya—for the whole of reality. All of us act on the basis of what we take to be real. Bob acted on his perception of what he took to be real, and his actions had consequences. Actions and the fruit of action—known as karma—together constitute one of the most important principles in Hindu thought.

Terry's Story

Terry, a capable young woman lawyer in her mid-30s, came to her first appointment wearing power clothes: navy-blue suit, white blouse, discrete gold jewelry. Her hair and makeup were impeccable, although I did think she looked a bit thin and her cheekbones seemed a bit too prominent, as though she had been ill and was not fully recovered. She had told me on the phone when she made her appointment that she was depressed and angry.

In our first session, Terry said she hated her career in law, and had been suffering from an eating disorder for many years. Although she was a respected lawyer and performed well on the job, her private life was desolate. When she was not working, she would spend days in bed with the covers pulled up over her head, often crying. Her eating disorder dated from her high school years, and, although she had been in treatment for it from time to time, it persisted unabated, as did her depression and the intense anger she felt, but could not express.

Terry's father had wanted a son who would study law, something he had hoped, but had been unable, to do. Terry had always known that the relationship between her parents was strained and felt responsible for her father's emotional survival. In high school, she had excelled in athletics because sports were important to her father. He had encouraged her to go to law school. Seeing how disappointed he was at her lack of enthusiasm, Terry had—once again—overriden her authentic interests and followed the path her father envisioned. "I felt I had to keep him alive," she said. "He'd die if I didn't." Throughout high school, college, law school, and her law practice, Terry hated herself, but couldn't challenge her fear that her father would die if she disappointed him by doing what she wanted.

Over the course of several months, Terry talked about how meaningless and empty her life felt. She had fantasies of other kinds of work she might like to explore, but couldn't bring herself to give up her high-paying position in the law firm. Her eating disorder abated somewhat as she was able to express her likes, dislikes, thoughts, and needs more often. Cautiously, Terry started to tell her father things she feared would devastate him. In fact, although he was sometimes obviously disappointed, he has been able to acknowledge Terry's right to choose how to live her life.

Terry's choices illustrate the workings of the law of cause and effect called karma. By choosing to please her father rather than following her natural inclinations and developing her own interests, Terry set in motion a chain of events with consequences that have plagued her, generating her depression, her eating disorder, and her self-loathing. This is the basic idea of the law of karma.

Terry continues to face fears she recognizes as irrational, although it is still a struggle for her. Her relationship with her father is much improved. She still hates her job, but is exploring other professional possibilities that would feed her soul more than the practice of law. Since she has realized that not eating was her way of refusing to take in emotional things she "couldn't swallow" and "couldn't stomach," she eats more regularly. Equally important, Terry can now recognize that, when she feels revulsion at the thought of food, she needs to pay attention to what has been going on around her that is emotionally toxic. She can then deal with it rather than avoiding the possible conflict she fears. Terry is retiring the karma she created in her relationship with her father.

KARMA, THE TEACHER

Karma is a Sanskrit word meaning "action." The law of karma implies that the universe reflects an eternal moral order. Behind the apparently blind mechanical forces governing the cosmos, there exists a cosmic intelligence, a power that controls the operations of nature and guides the destiny of humankind. Karma emphasizes the freedom of choice: by the choices we make today, we retire the consequences of past actions and lay the foundation for the future. According to the law of karma, even though our future holds the expectable consequences of our past actions, we can still choose which actions to take in the present. When we understand the law of karma, we find that destiny, properly understood, is not incompatible with human creative freedom. Rather, it is the outcome of the actions we chose in the past whose effects create our present. Likewise, by our actions in the present, we create our own future. As we grow and evolve along spiritual lines, we have the opportunity to set in motion courses of action that bring beneficial, rather than painful, consequences.

Although we may believe that our present actions serve our best and highest interests, these very same actions may either be guided by and serve maya, or may lead us further along the path to the soul. In the first case, actions that serve maya are called mayic karma, and while these may achieve the goals of maya, they may also leave us with the karmic consequences of a neglected inner, spiritual life. These karmic consequences may create our jail or our castle, and are the cause of suffering or the fulfillment of our goals. The thrill of our achievements can seduce us into more mayic actions with their necessary mayic karma.

When the suffering outweighs the seduction of achievement and acquisition, however, life forces us to look for deeper meaning. At this point, we can choose to undertake spiritually informed action that leads us toward the soul. The spiritual principles that guide our karmic action toward the soul are guided by dharma (which I will discuss later). First, however, it is important to distinguish the notion of karma from several other concepts.

The law of karma is not the same as the law of causality in science, the idea of fate in ancient Greek philosophy, or the Islamic theological concept of *kismet*.[6] Causality is the law of cause and effect. It is similar to the idea of karma in the sense that past actions bear subsequent consequences. The law of karma, however, implies that we have the opportunity to modulate the impact of the past by our present choices and actions. Present actions grounded in moral and ethical choices not only atone for the past, they lay the foundation for the meaningful and spiritually fulfilling future course of our lives.

Karma also differs from the Greek philosophical concept of fate. Fate is an irresistible supernatural power that controls our destiny. The Greek tragedies tell us that, in spite of their inner strength, heroism, and supreme moral qualities, humans were dashed by the inscrutable whims of the gods. In both karma and fate, individuals have their lives determined by an invisible force over which they appear not to have much influence.

Karma is not some invisible force that controls us as an external, supernatural power with which we have no organic connection. Rather, the force of karma is the outcome of various actions we chose to perform in the past. We are the architects of our own virtues and vices. What we chose in the past has contributed to the formation of that invisible force that holds sway over us today. Whereas the concept of fate leaves no room for creative freedom, the law of karma directly links our freedom to choose and to act with inevitable consequences, for better or worse.

Karma also differs from *kismet*, the Muslim belief that the life of each individual is rigorously and rigidly predetermined from cradle to grave. Kismet is neither a blind, invisible, natural force, nor a supernatural power independent of humans. Rather, the

---

6. This and the following discussion of fate and kismet are drawn from Haridas Chaudhuri, *The Essence of Spiritual Philosophy* (New Delhi: HarperCollins India, 1990), p. 56ff.

force of kismet is rooted in the will of all-powerful Allah. Humans simply have no freedom.

Let us return for a moment to Bob and Terry. When we are captive to maya, we base our choices and actions on our perception of a partial reality. We fit ourselves to the world we perceive, and present ourselves accordingly. That is, we develop our persona. Usually, we neglect or suppress substantial aspects of our authentic self and our potential (which accumulates as shadow). The choices we make lead to the consequence aspect of karma, which, sooner or later, will have to be addressed, acknowledged, and retired.

As I said earlier, action undertaken in the service of maya is called mayic-karmic action. The predominant action aspect of Bob's mayic karma was his compulsive working. The consequence aspect of his mayic karma was exhaustion, irritability with wife and children, and the feeling that people wanted him only for what they could get from him. (This was, in fact, unfounded: Bob generalized his father's expectations of him and believed other people had expected what his father expected.) Bob's emotional belief system—his maya—trapped him in a vicious circle of action and outcome that was self-perpetuating.

Terry's maya was grounded in her emotional belief that she had to keep her father emotionally alive by doing his bidding, whether or not it suited her interests and inclinations. As a consequence, when she acted on her father's designs for her—the action aspect of her mayic karma—she developed an eating disorder, depression, and self-loathing.

As we have seen in these two examples, karma means that our action bears fruit that may be bitter. Better-informed action can bear sweeter fruit. We may like or regret the results. We are not, however, condemned to repeat our patterns eternally. As I discussed earlier, we always have the possibility of choosing our actions and thereby influencing the consequences of our choices. When the karmic consequences begin to disturb us, and we start to question the assumptions that underlie our seemingly self-evident path, we have taken *the* major step toward interrupting the vicious cause-and-effect circle of mayic karma. As our consciousness widens, we have the possibility of making new choices in old situations that will lead to different, and hopefully more desirable, outcomes.

By questioning the absolute reality of our maya, our consciousness develops into a karmic consciousness: becoming aware of our mayic patterns and karmic consequences empowers us to change our self-defeating ways. With this shift in consciousness we open ourselves to Vishnu/Laxmi and Shiva/Shakti, two members of the Trimurti who represent the transpersonal forces that work to maintain right order and destroy our limited mayic consciousness.

We first become aware of one aspect of the Trimurti—Shiva/Shakti, the force that destroys the tyrannical hold of maya—when the system breaks down, the relationship doesn't work, or medical, psychiatric, or emotional symptoms hint that what we thought was our castle has turned out also to be our jail. We hope that there is a world beyond the walls we now see surrounding us.

Shiva/Shakti presides over the creation of a spiritual attitude that can lead to a new order, a new/renewed life after the destruction of the old. The mystery of Shiva/Shakti is that destruction *always* holds the potential and promise to renew life and remove obstacles that keep us from actualizing our spiritual potential. We can, for example, view the painful consequences of our choices as Shiva/Shakti trampling us underfoot. We can learn to see people who confront us or who force us to look at ourselves and our actions as Shiva/Shakti's agents. Or we may have a dream that shows something being destroyed.

Karmic consequences inform us of another dimension of reality. Gradually, we sense a life beyond our maya. The latent life beyond the manifest, mayic world awakens us to the hidden meaning and mystery of our lives—our dharma. To make the transition from a mayic to a dharmic attitude, however, we must first develop a karmic attitude. That means we recognize that our actions have created—and will continue to create—much of the reality we confront. With our karmic attitude in place, our dharmic awareness grows in scope and depth as we tune into the whispers of the soul. Having prepared the soil for our new lives in this way, it is the task of Vishnu/Laxmi to guide our steps into the realm of dharma.

Vishnu, called the "All Pervasive," "The Preserver," represents the cohesive force that maintains the continuity of existence and the timeless order of nature that interconnects all that exists. Laxmi is the patron goddess of wealth, prosperity, and peace, the prerequisites for maintaining the dharmic order in the world. Periodically, when necessary, Vishnu reincarnates in one of his several forms *(avatars)* to reestablish the timeless order. Vishnu/Laxmi can work through the sage and time-tested advice our friends may give us. We may experience Vishnu/Laxmi speaking through wisdom books such as the Bible, the Koran, the *Tao Te Ching*, or the *Bhagavad Gita*. They may appear in dreams as the wise old man or woman, as the animal that speaks to us and guides us, or as a talking stone or tree. Sometimes, Vishnu/Laxmi confronts us with our dharma—our spiritual tasks and path—in a life-threatening or near-death experience. Working together, Shiva/Shakti and Vishnu/Laxmi speed us on the dharmic path to the soul.

DHARMA, THE LESSON

In the Bhagavad Gita, the centuries-old exemplary text of Hindu culture, Vishnu, in his incarnation as Krishna, instructs Prince Arjuna, addressing him as Bhàrata:

> *For whenever there is a decrease in* dharma, *O Bhārata,*
> *And a rise in* adharma,
> *Then I send forth myself.*
>
> *For the protection of the good and the destruction of evil,*
> *For the purpose of the establishment of* dharma,
> *I am born from age to age.*[7]

---

7. *Bhagavad Gita*, chapter 4, verses 7–8, p. 48.

Vishnu represents the archetypal tendency that holds the universe together, the cohesive force that maintains the continuity of existence. When he speaks of the "standard of sacred duty," he is referring to dharma.[8] In his Krishna form, Vishnu tells Arjuna that he reincarnates whenever *adharma* (the opposite of dharma) prevails over dharma. He is revealing to Arjuna that he reappears in a form that will sponsor individual or community actions (karma) that are needed to move us out of our waywardness in maya and back onto the path of dharma. Hence, at all the crucial moments, Vishnu appears in some form to guide the evolution and destiny of the different orders of creation, species, forms of life, and people.

Another way to describe the "timeless order of nature," dharma, is as archetypal patterns and natural laws. By archetypal, I mean those innate "natural laws" that structure and govern instinct, development, behavior, emotion, and imagery in all forms of life. The various archetypes are analogous to the natural laws in the physical sciences. In terms of dharma, there are four principal aspects, or archetypal dimensions, ranging from the individual to the cosmic.

SVADHARMA: THE FIRST LESSON

The first lesson that maya and karma teach us is that our innate, individual pattern finds expression in our particular physical, mental, and emotional nature. Svadharma is the calling to honor and actualize our individual uniqueness. A metaphor is helpful here. If you are an oak tree, be content to grow acorns and let the peach tree grow peaches. The fairy tale, "The Tree that Wanted Other Leaves," points to the same truth: we can realize the other three dharmas only through being what we actually are. Hence svadharma is dharma individualized. It depends on one's

---

8. The term *dharma* has been translated in many ways, often as "divine law," "law of being," "way" or "righteousness," "religion," "duty," "responsibility," "virtue," "justice," "goodness," and "truth." Some of this reflects the concretization and literalization that befalls profound insights as people attempt to grasp the relevance of the insight for their lives.

karma, gender, race, community, physical characteristics, health, intellectual endowment, emotional constitution, desires and interests, and strengths and weaknesses. The astrological birth chart, for example, diagrams our svadharma, clearly indicating the interrelationship among our assets and liabilities. Within the limits set and the challenges posed by our svadharma, we fulfill the other three dharmas.

ASHRAMA DHARMA: THE SECOND LESSON

Ashrama dharma refers to the necessary developmental tasks of each of life's several stages—the calling to fulfill the responsibilities life presents us as we mature. Throughout life, new developmental stages challenge us to grow beyond ourselves. Adolescence transforms the child; marriage and family transform the single young adult into parent and householder. When the children leave home and the nest is empty, we enter another developmental stage that calls us again to change and transform from parenting children to mentoring younger adults, often other people's children, often also younger colleagues and coworkers. And as we look forward to our later decades, we become more concerned with the meaning of life and spiritual issues than with the day-to-day affairs of the world.

VARNA DHARMA: THE THIRD LESSON

Varna dharma calls us to fulfill our responsibilities to community. Our needs for one another are non-negotiable beyond a certain point. That is to say, our social needs are part of our human constitution, not completely a matter of our personal choice. Varna dharma, "the law of one's kind," defines our interpersonal responsibilities within family, community, class, occupation, society, and nation.

RETA DHARMA: THE FOURTH LESSON

The lesson of *reta dharma* is clearly the most spiritual of the four. Reta is the calling of the divine principle and law underlying all things. At the level of the human individual, *reta dharma* is that archetypal drive to relate to a "higher power." We can think of reta dharma as honoring the transpersonal powers that move in us by giving appropriate expression to those powers, each of us in our unique way in accord with our svadharma and in the context of our ashrama dharma and our varna dharma. In other words, spirituality and caring for the soul is part and parcel of being human.

Actions, Outcomes, and Dharma

The four facets of dharma are intertwined and interdependent. However, actualization of our innate potential (our svadharma) depends on adequate fulfillment of our developmental tasks (ashrama dharma) at each stage of life. Together they constitute the foundation that supports our endeavors to fulfill our responsibilities to our fellow creatures (varna dharma) and to manifest our spiritual instinct (reta dharma). In other words, if we aren't living our authentic selves in an age-appropriate way, our relationship to our community and to our spiritual life will suffer.

We can see the interdependence of the four facets of dharma and the karmic actions and outcomes in Bob's life. Bob's maya centered around his need for his father's approval. To obtain his approval, Bob tried to live the life his father had both modeled and insisted on: unrelenting work and the accumulation of (material) wealth. However, in this narrow scope, pursuit of material wealth and slavish attachment to the personal parental dimensions of maya, Bob lived in the relative, limited, or provisional manifest reality that concretely surrounded him. His pursuit of the fourfold good was likewise limited.

Chaturvarga: The Fourfold Good

Chaturvarga refers to the four pursuits of human life in which we may legitimately engage. Dharma is the steady guide for the other three: artha (wealth), kama (pleasure, love, enjoyment), and moksha (liberation).

The most primal of human activities are in pursuit of artha—the wealth and prosperity necessary for security and survival, and kama—the pleasure that gets us into relationships, fosters procreation and new life, forges our attachments, and ensures the continuation of our species. In the Hindu view, however, wealth (artha) is guided by dharma and therefore encompasses much more than material possessions. Artha includes the basic needs—food, money, clothing, and shelter—and extends to the wealth required to maintain a comfortable home, raise a family, fulfill a successful career, and realize our spiritual tasks. In its broadest sense, artha includes the blessing of worthy children, good friends, leisure time, trustworthy colleagues, and the means to support worthy causes.

Bob's slavish attachment to his father was an aspect of the desire for pleasure, kama. Kama is likewise a broad concept that includes the sensual pleasures (earthly love, sexuality), aesthetic and cultural fulfillment, the joys of family, intellectual satisfaction, and the enjoyment of security, creativity, usefulness, and inspiration. As we saw, Bob's single-minded quest for his father's approval and the satisfaction and joy that would offer him eclipsed many other dimensions of kama in his life.

Bob's actions—compulsive work done to win his father's approval by accumulating material wealth—kept him locked in the realm of maya. He continued to engage in mayic-karmic actions that perpetuated the vicious mayic-karmic circle of consequences of his life with his dark moods, angry outbursts at home, and feelings of being exploited by one and all. Bob's plight prevented him from actualizing other aspects of his innate potential (his svadharma, particularly his sculpting talent) and his development into an autonomous adult (the next stage of his ashrama dharma). Fortunately, Bob has developed a karmic consciousness—an awareness that the means he has chosen are not leading him to the goal he seeks, a sense of himself as a worthwhile man in his own right, not dependent on others for his emotional well-being, an identity free from the tyranny of his overbearing father.

Like Bob, Terry was also caught in a mayic-karmic loop. Her codependent imperative to keep her father emotionally alive by attempting to fulfill his plans for her was only one, limited yet concrete, facet of kama, pleasure. She tried to please him (mayic-karmic actions) so that she could feel pleasure in his emotional presence. Since Terry has recognized that she was caught in a vicious circle, she is mustering the courage to break out of it. She sees that her father does, in fact, emotionally survive her acts of self-assertion and autonomy. As she challenges her emotional belief (maya) by following her inclinations and interests, she is actualizing more of her innate potential (svadharma), and, at the same time, furthering her transition from dependent (codependent) child to mature adult (the next stage of her ashrama dharma).

As we can see, Terry's and Bob's attachments blinded both of them to other possibilities that life offers, and kept them stuck in a pre-adult level of development (the mayic-karmic consequences), so they could not move on to the independence and autonomy appropriate to the adult stage of ashrama dharma. As we progressively actualize the possibilities and potential in ourselves, we diminish our identification with our persona, the face we turn to the world, and reclaim aspects of ourselves from our shadow. These steps lead us toward the soul and the freedom from entanglement in maya that Hindu thought calls moksha.

Moksha: Caring Detachment

All individuals have the potential to achieve the state of *moksha*, liberation from the misery of the human condition and the repetitive cycles of maya and karma. Moksha comes through the fulfillment of dharma, artha, and kama. In other words, when we have lived life to the full, and have actualized our innate potentials, then our desires for artha and kama (wealth and pleasure in their various forms) no longer drive us. We are no longer attached to worldly joys or sorrows. This does *not* mean, however, that we have become indifferent to life on this planet.

In Hindu teachings, we are free from the cycles of reincarnation when we reach the full state of moksha. While I do not propose to discuss the intricate subject of reincarnation and its clinical and metapsychological implications here, it is important to point out that we are symbolically reincarnated in many cycles of maya and karma in our current lifetime as Vishnu/Laxmi, the transpersonal force that maintains the right order of the universe, guides us toward realizing our dharmic potential.

Metapsychological perspective aside, the best empirical, pragmatic, and clinical description of moksha—for me personally and in my work with individuals—is that of "caring detachment." Caring detachment comes from living life fully, not from avoiding it. The caringly detached person is a very active participant in the affairs of self, family, community, and the spirit, yet detached from the outcome of his or her endeavors. Work and life then become God's work, not a personal quest. Moksha is the detachment from the *outcome* not from *engagement* in the enterprise itself, since, to fulfill life, we must live it as duty to the spirit and to God, however we may conceive that higher power.

In the Bhagavad Gita, Lord Krishna counsels his protégé, Arjuna, to do God's work. Arjuna is ambivalent about fighting the war to restore the right order. In several passages, Krishna aptly conveys the inner state of an individual who has achieved moksha, which is the attitude Arjuna needs to develop in order to fulfill the task set him:

> *Seers know "renunciation" to be the giving up*
> *of acts of desire;*
>
> *"Detachment" is the relinquishing*
> *of the fruit of all action.*[9]

We all have the possibility of attaining moksha, or at least some degree of it, provided that we let our life experience temper our willfulness and fear. When we can care in a detached way, we can be deeply involved in the enterprise without worrying about the outcome. Our participation is intense—full of integrity and concern for what we have undertaken. Caring detachment is like the love of a grandparent whose parenting is intense, full of love and integrity, but free from preoccupation with the outcome of parenting. When in the company of such people, we feel as though we are in the presence of a silent deep ocean. The life and story of Mahatma Gandhi, as one such individual, has always inspired me.

---

9. *Bhagavad Gita*, chapter 18, verse 2, p. 117.

Gandhi

Gandhi's life exemplifies a living dharma. In Mohandas Gandhi, the Mahatma, we recognize the evolution of an individual soul and its profound effects on the evolution of our living together on this small planet.

After Gandhi had completed formal training to be a barrister in England, he was unsuccessful in establishing a thriving practice there or, later, in India. Like many Indian professionals of his time, he decided to try his fortune in South Africa. At this point, Gandhi's life was directed by the callings of maya: the wish for professional success, artha, and for the pleasure of his father's approval, kama. This led to the mayic-karmic actions of leaving his homeland, and migrating first to Great Britain for barrister training, and later to South Africa to establish his law practice.

In South Africa, Gandhi's destiny and dharma had other plans in store for him. A trivial but significant event changed the course of his life, and eventually that of human consciousness worldwide. Traveling by train on a first-class ticket he had purchased by mail order, he was fifty miles into his journey when a white passenger objected to sharing his compartment with a non-white. Because Gandhi was a brown man in white-dominated South Africa, he was not permitted to travel in the first-class compartment. The passenger and a railroad official forcibly ejected Gandhi at the next station, strewing his belongings all over the platform.

Gandhi felt humiliated and dejected. He had just experienced the dark side of human nature and the ugly face of racism. He sat on the platform till dawn, thinking about how he would seek justice from his white oppressors. By morning, he had his inspiration and his answer. He would seek justice and fair treatment, but in *his* way—the nonviolent way.

This hurtful event turned out to be a transformative experience, a major step in his evolution as an individual and a soul. It launched him on his lifelong quest for Indian independence from the British, and, more importantly, for the liberation of humankind from its dark side. As his tactic, Gandhi embraced the ancient Hindu principle of *ahimsa*, usually rendered in English as "nonviolence." As we know, Gandhi's protest and his doctrines became the spiritual and tactical framework for the Reverend Martin Luther King's movement for equality for all races in America. Gandhi's approach seeded a whole new consciousness-raising movement throughout the Eastern and Western worlds. Gandhi was propelled into his svadharma—his selfhood—by his own mode of protest, which was soulful, not spiteful. Simultaneously, he continued to fulfill his ashrama dharma by maintaining his law practice, but more to enable him to act as a spiritual than as a legal guide to his fellow South Africans. More importantly, he was impelled into his varna dharma by providing a spiritual framework to guide both the oppressor and the oppressed in South Africa toward a spiritually informed engagement with each other. This template became the foundation and cornerstone of Gandhi's philosophy and his legacy to the community, his ultimate varna dharma, encapsulated in the following four principles.[10]

1. *Satyagraha* (Sanskrit; *satya* = truth, *agraha* = insistence) is the principle of pursuit of and insistence on truth at any cost. Eventually, this became the cornerstone of contemporary Indian philosophy, as *Satya Mave Jayate* (Hail the truth).
2. *Ahimsa* (*a* = lack of, *himsa* = violence) is the principle of nonviolence. Gandhi's principles advocate prohibition of physical, emotional, or spiritual violence against self or an adversary. One may confront the dark side of the self or the other, but only with love, and with an awareness of the humanity of self and the other and their underlying goodness.
3. *Trusteeship* implies that our personal strengths, skills, assets, and potentialities are merely in our safekeeping on behalf of the community. While we may enjoy our gifts for personal

10. Personal communication from Arun Gandhi, grandson of Mahatma Gandhi, September 24th, 1995.

survival, eventually they must be used for community good, as directed by our inner, spiritual instincts. To me, trusteeship implies a movement away from a mayic mode of existence, in which we use our gifts for personal survival, toward the ashrama dharmic mode, in which we use our gifts and assets for family and others we love. Finally, we use our potentialities for our individual maturation (svadharma), community service (varna dharma), and for God's work (reta dharma).

4. *Constructive action* addresses the issue at hand in a manner that honors the humanity and morality of the adversary, and yet highlights the injustice of the situation in a way that restores the right and dignity of the oppressed. This mode of action abstains from generating negative karma, even with one's adversary, and provides the opportunity to the other to accumulate positive karma, and perhaps even ascend to the dharmic level of consciousness by doing right in spite of apparent might.

The ejection of Gandhi from the train, a small, rather common event in the lives of many minorities in South Africa at the time, became a call to Gandhi to undertake his life's work. Starting a revolution was not something he had planned to do; rather, it was fidelity to the law of his being, the orderly fulfillment of his inherent nature (svadharma) that recruited him as an actor to play out its script. Gandhi's decision on the station platform led to a globally significant shift in human social consciousness that has altered the way we live together in the world.

Gandhi's decision, after his night of soul-searching on the train platform in South Africa, was dharmic. His frustrated attempts to build a law practice (mayic-karmic action), his purchase of a first-class train ticket (again mayic-karmic action in the service of kama and artha), and his subsequent rude ejection from the first-class compartment (karma consequence) imply that his initial desire was not in accord with dharma, his vocation or calling. Apparently, it was not Gandhi's lot in life to find a niche in the established order. Rather, his dharma had other plans for him.

To live out our dharma, we are called upon to make a sacrifice of our maya and karma. Taking Gandhi as our example, we can see that, initially, he lived at the level of mayic consciousness. He wanted to succeed as an attorney in his professional life. Because of the traumatic experience of making a railway journey in South Africa, he might have chosen to devote his professional life as a lawyer to furthering the cause of civil rights in the British Empire. That would have been very commendable in itself, and it would have meant that he had then moved from a mayic to a karmic level of existence.

But his vocation was of the highest nature: he was called upon, not only to advocate for the rights of minorities in the British Empire, but also to establish a whole new mode of moral and spiritual protest against the forces of the dark side of human nature, both British and Indian. Through the movements he initiated for nonviolent protest and civil disobedience, Gandhi became a great advocate for oppressed Indian minorities and women within Indian society itself. One of the causes dearest to his heart was the plight of the so-called untouchable castes in India—people who were relegated to the bottom of the ladder of the highly stratified caste-conscious Indian society.

What Gandhi launched was far beyond even his own individual ethics and karma. His actions were spiritually informed, an example par excellence of dharmic karma: spiritually informed choices and actions. His was an entirely new mode of morality and cultural dialogue. That was the call of reta dharma working through his svadharma. Fortunately for him and for the rest of the human race, he was able to respond to the call and live a dharmic existence that advanced civilization to a new level of maturation and consciousness. In the final analysis, while Ghandi's life served the human community by enhancing its spiritual consciousness, it also served to reassert the rule of God over the rule of humanity, the reta-dharma consciousness.

At the end of his life, Gandhi's worldly possessions were worth less than two dollars. Gandhi had achieved a great degree of moksha, of liberation from the allure of the relative reality we experience as the world about us that Hinduism calls maya.

Sara, the Rock Lady

While Gandhi's life is history and the stuff of legends, I have been privileged to work with many individuals who have made journeys no less courageous than Gandhi's, but who are not well-known. One of my patients who has achieved moksha in many areas of her life is Sara, the Rock Lady.

When I met Sara, I felt as though I were in the serene, meditative, and peaceful precinct of a holy temple. She had a quietly reassuring inner strength about her. Yet Sara was troubled. She was depressed and lacked joy in her life. She felt overburdened by her work and tremendous family obligations. She had assumed responsibility for her demented mother, who was in a nursing home, the care of her two daughters, who were in the throes of serious mental illness, and was concerned about an alcoholic brother who denied his addiction and refused treatment.

Sara was in her 50s. A highly regarded professional, she worked as an advocate for disadvantaged children. She was the oldest child from a large family with an alcoholic father and depressed mother, and she had been the designated caretaker of her younger siblings. She never had much time for herself. Indeed, she was codependent in her focus on taking care of others to assure her own self-esteem. Sara's web of excessive attachment to her family had the inevitable consequence of making her emotionally alienated from her husband; she was unable to enjoy her professional success and passion for her work, and she was depressed.

Although she suffered from it, Sara likewise believed, at an emotional level, that she had to take care of anyone and everyone; she felt she had to be serene, infinitely patient, never expressing displeasure, or fatigue, or disagreement. Sara knew she needed help.

Sara's persona—her passion for helping abused children, her commitment to her family, and her serene, meditative, and peaceful appearance—exhibited authentic traits of her character. Since her persona ruled unchallenged, however, Sara had little choice in the way she related to people and situations. She felt she *had* to be serene, *had* to take care of her depressed mother and her alçoholic brother, just as she *had* to take care of all her younger siblings as a girl in her parents' home. What Sara's persona—the face she turned to the world—did not show was her depression, the lack of joy in her life, her feeling of being overburdened.

When I looked at Sara's shadow, I found a frustrated natural drive for self-assertion, competence, and autonomy, as well as a deep but hidden spirituality and a very well-concealed anger at feeling trapped in her family circumstances. Sara's frustrated, positive shadow qualities expressed themselves as lack of energy, low self-esteem, and depression that was further fueled by her hidden anger. Although active in her church, Sara felt that she did not have adequate opportunity to express her spirituality.

Then she had the following dream, which she reported in a crucial session. *"I am lying down and there is a large rock on my chest."* (There were a lot of additional details in the dream that are not relevant to the present discussion.) We analyzed this dream at length. Dreams are the whispers of the soul and relay crucial information that prompts us on the path to spirituality. So what was Sara's dream encouraging her to do?

As is turned out, this dream was a turning point in her life, calling her to move from maya to dharma. The rock was on the right side of her chest. Sara had a history of cancer of the left breast, which had been successfully treated surgically five years earlier. This dream concerned me, because I feared that it might be indicative of some problem with the right breast. Sara agreed to a consultation at the Mayo Clinic. Fortunately, we were in good time for preventive intervention and she was started on prophylactic Tamoxifen therapy for prevention of breast cancer. The dream was also giving us a deeper signal, however, one that went beyond the medical warning. The rock was reminiscent of the crushing feelings of depression with which Sara was struggling. But what was she to do about them?

In psychotherapy, Sara started to explore the rock as a symbol of her mayic-karmic actions. The karmic consequence of her choices was the burden of codependency she carried all her life by taking care of others who were now in a position to take responsibility for themselves. Now she began to ponder karmic choices based on dharmic goals.

She started developing an attitude of caring detachment. One weekend, she decided to go to a professional conference in Chicago rather than stay on call for her mother, who had an army of nursing home staff to assist her. Sara was, after all, only ninety minutes away, as well as being accessible on her cell phone in case of emergency. Sara started to reclaim her life in incremental steps, while still staying available to her family when really needed.

Now that the mayic-karmic consequences of her rock burden are retired, Sara and her husband have rekindled the fire of their companionship, romance, and sexual and spiritual intimacy. Where does the rock want her to go next? What is the dharmic message of the rock? We have been working on the symbol of her rock for several months to realize its full potential. At this point, she has broken the web of mayic attachments and retired the negative karmic consequences created between herself and her husband. What is to be her future dharmic path?

One of her further associations is to the "Rock of Gibraltar," a symbol of strength and stability. Sara and I have continued to research the mythological context of the rock image. Of the several myths she has discovered, the myth of the Mithra touches her the most. Mithra is the god of the Mithraic tradition, well-known for his strength. Mithra was born out of a rock. He was a warrior and protector of the weak and the just. Is this perhaps part of Sara's dharma? This has turned out to be precisely the case.

Sara has freed herself from the throes of her mayic attachment and the tangles of her codependent caretaker role in her family of origin. She has retired her negative karma with her husband and restored her intimacy with him. Now she feels free to achieve her dharma as a rock-solid individual and professional. She enjoys her work with renewed passion. At age 40, she had gone back to school to complete her professional training. Now, more than ten years later, she is harvesting the fruits of her enterprise. This is her svadharma, her duty to herself to honor her own innate potential. She had more than retired her ashrama (or family-life stage) dharma, not only through helping and caring for her family of origin far beyond the call of duty, but also had launched her own children as best she could. Now she is responding to numerous invitations to be on community agency boards, not for self-aggrandizement, but motivated by a deep desire to serve.

She is passionate about her causes; she does volunteer work that expresses her community or varna dharma. Sara is fully living out her life symbol and is a true rock of strength and service in her community. Her life now marches to the tune of her spiritual calling. She is connected to her soul and to that spiritual calling—her reta dharma—doing not only her own, but also God's work. As it says in the Christian scriptures, "Let Thy Will Be Done."[11]

I am deeply moved by Sara's selfless service to her community and to her God. Sara takes seriously Christ's words as recorded by St. Matthew:

> *Then the King will say to those at his right hand, "Come, you whom my Father has blessed, take for your heritage the kingdom prepared for you since the foundation of the world. For I was hungry and you gave me food; I was thirsty and you gave me drink; I was a stranger and you made me welcome, naked and you clothed me, sick and you visited me, in prison and you came to see me." Then the virtuous will say to him in reply, "Lord, when did we see you hungry and feed you; or thirsty and give you drink? And when did we see you a stranger and make you welcome; naked and clothe you; sick or in prison and go to see you?" And the King will answer, "I tell you solemnly, in so far as you did it to one of the least of these brothers of mine, you did it to me."* (Chapter 25:34–40)

Sara is a Quaker and an active participant in the Quaker Prison Visitation Committee. The committee meeting consists of sev-

---

11. In his translation of the Lord's Prayer from the Aramaic, Neil Douglas-Klotz renders this line with eloquence and deep psychological insight: "Create in me a divine cooperation—from many selves, one voice, one action." Neil Douglas-Klotz, trans., *Prayers of the Cosmos: Meditations on the Aramaic Words of Jesus*, foreword by Matthew Fox (San Francisco: HarperSanFrancisco, 1994), p. 22.

eral members who go to a regional correctional institution every month to visit between five and twenty-five inmates. They go in friendship, but not to convert anyone. The visits usually begin in typical Quaker silence with all sitting in a circle. After about fifteen minutes, they begin a Quaker worship sharing. People respond, and the hope is that they speak from their hearts. Angry talk or arguing is discouraged. Responses to queries reveal information about beliefs, behaviors, and life experience. Some of the group respond in depth, some superficially, depending upon their trust levels. Some inmates grow in sensitivity, in their ability to manage conflict, and in their insight into others' opinions about themselves. The meetings act as a catalyst for positive and adaptive change, not just for the inmates, but also for the participating Quaker volunteers. Sara's participation in the Quaker Prison Visitation Committee is a commendable example of varna dharma, her relationship to community. For Sara, however, it is also an opportunity to express her innermost essence—her svadharma—as well as to do God's work, reta dharma.

Restoring Right Order: Maya, Karma, and Dharma as a Path to the Soul

Whenever my grandmother responded to my complex problems with the simple three-step maya-karma-dharma approach, I was outwardly respectful, but inwardly skeptical of such a primitive formula for approaching the intricacies of human life. Sensing this, from time to time she would tell me the story of Vamana, the dwarf incarnation of Vishnu.

Bali, the son of Virochana and the grandson of Prahlada, was the king of the *asuras*, evil spirits that can and do interact with the physical plane, causing all sorts of problems in people's lives. (In our lives, Bali represents our shadow tendencies that attempt to usurp our spiritual potential for personal, mayic gain.) By his sacrifice and valor, Bali became very powerful and gained dominion over the three worlds—the Earth plane (the *bhuloka*), the astral plane (the *antarloka*), and the plane of the gods (the *shivaloka*)—thereby depriving Indra, King of the Celestials, of his abode. Bali's power threatened the right order of the universe. Indra and the demi-gods propitiated Vishnu, begging him to come to their rescue, as there was danger of the three worlds being overrun by the asuras. Aditi, Indra's mother, was pained, and she asked Vishnu to be born of her and kill Bali. Vishnu agreed and was born as Vamana, the dwarf, in the home of a Brahman.

On reaching boyhood, Vamana went to King Bali and begged him for alms. The priest of the asuras warned Bali that the beggar was Vishnu. Bali was generous, however, and readily agreed to give the beggar whatever he wished. He even boasted that, if Vishnu himself should come to him as *Yajna purush*, the divine embodiment of sacrifice, and ask for a favor on the occasion of the sacrifice, Bali would consider it to be the greatest honor that could be shown to him.

Vamana asked for space equal to three of his strides. When Bali assured Vamana that his wish would be granted, Vamana grew to tremendous size and, in two strides, covered Earth (the bhuloka) and the space between heaven and Earth (the antarloka). Since there was no space left for Vamana's third stride, Bali offered himself, and Vamana placed his foot on Bali's head and pushed him down into the netherworld, thereby saving the three worlds from the atrocities of the asuras.

This story had always intrigued me. When we have lost our sense of dharma in the maze of life and gotten inflated, like King Bali, with our conquests and power in the world of maya, we sow and eventually reap tons of negative karmic consequences: toes stepped on, relationships compromised, life unlived, potentialities ignored. When this state of psychic imbalance prevails, the healing part of the psyche, what the Hindus call Lord Vishnu, is activated to set us back on the path to the soul and to restore balance and order, that is, dharma.

The Vishnu dimension of the psyche awakens when the allure of maya and the effects of karma divert us from the spiritual life and the path of dharma. Then Lord Shiva, the Destroyer, appears to eradicate the imbalances in our lives that may manifest as medical or psychiatric illness, relationship problems, or a loss of joy and passion about life and its gifts.

In subsequent chapters, I will discuss many such states of dharmic imbalance and the loss of soul. Modern psychiatry, as well as timeless Hindu templates, help us understand what we experience, and aid us in reclaiming our souls and reconfiguring our lives so that we reestablish the guiding presence of dharma on the path to the soul.

POINTS TO PONDER

1. How would you describe the mayic goals of your present life? How do they manifest in the sectors of your personal and your professional life?
2. To what extent have you mastered mayic goals in your life? How adequate and successful do you feel in the areas of work, relationship, material possessions, accomplishments, and social skills? How secure are you in terms of your basic survival?
3. How well does your mask (persona) mediate between your inner sense of yourself and the world in which you move?
4. What would you identify as your unlived life (shadow)? How does it manifest—as regrets, as latent talents, as envy toward others, as a certain part of your personality you do not like and would be uncomfortable presenting to others?
5. Which of your past actions carry major consequences for your present life?
6. What are you doing to undo the consequences of past actions?
7. What choices can you make in your life today that are likely to have a positive impact on your future life and relationships?
8. What are you doing in your life today to make you feel safe, successful, and secure?
9. Which area of your life's responsibilities (to family, community, personal growth, higher power) is presently your primary focus of attention and effort?
10. As you reflect on the course of your life, what patterns do you recognize involving maya (your percep-

tion of what you took to be reality), karma (your actions and their consequences), and dharma (your attempts at realizing or approaching some central, governing meaning)?

11. From your cycles of maya, karma, and dharma, what have you learned to date about your perception of "reality," the results of your actions, and the central core of meaning attempting to inform your life?
12. In chaturvarga (the fourfold good), dharma (the central core of meaning) governs the other three aspects, artha (wealth), kama (pleasure), and moksha (liberation). How would you assess the following: artha (your achievement of material, financial, emotional, and relational wealth); kama (your level of pleasure, enjoyment, love, intellectual, aesthetic, and cultural fulfillment); and moksha (liberation or detachment from the allures of maya and the freedom to make choices that create "good" rather than "bad" karma).
13. In your personal experience, cite an example of a person you know who you believe has lived a dharmic life (it doesn't have to be a famous or rich or powerful person).

chapter three

Physical and Emotional Symptoms as a Portal to the Soul

. . . if we can reconcile ourselves to the mysterious truth that the spirit is the life of the body seen from within, and the body the outward manifestation of the life of the spirit—the two being really one. . . .

—C. G. Jung[1]

Mr. Powers, a very successful executive who consulted me with complaints of depression, said in a session one day, "The depression is getting in my way"—in the way, that is, of success in his business. I commented that, from what I knew about his life circumstance, depression was the only way to his healing, and to wholeness and balance in his life. This was a very accurate interpretation on my part. Whenever he got depressed, he was less compulsive about work. He spent more quality time with his wife and children, took time to read, reflect, and meditate on the meaning, direction, and purpose of his life. In the past, whenever his depression lifted, he again got overinvolved in work. By "robbing" him of energy, his depression compensated for his workaholic excesses.

Depression is one of the most frequent, painful, and medically treatable of psychiatric disorders, and it can be aggressively treated using both medication and psychotherapy. Therapists and patients alike, however, consistently bypass the soul-healing

1. C. G. Jung, "The Spiritual Problem of Modern Man," in *Civilization in Transition*, CW10 (Princeton: Princeton University Press, 1970), ¶195.

aspects of depression. Depression is often a messenger of the soul that arrives with the script for reestablishing balance and wholeness in life. Medical and psychiatric conditions are Janus-faced: they look both to the past and to the future.

THE JANUS FACES OF MEDICAL AND PSYCHIATRIC SYMPTOMS

Janus, the Roman god of beginnings, was always depicted facing two directions. He appears to have been one of the most ancient of Roman deities, one of the original *numina*, which means "powers."[2] Janus presided over transitions: the first hour of the day, the first day of the month, the first month of the year (January), and, of course, over thresholds and doorways. His symbols were keys and a doorkeeper's staff.[3] Like Janus, who looks to the past and the future, medical and psychiatric symptoms arise from causes in our personal history but also attempt to alter the present direction of our lives, pointing us toward something new in the future. Symptoms are the soul's messengers.

In my role as companion and guide to individuals who have undertaken the journey to the soul, I am repeatedly awed and amazed that the problems or symptoms my patients initially present are the very key to their unlocking the door to the mystery of their soul and the dharmic reason for their existence. The tendency to pathologize the manifestations of mental anguish and physical illness distracts from the numinous healing potential of symptoms. Symptoms can be signposts on the road map of dharmic transformation.

Mental health professionals in general, and psychiatrists and other physicians in particular, are often prone to regard the so-called symptoms of mental and physical distress merely as indications of disease. Physical and emotional symptoms are not only signs identifying known conditions, but may also be images conveying nonliteral meanings. Physical and emotional symptoms are

---

2. Edith Hamilton, *Mythology* (New York: New American Library, 1942), p. 44.
3. *Larousse World Mythology*, Pierre Grimal, ed. (London: Paul Hamlyn, 1965), p. 178.

the building blocks of diagnostic entities. The currently dominant psychiatric and medical approach to emotional and physical distress holds that eliminating the cause of the symptoms cures the illness. This approach, however, fails to take into account the reciprocity between mind and body.

The Principle of Reciprocal Action

The distinction between mind and body characteristic of Western thinking for hundreds of years oversimplifies the complex organism that we, in fact, are. Conceptualizing the human organism as a holarchy—a hierarchy of functional units that constitute a greater whole—enables us to consider the reciprocal action among various systems in the organism. In the present context, we are interested in the reciprocal action between mind and body.

Most of the time, we are not aware of much that is going on within us. A lot takes place outside our awareness. So long as the body or the psyche functions smoothly and maintains a dynamic self-regulation, we take little or no notice. Often, we begin to pay attention only when a distress signal forces us to stop and take notice. Physical symptoms, such as pain, fever, fatigue, hunger, thirst, or emotional symptoms, such as fear, anxiety, depression, or anger, alert us that something is not working as it should. When we perceive and respond appropriately to this kind of information, we take the necessary actions to remedy the situation or condition. Then the distress signal shuts down, and we continue on our way. The reciprocal action between consciousness and the rest of the organism—the self-regulation that sometimes involves the participation of the conscious mind—has functioned satisfactorily. Many people pay attention only to what is in their conscious minds and remain largely unaware of everything else that goes on. This "everything else" is usually called "the unconscious."

Many modern individuals struggle with an attitude of contempt and suspicion toward "the unconscious." Many trivialize whatever lies outside the range of the conscious mind and overvalue rational and conscious thinking. This, of course, is their choice. In my clinical and personal experience, however, I have found that what we loosely call "the unconscious" treats us as we treat it. When we start taking the whispers of the unconscious seriously, when we take time to tune in to them, record them, and treat them with respect, they provide us with information that is not only useful for our physical and emotional health, but also valuable as karmic and dharmic messengers. What is called for is not the dictatorship of the ego or of "the unconscious," but a democracy in which both have an equal voice, in which both viewpoints are considered and, through negotiation, strike an ethical compromise in dealing with the vicissitudes of life. Tom's depression illustrates the reciprocal action of which I speak.

Tom's Depression as Path to His Soul

In our extroverted Western culture, depression is often one of the psyche's last stratagems for putting the brakes on an individual's overinvolvement with the mayic side of life and enforcing a necessary introversion. For the extroverted attitude, the locus of value, the yardstick against which to measure the worth of our interests and actions, is the manifest world of people and things (maya). The introverted attitude takes as its reference point the needs, interests, and realities of what has been called the "inner" world. One group of introverted factors consists of our psychological makeup: our interests, abilities, and basic nature (svadharma). Another group comprises our development through the stages of life (ashrama dharma). Yet another consists of the relationships with other human beings that makes our lives together possible (varna dharma). The last is made up of the spiritual laws that govern all of creation (reta dharma).

Tom's depression illustrates the principle of reciprocal action. The effects of depression are both somatic and psychic. Depressed people have a poor appetite or overeat, suffer insomnia or hypersomnia, experience fatigue and a low energy level, and don't think well of themselves (low self-esteem). Their ability to concentrate is impaired; they have difficulty making decisions and often feel hopeless and helpless. These symptoms cause significant distress and often impair social, occupational, or other important areas of functioning.

Here we see changes affecting both mind and body. Because of Tom's overinvolvement with work, his life was out of balance. Because Tom couldn't do the psychological work of recognizing the imbalance consciously, he couldn't choose how to change his ways. Therefore the problem dropped down to the physiological level, the next level of reciprocal action: depression that sapped his energy. For Tom, depression was a message that was not only a symptom of a somatic and psychological condition but also a symbol. What is the difference between symptoms and symbols?

Symptom, Sign, and Symbol

The words "symbol" and "sign" are frequently used interchangeably. I make an important distinction between them, however. "Sign," as I employ the term, designates something known, without hidden meaning. Typical examples are street signs that state the name of the street, or signs on buildings identifying the occupants or businesses, or signs of the changes of the seasons (such as the reappearance of robins in spring, or the migration of geese, or the sprouting of crocuses).

A symbol, however, means more than it literally is. A symbol is the best possible expression for things *not* fully known. Signs may inform us, amuse us, or arouse our curiosity, yet they are not mysterious. When something stirs emotions in us that we cannot fully explain, we are responding to a symbol. One person's symbol may be only a sign for another person. Collective images, like the flag, or the Christian cross, may be symbols for some people, but only signs for others. It all depends on the way the image affects us, and whether or not we can fully explain the meaning in the image.

We can view medical and psychiatric symptoms as signs and as symbols. When we ask what caused the symptom and trace its history, we are viewing it as a sign. When a symptom persists after we have eliminated the cause, we probably are dealing with a symbol. Symbols point to something more than what caused them—to a goal, to some future condition—and therefore are stepping-stones on the path to the soul. Symptoms have histories, of course. It would be irresponsible to neglect exploration of the origin of a symptom. Ignoring the possible symbolic dimension, however, is no less an error.

We need to interpret symptoms symbolically, as well as investigate them for their causes in the traumatic events of the past. In the symbolic view, psychiatric symptoms are symbols that point the way our development is trying to take us as we move toward our dharmic destination: the physical health and wholeness of our personality. In order to make this transition, we need to interpret and understand our symptoms, not only as signs of illness and dysfunction, but also as symbols of transformation.

When viewed as a sign, Tom's depression is a chemical imbalance treatable with the appropriate medications. While depression does, of course, alter Tom's physiology, there is more to the story: a symbolic dimension that holds open the possibility of additional meaning that Tom cannot consciously access from his usual conscious point of view. Since Tom can't get at it consciously, the message is "translated" into physical and emotional language according to the principle of reciprocal action. The symbolic meaning may not be exhausted by simply translating it into an admonition, "Slow down!" although that is certainly a part of it. Tom could, of course, slow down and do nothing but sit around watching television. That in itself, however, would not necessarily bring his life more closely in tune with dharma. Tom's depression, broadly stated, signifies that his life is dharmicly out of balance—one-sided.

SYMPTOM, SYMBOL, AND EATING DISORDERS

Eating disorders offer another vivid example of the purposive aspect of emotional and physical symptoms in which the soul speaks through the body. Anorexia and bulimia—refusal to eat, and vomiting what has been eaten—pose serious medical risks at the physical level. When we consider the purposeful dimension, however, we realize that the body is speaking in metaphor: "I can't swallow it." "I can't stomach it." "It's enough to make me puke." Of course, the "eating," the taking in, does have something to do with food for the body. Many anorexics are terrified of their physical size (which, as I will point out in a moment, also has a symbolic component). We also have to find out what the anorexic or bulimic is "being fed" or "feeding on" emotionally if we are to discover what the symbolism of the eating disorder is trying to tell us.

Eating is an image of taking something, ostensibly nutritious, into the body. In vomiting, the body expels noxious and indigestible substances. When we examine the life experiences and situations of people suffering from eating disorders, we usually discover toxic emotional atmospheres and noxious interpersonal relationships. But we also find something else: a conscious or, more often, unconscious prohibition against recognizing or openly confronting the destructive forces at work. When the voice is prevented from speaking, the body often enacts the message. Then we must consider the symbolic aspect of the symptom.

In eating disorders, the waking mind of a person suffering from anorexia or bulimia does not see the connection between the food and the symptoms of self-starvation or vomiting. Although they may realize that they do not like the quality of the relationships in their lives, they believe they are unable to change or to leave. Another person observing the anorexic's or bulimic's life might indeed see the connection between the eating disorder and those life circumstances, and might, therefore, be able to say, "You can't swallow all that emotional stuff; it's enough to make you puke." For the outsider, the symptoms might not be a symbol at all; yet for the sufferer, who does not know what it means, the symptoms have—or can have—symbolic value. When people suffering from an eating disorder are able to grasp some of the meaning that the disorder is symbolizing, they discover the possibility of again taking up the dharmic journey.

Once More, Dharma

The four aspects of dharma I have discussed are, sva dharma (the law of one's own being, the individual uniqueness that strives for actualization within the context of one's family, society, place and time in history); ashrama dharma (the stages of life with their various culturally-shaped archetypal patterns to fulfill and the attendant responsibilities); varna dharma (the typical patterns of behavior, attitude, and emotion of one's species); and reta dharma (universal spiritual and physical laws). As we have seen several times, a person's life can be out of dharmic balance—an excess here, a deficit there. When this is the case, the principle governing the organism's adaptation to outer circumstances and the inner necessities of dynamic homeostasis and self-actualization attempts to restore the equilibrium.

When the conscious mind either does not or will not cooperate, for whatever reason, the self-regulatory and self-actualizing authority has to resort to ever more emphatic messages. Margaret's cancer dramatically illustrates the reciprocal action between body and the psyche.

Margaret's Cancer

Margaret died of cancer of the liver. Maybe she could have had a different and less painful death if she had been able to honor and act on emotions of which she was well aware. Her personal doctor referred her to me because Margaret became depressed and anxious following her cancer diagnosis. Her husband died six years earlier, when she was 67. For two years, Margaret lived alone on the family farm. The final chapter of Margaret's life began when her youngest sister, Dottie, came from another state to live with her following the death of Dottie's husband.

Throughout her life, Margaret had difficulty maintaining her boundaries. Other people could impose their wishes and demands on her, and, although she would feel overburdened and sometimes complain, she could seldom say "no" before she was exhausted. In a word, she wasn't able to mobilize the appropriate aggression to guard the gates of her soul, so her body had to try to digest the overload that her consciousness couldn't manage.

When Margaret got to the point of exhaustion, she often suffered what she called "a liver upset"—severe indigestion, nausea, vomiting, headache. Like a person with an eating disorder, Margaret was taking in ("swallowing") too many demands from other people, but was unable to refuse them. Since she could not act consciously, her body had to react in order to protect her. Actually, Margaret told Dottie she could stay with her until Dottie got settled in the community. However, Dottie stayed and stayed.

She made no gesture toward finding her own home. Apparently, Dottie never knew how upset Margaret was getting. Margaret's son knew she was unhappy and heard her grumbling, but he was unable to persuade Margaret to take the necessary action, which would have been to set a deadline for Dottie to find her own apartment or little house.

It was very difficult for me to work with Margaret. She elicited a powerful response in me. She reminded me so very much of my own mother that it was hard for me to get out of the son mode with her. Consequently, I had trouble detaching myself and confronting her with the psychological and spiritual realities I saw. When I was able to break out of the son mode and focus our attention on the lifelong pattern of anxious compliance and angry submission to others that was again playing out with her sister, her eyes filled with tears, her throat tightened, and she wrung her hands.

The message from Margaret's soul was clear: your liver is destroying itself in its attempt to heal you. Most people know that the liver secretes the bile that is necessary for the digestion of fats. What is not so well-known is the liver's function as a detoxifier. The liver combines toxic substances (including metabolic waste products, insecticide residues, drugs, alcohol, and other harmful chemicals) with substances that are less toxic. These substances are then excreted via the kidneys. From a kundalini perspective (which I will discuss in detail in the next chapter), Margaret's liver was attempting to do the third-chakra work that she should have done consciously and deliberately by exercising her personal power to establish autonomy. Her tears expressed the sixth-chakra issue of her failure to achieve ego integrity, and her choked-off voice eloquently witnessed her inability "to voice" the distress she experienced, as well as the necessary remedy (that is, telling her sister to move out).

According to the principle of reciprocal action, we can regard Margaret's cancer as the body's way of getting her out of an intolerable situation that she could not address deliberately. Psyche and body work together in powerful ways to heal the distressed soul or to rescue it from intolerable situations. Margaret's rescue was death.

The Dharmic Dimension of Robert's Lust

Robert, another of my patients, was more fortunate than Margaret. With my help he was able to respond to the symbolic message in his symptoms.

Robert is an extremely successful attorney, who is afflicted with manic depressive disorder. He rapidly achieves the zenith of whatever he sets out to do, but, once at the top, his grandiosity and lack of impulse control (the manic energies that ceaselessly propel him) quickly sabotage his accomplishments. Each time he loses his professional footing, however, he ends up in a more prestigious firm. The same pattern repeats in his relationships with women. Presently, he is in his third marriage. Between marriages he has had concurrent multiple relationships.

Initially, Robert's story seems like the typical saga of a manic depressive, with peaks and valleys in his professional and relationship life. A closer examination of his problem, however, revealed a different theme. What at first looked like impulsivity became the most illuminating guide in the darkness of his problems. Gradually, Robert and I recognized that he continued to sabotage his professional success because he was most uncomfortable dealing with a large corporate clientele. Although his work was brimming with the mayic trappings of fiscal success and prestige, it did not feed his soul. He yearned to return to work for the "small people," people like his parents and their friends from the earthy, wholesome neighborhood of his childhood. Robert decided to quit the high-powered firm and establish his own small practice working for the underdogs. Still, he felt something was missing.

Then, in one session, he reported that he was ashamed and troubled by continuing to lust after women in spite of a deep and sincere attachment to his wife. I knew that Robert's commitment and devotion to his wife were deep and that his mania medications were well-stabilized. Therefore, his residual symptom of lusting after women was a bit puzzling—not that any of us is immune from our own sexual shadow. Robert, however, felt his preoccupation with women was excessive.

It dawned on me that Robert's lust might be more than just a symptom to be studied from a causal, historical viewpoint, but a symbol to be understood as the best possible expression of something Robert could not otherwise make comprehensible. Taken as a symbol, Robert's lust might be showing him and me something about his dharma.

By this point in his life, Robert had adequately retired the karma resulting from his past indiscretions. Leaving the prestigious firm and establishing his small neighborhood practice had been a dharmic choice. He was ready to further realize his dharma. What was his lust saying? Toward what was it pointing? Was this the answer to Robert's feeling that there was a missing piece in his professional re-engineering?

This turned out to be precisely the case. I suggested to Robert that, instead of denying or pathologizing his lust for women, he try to see it as a symbol pointing the way to his destiny. If he loved women so much, why not honor his love and let love and devotion emerge out of his lust? If he could hold the tension between his restraint and the urgency of his sexual impulses, something new would emerge from his intense frustration.

As he pondered my proposal, the dharmic way emerged for him. He decided to devote all the professional prowess he had so far employed in the service of maya and large corporations to women and women's organizations. Robert continues to make a highly significant contribution to women's rights and issues in the community.

Why was my suggestion to Robert not just a lucky guess? To answer this question, we will have to review symbol formation.

Symbol Formation

The symbol transforms instinctual energy by channeling it into a socially useful and acceptable activity. In Robert's case, his sexual lust sought release and satisfaction; by working for women's rights and causes, his "intercourse" with them moved from the instinctual to the social level. Not all of our biopsychic energy is consumed by the various functions needed to sustain the regular course of life. We can use some of it for noninstinctual purposes, for example to fulfill our varna dharma (the interpersonal responsibilities we have to one another as social creatures). The fact that the symbol makes it possible for us to create artifacts, relationships, and institutions cannot be explained—or can be explained only very inadequately—as the result of merely natural conditions. In other words, an idea or an image can give equivalent expression to our biopsychic energy and channel it into a form different from the original, instinctual one.[4]

To return to Robert, viewing his lust for women as a symbol meant seeing it as more than mere instinctual discharge. Consciously, Robert did not want to chase women, but his sexual energy found no more satisfying outlet until he recognized service to women and to women's causes as an adequate symbol.

Images that grip us deeply and irresistibly are symbols, the stepping-stones to new activities that must be called cultural in order to distinguish them from the instinctual functions. A symbol cannot form, however, until we have dwelt long enough on the elementary facts and exhausted the literal, concrete experience.

Robert was ready for this transformation of energy. We had long discussed the conflict between the urgency of his lust and his conscious devotion to his wife. When I suggested that his insatiable urges might mean more than literal sex, the symbolic dimension came alive and became effective as he was gripped, fascinated, and awed by it.

THE BRIDGE BETWEEN SYMPTOMS AND DHARMA

We live at least two existences, conscious and unconscious. Our health and wholeness are contingent upon the degree of relatedness between these two aspects of existence. When these two disconnect, another bridge appears to connect them: this bridge is a symbol. It may appear in a dream, a fantasy, or a relationship; as enchantment with a certain myth or fairy tale; or as a medical or a psychiatric illness. When understood in a symbolic context, these phenomena reconnect us with our inner unconscious life and reestablish health, healing, and wholeness.

---

4. C. G. Jung, *The Structure and Dynamics of the Psyche*, CW8, ¶92.

Understood in this way, illnesses are not only afflictions. Illnesses can transform our attitude, goals, and life direction in a soulful direction when we awaken to all that pulses and moves in us, and when we become aware of more than just our conscious goals and wishes. An illness can force us to see the true meaning and mystery of our journey through life. The new life does not always fit in neatly with our outer circumstances, but it is more attuned to our inner, dharmic goal.

Viewed in this light, we may see our medical and psychiatric illnesses, not as major inconveniences to be quickly remedied, but as signals and symbols from the depths of the soul challenging us to discover a different path through maya to dharma. If we understand and honor the message of the illness, it deepens and heals our awareness, makes our superficial, lopsided, and maya-ridden existence whole, and elevates our life to its dharmic richness. Illness is then a gift to be treated with devotion and reverence for its potential to unlock the deepest purpose of our life journey.

Medical conditions manifest in specific bodily locations and organs. Do they correlate with emotional symptoms, and if so, how? The ancient system of Kundalini Yoga, the subject of the next chapter, provides a key to the relationship of body and emotions.

POINTS TO PONDER

1. What have been the significant medical or psychiatric symptoms in your life to date? How have you assessed the message these symptoms were trying to convey to you about your inner life?
2. How have your symptoms complicated your life, and in what ways do they force you to change business-as-usual in managing your life?
3. When your symptoms force you to change the way you conduct your life, how does this new path feel?
4. List the soul-healing and spiritual-awakening aspects of your illness and symptoms.
5. How do your symptoms put you in touch with your unlived life? How do the symptoms point in the direction of a new way of living your life?

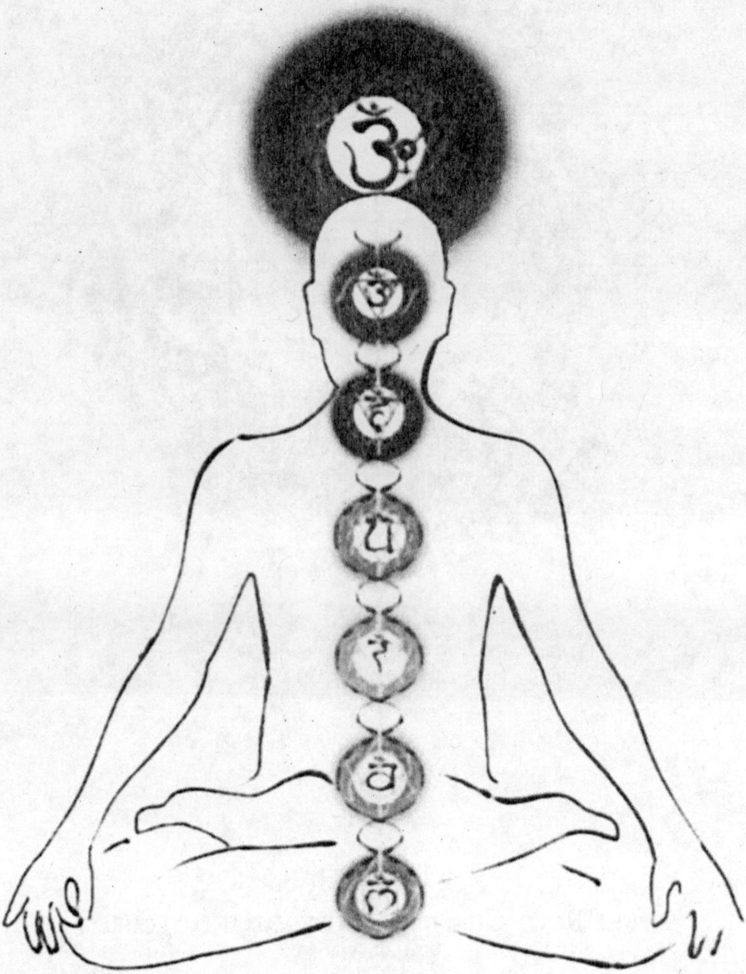

THE SEVEN CHAKRAS
OF KUNDALINI YOGA

Muladhara

The Root Chakra of Survival and Security

SVADHISTHANA

THE PELVIC CHAKRA OF GENERATIVITY

Manipura

The Naval Chakra of Autonomy

Anahata

The Heart Chakra of Intimacy

Vishudha

The Throat Chakra of Initiative

AJNA

THE EYE CHAKRA OF INTEGRITY AND LEADERSHIP

SAHASRARA

THE CROWN CHAKRA OF SPIRITUALITY AND MOKSHA

chapter four

Kundalini Yoga as a Path to the Soul

The yogas that do concern us are those designed to unite the human spirit with the God who lies concealed in its deepest recesses.

—Huston Smith[1]

In the previous chapter, we explored what happens when we get caught in maya and ignore the calling of the soul: the soul sends out emergency signals in the form of medical and psychiatric symptoms to remind us of our dharmic potential and alert us that we need to reestablish the bridge to the soul. But how does the soul choose its signal? Why do some get depressed and others develop schizophrenia as a connection to the soul? Why do certain individuals get stomach ulcers, while others suffer from cardiac problems? Why do each of us have to make our own unique journey to achieve our dharmic potential? What are the signposts that guide us on this crucial journey? How do we know that we are on the right path?

Dreams are one of several ways in which the soul whispers to us. The following dream of mine addresses some of the questions about our bridge to the soul and how to know whether or not we are on the right path.

---

1. Huston Smith, *The World's Religions* (San Francisco: HarperSanFrancisco, 1991), p. 27.

THE DREAM OF GODDESS AMBA

The night before I was to lecture on medical and psychiatric symptoms as a portal to the soul, I had a dream about taking my two cats to the vet that answers some of these questions:

> *I take my two cats to the vet's office to have them checked out. The vet says that I have to wait in the examining room because she has another important client who needs to be taken care of and that she will need some time. And I say it's okay, go look after your critical client. So she welcomes me to the inner sanctum, the examining room. There sits a huge cage, and in this cage is a tigress, a talking tigress commenting on day-to-day life. Nothing profound, just like the TV show Mr. Ed, the talking horse. The tigress was a little bit like that. I was amazed and amused at this talking tigress. And she wasn't locked in the cage, just kept in the cage. So I asked the vet why the cage was not locked. She said this was a very harmless tigress. The cage was meant mainly to reassure those who look at her so they won't get frightened. "So," she said, "I improvised this cage for the tigress."*

This dream, and the events preceding it, brought my presentation into sharper focus.

On the day prior to my lecture, my daughter, who has seasonal allergies, had a rather nasty asthmatic attack. I quickly switched from father mode to M.D. mode, made a medical diagnosis, and prescribed the treatment: she should return the two beautiful cats to the friend who had given them to her! In my medical opinion, they were exacerbating her asthma. Obviously and rightfully, she retorted that I should keep my medical opinion to myself, particularly since I had two cats and two dogs of my own! That night, prior to my presentation, I had the tigress dream.

As I always do in the morning, I pondered this dream and, of course, consulted my wife about it. We were playing with what the tigress might mean. Later in the morning (before my presentation), it dawned upon me that, throughout my preparation, I had completely omitted the role of the feminine and the

Kundalini Shakti. I remembered that the tigress is the mount of the goddess Amba, who is Shakti and Kali in her benevolent form. Moreover, in Chinese mythology, the tiger is the symbol for Yin, the universal feminine.

Humbly, I became aware that I had not acknowledged the healing power of the Goddess Kundalini Shakti. The dream was a reminder. The Goddess Shakti, the healing Great Mother, appeared to me in the form of a tigress before my first public presentation of my ideas on kundalini. Let me now present my thoughts and observations concerning the healing power of kundalini.

The Answer to My Questions

To answer the many questions I had about the specifics of each individual's path to the soul, I sought a template that my patients and I could use to help reconfigure their lives in accordance with their dharma, so that they could lead a spiritually fulfilling life. As I discussed in the first chapter, the concepts of maya and karma clarify the relationship among actions and consequences, and whether our life is more a vicious cycle of karmic consequences or a path leading to the fulfillment of the four aspects of dharma. All this was fine, but I still could not account for the frequent correspondence between medical conditions and symptoms on the one hand, and psychological and emotional phenomena on the other. After much trial and error, I came to the surprising realization that the ancient Hindu wisdom of Kundalini Yoga held many of the answers I was seeking to most of these questions. I learned that people could better understand themselves when we added the kundalini perspective to the overall picture of their suffering and life journey.

The seven-chakra system of Kundalini Yoga gave me the template that effectively integrated my understanding of maya, karma, and dharma with medical and psychological problems in a clinically useful manner (see figure 1, page 87). The system of the seven chakras is particularly inviting, since it corresponds to the wisdom of the body and the nervous system in such a clearly analogical manner.[2] More importantly, it works for me and my patients. I can't argue with the evidence of its pragmatic success.

In this chapter, we'll discuss some thoughts on the integration of Kundalini Yoga with medical conditions, contemporary psychiatry, and depth psychology. This presentation is intentionally simplified and preliminary to facilitate the understanding of this complex model. However, I do wish to emphasize that this basic information on the seven chakras is not intended as an alternative to available and well-established medical, psychiatric, and psychological treatment, but rather an adjunct to it, enhancing the treatment and prognosis of many conditions that can be understood using the chakra system in conjunction with the concepts of maya, karma, and the four aspects of dharma.[3]

---

2. Two major inspirations for my understanding of the chakras are E. H. Erikson, *Childhood and Society* (New York: W. W. Norton, 1950), and Ambika Wauters, *Chakras and Their Archetypes: Uniting Energy Awareness and Spiritual Growth* (Freedom, CA: Crossing Press, 1997).

3. The Hindu Tantric system of Kundalini Yoga prescribes a complex and intricate system of exercises and rituals for the initiate to practice to awaken and raise the kundalini through all seven chakras. The present discussion does not discuss these exercises, but rather focuses on the medical-psychological-spiritual dimension. It is essential to have a good basic understanding of the spiritual and dharmic aspects of Kundalini Yoga and start to reconfigure one's spiritual understanding and soul journey in accordance with some of its basic tenants before one dabbles in the mysterious complexities of Tantric ritual. For those who attempt Tantra before understanding the spiritual road map to the soul, the danger is that most such individuals get seduced by the exotic practices and miss the bigger picture. That puts the cart before the horse. Such individuals gain psychophysiological mastery of their medical, physical, sexual, mental, and relationship problems before they know where they are going spiritually. Usually, such travelers get stuck on the way at some comfortable rest stop rather than fulfilling their dharmic potential and reaching their soul destination.

Another common misperception of the Tantric rituals of Kundalini Yoga in the popular Western media is the confusion between spirituality and sexuality. While the initiated Tantric masters are able to prescribe Tantric sexual rituals to awaken kundalini energy in each of the seven chakras, often, the uninitiated get seduced into and then stuck in experiencing kundalini as mere sex. The Tantric sexual rituals are designed to capture the reflection of one's own soul in the mirror of a loving partner committed to mutual spiritual growth.

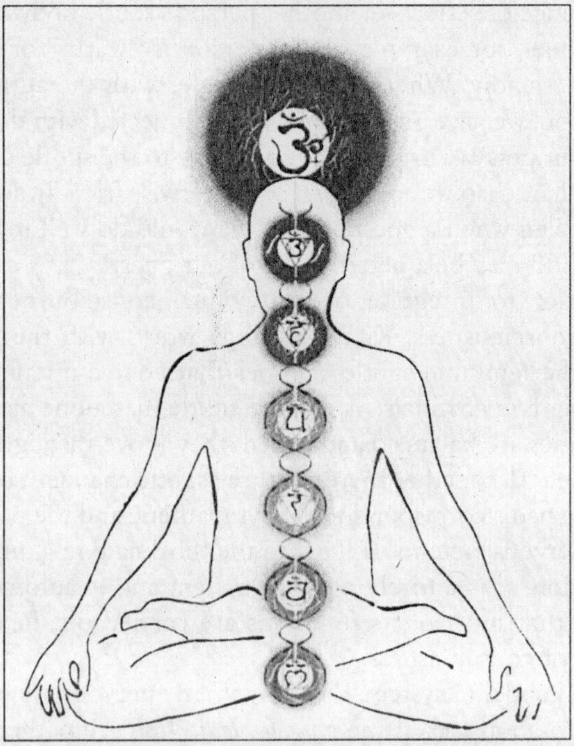

Figure 1. The seven chakras.

Basics of Kundalini Yoga

The word *yoga* means to "yoke," to "join together." Kundalini Yoga aims at integrating our individual consciousness with dharmic consciousness, the individual soul with the Great Soul. As is true for all attempts to mature and grow emotionally and spiritually, we must cultivate moral imperatives: noninjury *(ahimsa)*, truthfulness, self-control, the discipline to scrutinize ourselves, and the desire to reach the goal.

In addition to cultivating these moral imperatives, we must balance the subtle masculine and feminine energies that move through the body along specific pathways. "Subtle energy" is the energy of the nonphysical body, also known as the astral body or subtle body, that appears to clairvoyants as the aura surrounding a person's physical body. Whether or not we see the human aura, we experience the effects of another person's subtle body, or aura, when we feel, for example, that a person is "warm" or "cold," hostile or friendly. When our aura mingles with the aura of another person, we have a sense that we are connected with this other person. Our pets are usually more sensitive to the subtle energies that we radiate than we are. When our otherwise friendly dog hides under the bed when a guest arrives, we would do well to pay attention: Fido may be a better judge of our guest!

In order to integrate our individual consciousness with dharmic consciousness, Kundalini Yoga works with the masculine and the feminine subtle energies that course up and down the spine in two channels. When the subtle masculine and feminine energies are balanced and yoked, they move through a central channel. All together there are three subtle channels, or *nadis*. Two of the nadis correspond to the sympathetic and the parasympathetic nervous systems. (I'll get to the third nadi in a moment.) By definition, it is entirely a motor system and is automatic, in the sense that most of its functions are carried out below the threshold of consciousness.

In the kundalini system, the sympathetic nervous system corresponds to an aspect of the *pingala nadi*. The sympathetic nervous system is the "hot" system, in that it prepares the body and the individual for the fight-or-flight response. In general, it excites the heart and blood vessels, increasing blood pressure, slowing the gastrointestinal system, and increasing the metabolism of essentially all the cells of the body. Pingala is the carrier of solar currents and intellectual-mental energy. It makes the physical body more dynamic and efficient, and provides increased vitality and "male" power. Pingala has a purifying effect, but its cleansing is like fire.

The *ida nadi* corresponds to the parasympathetic system. The parasympathetic is the "cool" system that is responsible for calming, soothing, and renewing. It has a more discriminative, organ-specific response pattern compared to the sympathetic nervous system's global fight-or-flight style. In general, it calms the heart, may lower blood pressure, enhances the gastrointestinal system, and is responsible for sexual stimulation and function. The ida nadi carries lunar currents, and is the channel of physical-emotional energy. It is "feminine" in nature, and the storehouse of life-producing, maternal energy. Ida nourishes and purifies, but its purification is gentle.

Kundalini flowing primarily in one or the other nadi results in an energy imbalance, which correlates with the Type A or Type B personalities. When energy moves primarily in the "hot" pingala nadi, the result is the well-known Type A personality who is always on the go. Type A people are characterized as competitive and hard-driving, impatient, verbally aggressive, and prone to anger and hostility. These characteristics appear to be associated with increased risk of cardiovascular disease. From the kundalini point of view, the pingala nadi is overly energized. When kundalini moves primarily in the "cool" ida nadi, the personality shows Type B characteristics. Type Bs tend to be cooperative, easygoing, patient, and have a generally mellow temperament.[4] The desirable condition is for neither nadi to dominate, but rather to flow naturally as a balanced energy in the third nadi, the central channel called the *sushumna*.

There are two ways in which a balance can be achieved. We can consciously and intentionally strengthen the flow in one nadi and decrease it in the other; or we can experience a transformation so that the energy flows in the central nadi, the sushumna. Maintaining the tension between pingala and ida demands consciousness and self-discipline. Eventually, the tension may resolve when the energy begins to flow through the central nadi, the sushumna. In the case of the Type A person, we may see a decrease in the compulsive quality of self-assertion, for example, replaced by more freedom to choose how to address issues and

4. Most sympathetic nerve endings secrete a hormone called norepinephrine that excites most of the visceral structures and inhibits a few. The parasympathetic nervous system secretes acetylcholine, which, like norepinephrine, stimulates some organs and inhibits others. Modern antidepressant medications have considerable impact on neurotransmitters like norepinephrine and acetylcholine, and thus impact the autonomic nervous system tone. This, in turn, impacts the pingala and ida nadis and may maintain or disrupt the kundalini homeostasis. Before one uses medications to manipulate the kundalini energy system, it is preferable to use the inherent self-correcting and balancing potential of kundalini to establish healing, health, and psychic and spiritual wholeness.

situations. The Type B person may still be laid-back and easy-going, but also assertive when situations call for a more energetic response.

I had approached my lecture on medical and psychiatric symptoms as a portal to the soul in the pingala nadi, "hot" energy, manner. My dream and my daughter's rebuke pointed out my one-sided attitude, and I was able to correct the imbalance by integrating the ida (feminine) perspective. This will become clearer as I discuss the energy channels, the nadis through which subtle energy flows.

THE NADIS, THE CHAKRAS, AND THE DYNAMICS OF IMBALANCE

The nadis are linked with the chakras, the subtle energy centers of interchange between the physical, emotional, psychological, mental, and spiritual dimensions. Medical and psychological symptoms often indicate that one or more chakras are over- or underenergized, and that we are stuck either in the ida or the pingala nadi in one or more chakras. The Greek myth of Icarus offers a vivid analogy to the dangers of excess in either nadi.

Icarus's father, Daedalus, built a labyrinth to house the Minotaur, the half-bull, half-man monster. Daedalus, however, then longed to escape from the labyrinth he himself had built. This is analogous to the web of maya we all build for ourselves that imprisons us and our loved ones. To escape from the labyrinth was not easy, since King Minos kept all ships under military guard. But Daedalus made a pair of wings for himself and another for his son, Icarus, the quill feathers of which were held in place by wax. Having tied on Icarus's wings for him, Daedalus said, with tears in his eyes, "My son, be warned! Neither soar too high, lest the Sun melt the wax: nor swoop too low, lest the feathers be wetted by the sea." Then he slipped his arms into his own pair of wings and they flew off together. "Follow me closely," he cried. "Do not set your own course!"

This may be considered a situation closely analogous to the kundalini experience. The uninitiated may be seduced into letting their energy flow primarily in either the "hot" pingala nadi or the "cool" ida nadi. Either choice leads away from the optimal path and the journey may be hazardous.

As they sped away from the labyrinth, flapping their wings, Icarus disobeyed his father's instructions and began soaring toward the Sun, thrilled by the lift of his great sweeping wings. When Daedalus looked over his shoulder, he no longer saw Icarus, but only scattered feathers floating on the waves below. The heat of the Sun had melted the wax, and Icarus had fallen into the sea and drowned. Such can be the fate of those ruled by either the pingala ("hot") or the ida ("cold") nadi.

When we are living our life predominantly in either of these nadis, we are in the mayic mode. The unlived potential of the underenergized nadi then automatically finds expression, either via an illness or in projection onto a significant person in our life (e.g., a spouse, parent, employer, friend, or adversary). One kind of relationship problem illustrates how nadi imbalance manifests.

The heart chakra governs compassion and caring attachment. A dependent person, for example, may live primarily out of the ida nadi in the heart chakra. He or, more often, she will typically have difficulty exerting personal power and authority, and may project the authority and power drives onto a spouse or an employer. This creates a karmic relationship problem with the carrier of the projection—that is, reacting to aspects of themselves reflected to them by the person.[5] In fact, this is not really a problem between the dependent person and the projection carrier, but

---

5. Projection is an unconscious process; projections happen to us, we do not intentionally make them. Projection is a psychological mechanism in which we attribute to someone else the inner thoughts, feelings, emotions, ideas, images, and personal potentials that we do not recognize as our own. This may lead either to idealizing or devaluing the carrier of the projection. Moving toward maturation involves taking back our projections and integrating them with our conscious personality. This leads to growth in personality and a more realistic appraisal of the former carriers of our projections. Hence, we can have more authentic, reality-based relationships with others and a more realistic view of both our strengths and our weaknesses.

rather a problem of the dependent person's unlived energy that is projected onto and lived out by the significant other. The growth task is to become conscious of the projection system, reclaim the projected energy, and live it as actively, fully, and responsibly as possible.

In the example above, the individual—let's say, the woman—is stuck in the heart chakra. This may or may not be her native, dominant chakra, but rather the chakra most strongly developed by the forces that also shaped her persona. In order for her to get into the central, sushumna nadi of her dominant chakra, she may have to make a necessary detour through other, auxiliary chakras. This detour may involve withdrawing her projections: recognizing that she is permitting others to live that (projected) part of her potential for her. In this case, she has to discover how she surrenders her power and voice to others, and then reclaim it by learning to speak her truth and exercise power in her own right.

Symptoms of migraine headache and thyroid problems in women may be indicative of problems in the heart and head chakras. When a woman is stuck at the level of the heart chakra, the throat chakra compensates by asserting its presence in the form of thyroid problems, and the head chakra of intelligence speaks via headaches. The therapeutic task for this woman is to honor the needs of the throat chakra by finding an assertive voice for her viewpoints and claiming her authority of the head chakra by developing and expressing her intellect. Often, a woman in this situation is able to do this only in the second half of life, after she has fulfilled her karmic and dharmic chores of rearing her family.

Heart problems in many professional women and men may indicate an arrest in the naval chakra of personal power: the fire of ambition is excessive and the heart chakra protests through cardiac symptoms and conditions. Professional men who are stranded in the naval chakra of power, control, and authority do not rise above it to the next level, which is the heart chakra of compassion and intimacy. For these men, healing involves honoring the heart chakra by getting in touch with their feelings of loving attachment, sometimes possible only after they have their first brush with death in a heart attack or other major medical problem that helps them put their striving and professional success in perspective. After a major medical catastrophe, many such men learn to value love feelings and relationships.

SYMBOLS: THE BRIDGE BETWEEN SYMPTOMS AND DHARMA

Symbols are images, events, people, or things that, for us, are pregnant with meaning. Whenever we are fascinated by something whose meaning we cannot exhaust, try as we may, we are dealing with a symbol. Unfortunately, the term "symbol" is often used very imprecisely to designate any image. A company's logo, for example, is an image, a sign, but not a symbol, since its meaning is explicit and limited. The red octagon meaning "STOP" is likewise a sign. The essence of the symbol is that we can't say enough about it; if only we could find the words, we would say more. Its meaning seems limitless. It is the best possible expression for something we don't fully know or understand.

Symbols appear when consciousness and the unconscious are at odds. Health and wholeness are contingent upon the degree of relatedness and cooperation between our conscious minds and all those activities outside of our waking awareness that we call "the unconscious."

Viewing illness as a symbol can help us see the true meaning and mystery of our path through life. In this light, we may recognize our medical and psychiatric ailments, not as major inconveniences to be quickly remedied, but as signals and symbols from the depths of our psyche challenging us to discover a different path through maya to dharma. If we understand and honor the message of the illness, it can deepen, heal, and make whole our superficial, lopsided, maya-ridden existence, and elevate our life to its dharmic richness. The new life does not always fit neatly into our outer circumstances, but is more attuned to our inner, dharmic goal. Illness is, then, a gift to be treated with devotion and reverence for its potential to unlock the deepest purpose of our life's journey.

DOMINANT AND AUXILIARY CHAKRAS

The seven kundalini chakras are subtle energy plexuses where the somatic, psychic, and spiritual dimensions of our being intersect. Each and every person has a dominant chakra in which personal or individual dharma resides. The other six chakras are auxiliary chakras that inform, assist, and complete the optimal achievement of the individual's dharma situated in the dominant chakra. No one chakra is superior or inferior to the others. They mediate different aspects of energy and we need to be able to access each of them from time to time. However, our dominant chakra is the chakra in which our dharmic life will find its maximum potential. That is the chakra in which our unique psychological and spiritual endowment can realize its fullest expression. It is where we actualize what we are meant to be.

Our dominant chakra may not be the one we live out of most of the time. As I said earlier, the socialization and conditioning we experience shapes our persona and often influences which of the seven chakras becomes dominant in our first life. (Our "first life" is our life before we start developing our karmic consciousness and recognizing that our actions are circling us back into maya time and again, rather than advancing us toward actualizing our dharma.) Most of us may be socialized by parents and society to live our first life out of an auxiliary chakra in order to meet the demands of adaptation.

The developmental goal is to make appropriate use of all six auxiliary chakras as needed to consolidate our dominant-chakra management. The auxiliary chakras then become the consultants or advisors to our dominant chakra. If we ignore the auxiliary chakras, however, they become ferocious adversaries and create karmic problems in the form of projections, as medical or psychiatric conditions, or as complications piggy-backing on preexisting illnesses.

Over the last twenty-five years of clinical practice, I have observed that each chakra is the locus of both a mayic manifestation and a dharmic potential and task. There are, of course, many traditional attributes of the seven chakras, most of which I will not mention, because they are not fundamental to the present discussion.

THE DREAM OF YAMUNA— THE BLESSING OF THE RIVER GODDESS

For years, I have avoided writing about kundalini for fear that my medical and psychiatric peers and patients alike would consider my thoughts esoteric, unscientific, mystical, Eastern mumbo jumbo. Then certain events, images, and circumstances made it apparent that I had no real choice but to formulate my thoughts for more general discussion and publication. I did this with much ambivalence, however, stemming from the unpre-dictability of public response.

As my Amba dream had encouraged me to delve into the realm of kundalini, I wondered if my marching orders from the Healing Goddess were to integrate the kundalini framework subtly and imperceptibly into my practice, or to actually write about it and open it up for public discussion. In one intense week of incubation and creative outburst in the middle of August 1998, I wrote the bulk of this chapter. Then, on my last day of work, I had the following numinous dream.

I am visiting my alma mater, the B. J. Medical and Civil Hospital in my hometown in India, a city called Ahmedabad. It has been twenty-five years since I left India, and, when I left, I kept the master key to the college and the teaching hospital with me. I am visiting the hospital and college campus with my grandson, who is sitting on my shoulders.

As I walk around the campus and the hospital corridors, reminiscing about my student days, I come upon a large auditorium-like room that is actually an X-ray laboratory. A physician in a white coat is locking the door as I watch. Suddenly, I remember the old master key in my pocket and have an urge to try it to see if it still opens doors. All this time, the physician's back is toward me. I tap him on the shoulder and ask him to hold my grandson for a minute while I try my old key. He agrees and turns around to help me with my grandson, and, to my pleasant surprise, it is my medical school classmate and good friend, Dr. Yamunā.

My key works. I am excited that my old master key still unlocks the door of this modern X-ray laboratory with its big window. Through the window I see a beautiful stream leading to a river.

When I wrote this in my daily dream journal the next morning, it had a very soothing and reassuring feel to it. Since it had come on the last day of my work on the kundalini chapter, I tried to analyze it in kundalini context, especially since I was ambivalent and skeptical about openly exploring the subject in the first place. The dream stayed with me and, over the next few days, its message deepened.

First there is the meaning of my grandson's presence in the dream. As I thought about him, it became clear that my grandson symbolized my creative activity. My work as a psychiatrist, therapist, and physician is my child, my most immediate responsibility, I reasoned. But my grandson is the son of my son. That suggests that he is the offspring of my primary activity as a physician—in other words, of my creative understanding and scholarship. The writing of this book, and especially the kundalini chapter, is thus my grandchild.

The old master key from my alma mater unlocked a large, modern X-ray laboratory with a view of a stream leading to a river. It was Dr. Yamuna, my friend and classmate, who had access to that room. The X-ray laboratory can be considered a symbol of modern, contemporary, allopathic medicine, and, on the other hand, a symbol of the kundalini that reveals the invisible structures of our soma, psyche, and the soul. The key in my pocket reassured me that, even after twenty-five years, I had not lost the ancient kundalini wisdom, and could bring it to bear on present-day medical and psychiatric problems.

Both Yamuna and I have keys to this room. Yamuna is also the name of an ancient river in the Ganges valley that is considered the dark sister of holy River Ganges. Yamuna is the dark sister of the great Ganga, just as the kundalini healing art is considered the dark twin of the great healing traditions, only to be approached with caution and insight. If appropriately honored, both Yamuna and Shakti Kundalini have the potential to heal and nurture us.

In Indian mythology, rivers are considered holy in general, and the Yamuna and the Ganges are sacred in particular. They are the embodiment of the great healing mother archetype. To me, these dream images conveyed the blessing of the sacred River Yamuna, confirming that the kundalini system is still a valid paradigm that can unlock the mystery of turning illness to health. The old master key was the ancient healing wisdom from my motherland, India, which was still able to open doors to contemporary problems.

In this chapter, I have discussed some basic principles of Kundalini Yoga. The next chapter explores the mandala of each chakra in great detail and with case examples.

POINTS TO PONDER

1. What is yoga? To what does a yoga yoke you?
2. What is Kundalini Yoga?
3. What are the seven chakras of Kundalini Yoga?
4. What are the nadis? What are the ida, pingala, and sushamna nadis?
5. What are your dominant (primary) and auxiliary (secondary) chakras?
6. Have you been able to locate your dominant chakra before reading the next chapter?
7. What is a chakra imbalance? How does this manifest in your medical or psychiatric symptoms?
8. What is a nadi imbalance and how does it manifest in your symptoms or problems?
9. What is a symbol?
10. How do you understand the symbolic meaning of your symptoms, particularly in the kundalini framework?
11. If you have been able to identify your dominant chakra, what does this indicate about your dharmic life goals? In other words, do you have an indication as to which of the four dharmas presently call you—sva dharma, ashrama dharma, varna dharma, or reta dharma?

The next chapter will give you a much better understanding of some of these questions. While the questions at the end of this chapter may be seen as a pre-test, the questions at the end of the next chapter may be seen as post-test!

chapter five

The Seven Chakras of Kundalini Yoga

The chakras are the seven centers of the soul.

The seven chakras in Kundalini Yoga are centers of subtle energy situated along the spine from the tailbone to the crown. Each chakra is associated with specific bodily organs, typical emotions, characteristic attitudes, and levels of spiritual development. A totem animal is associated with the first four chakras. The three nadis, the subtle energy channels discussed earlier, penetrate the chakras like the cords on which beads are strung. The chakras, in other words, are focal points where the physical, emotional, and spiritual dimensions of our life intersect. Some basic understanding of the chakras is invaluable on the path to the soul.

Muladhara—
The Root Chakra of Survival and Security

The first chakra is called *Muladhara*, or the "root support." It is situated in the perineum, between the anus and the genitals. The ruler of the first chakra is Ganesha, the elephant-headed god, lord of all beginnings and remover of obstacles.[1] The totem animal associated with the Muladhara chakra is the elephant, which

1. The mystery of Ganesha is the subjugation of the rational mind, which is analytical and critical in nature, and the liberation of the nonrational mind, which is emotional, and necessary for any spiritual venture.

represents the life-long search for food for the body, the mind, and the heart.

The totem elephant has seven trunks representing the seven aspects and the seven types of desire that every person has to recognize in order to evolve in harmony with natural laws. These seven aspects include the five senses (sound, touch, sight, taste, and smell), plus sex and defecation. The seven types of desire are for security, procreation, longevity, sharing, knowledge, self-realization, and union.

Developing trust and an internal sense of emotional and material security is the task and goal of the first chakra. The person who has succeeded at this fundamental task will act in harmony with the natural rhythms of the body and the psyche, neither wasting energy nor polluting sensory awareness with over-indulgence. Such a person will act wisely and with moderation, able to explore body and mind as vehicles of liberation from maya and its allure.

The abbreviated story of one of my patients with root-chakra problems will provide useful background before I discuss the attributes of the root chakra in greater detail.

Paul's Survival

Paul is a physician whose life was characterized by chronic depression and difficulty in sustaining relationships with women.

While he enjoyed considerable professional success, his tendency to sabotage his work and his relationships led to a self-defeating life pattern. In kundalini terms, Paul's energy was "hot," flowing primarily in the pingala nadi. Unable to trust those around him and fearful they would abandon him emotionally, he tried too hard to succeed at work. He couldn't relax and open himself to others. This blocked the receptive ida nadi in which energy flow is "cool" and soothing. Had he been able to activate the ida nadi, he would have had a possibility of meaningful relationships with peers and women. But he could not commit himself to them for fear of being abandoned the way his mother had abandoned him emotionally as a child.

Both his work and his relationships had a chaotic, transient feel, without any sense of foundation or rootedness. His maya was compulsive work, rewarded with commensurate success, but his life was devoid of love, play, creativity, and spirituality. While he accumulated material wealth (artha) through his unceasing labor, he made no time for soulful relationships with friends or a lover. This was the negative karmic consequence he created for himself.

In the first chakra, the basic motivation is to establish security in its various forms. Attention is linear and follows a single-minded direction. At the mayic level, Muladhara is concerned with survival: food, clothing, shelter, and security. When this chakra is well-integrated, one has a sense of confidence in one's capacity to survive materially and emotionally and to use one's own abilities effectively. At the mayic level, a well-functioning root chakra forms the foundation for the first level of svadharma (selfhood), namely, sufficient security, worldly wealth, and success (the material aspect of artha) so that the individual can cultivate the possibilities offered by other chakras. Optimal attainment of the mayic goals of the first chakra not only creates personal wealth, but has the potential to enrich the community when the pursuit of wealth is informed by the second chakra of generativity and the seventh chakra of higher purpose.

Psychopathology manifests in the first chakra as disorders of basic trust or mistrust, and chaotic relationships based on needing significant others for basic physical or emotional survival. The prospect of losing basic emotional survival resources leads to fear of fragmentation or disintegration of the self, both psychologically and literally (as in death or suicide). The main problem for a person acting from first-chakra motivation is severe depression or violent behavior based on insecurity. That violence can turn against others or against the self.

In the search for caring and emotionally trustworthy survival resources, such individuals may often be attracted to fundamentalist movements and esoteric cults as substitute mothers. However, when their need for a collective mother is informed by the seventh chakra, the bridge to reta dharma, they can have an authentic connection to the spiritual dimension and to a transcendent mystery as a nurturing higher parent and life source.

The great bulk of my work with Paul entailed my being like an elephant, solidly holding my ground and confronting him about his issues of trust and his fear of losing basic emotional security in his relationships. Actually, there were many people in Paul's life who cared about him. Their steadfast emotional devotion was unwavering, but Paul could not see that because he expected other people to abandon him.

THE FIRST-CHAKRA DRAMA

When a person has accomplished the developmental task of the first chakra, she or he has a sense of emotional and existential security—a basic trust in life and self—that lays the foundation for realizing life's other possibilities. People who have balanced and well-functioning first chakras have usually had good experiences early in life with caretaking persons, most often the mother.

When either the pingala or the ida nadi dominates a person's energy flow in the first chakra, distrust rules, driving the individual to assume the role of the aggressor or the victim. When the ida nadi (feminine, "cool" channel) is predominant, we see people who are frequently victimized by others because of an inability to assert themselves. Those in whom the pingala nadi (the masculine, "hot" channel) is dominant behave aggressively in order to assure themselves of the material and emotional resources necessary for survival.

The experience of being in the victim or aggressor mode creates karmic complications in the realm of maya. Usually, the victim or the aggressor projects the other role onto a significant other—a partner, lover, or parent—creating a karmic problem for both of them. The victim has to find her or his courage to confront the aggressor, and thereby begin to integrate the projected self-assertion. The aggressor has to acknowledge and reconnect with the vulnerable, victim part, and work on withdrawing the projection to the other person in order to assimilate the victim shadow.

When the victim and aggressor aspects of the self experience are integrated, our energy flows in the central channel, the sushumna nadi. Then we experience the internal Good Mother as an active, reliable inner resource, as our capacity to secure our survival, and protect and nurture our basic physical and emotional security. In this way, we realize our artha (wealth) potential—emotional as well as material wealth.

The first chakra, Muladhara, is the foundation for our four dharmas. Without a solid base, our sense of ourselves (svadharma) is weak, and our ability to survive materially and emotionally is diminished. Progression through the stages of life (ashrama dharma) is seriously hindered if the root chakra is not well-balanced and developed. Our contribution to community (varna dharma) will be restricted if we have only limited emotional and material means. Attempts at doing God's work (reta dharma) may well be a flight to pseudo-spirituality to avoid dealing with a feeble root chakra.

When he first came to me, Paul was stuck in the pingala nadi of the root chakra, which manifested as untempered masculine enterprise. This excluded the ida nadi. In the transformative vessel of therapy, Paul gradually began to see the love and commitment he had received from those around him, which started to open his auxiliary heart chakra (fourth chakra). Little by little, he moved his energy into the sushumna nadi of the first chakra. This shift has enabled him to start diverting some of his work passion into interpersonal commitments. His relationships with his peers in general, and with his girlfriend in particular, are deepening.

She inspires him to use his considerable professional talent in a way that not only translates into personal success, but into community service as well. Her love (heart chakra) for him is healing his fear of emotional starvation (first-chakra problem), and this enables him to become truly generative in a life-stage appropriate way (thus honoring the auxiliary second chakra of generativity and its ashrama dharma of a fuller realization of who he potentially can be).[2]

Paul has become autonomous in his clinical practice (third chakra of autonomy and fuller actualization of self—svadharma). He takes more initiative in his work and in his relationships (fifth chakra of initiative and higher level svadharma). He has opened a specialized clinic (varna dharma) for certain medical conditions for which there is little treatment available in his community. His work is now also informed by a higher purpose than personal gain or success (seventh chakra of spiritual purpose). Paul is free of much of his compulsive striving for success, and he has gained some degree of moksha, liberation from the allure of maya.

SVADHISTHANA—
THE PELVIC CHAKRA OF GENERATIVITY

The second chakra is called the *Svadhisthna*, the "Dwelling-place of the Self." It is located in the area of the hypo-gastrum and bladder above the genitals. The totem animal of the second chakra is the croçodile (Sanskrit: *Makara*). The crocodile depicts the serpentine, sensuous nature of the person dominated by the second chakra.

The crocodile, an amphibian languidly floating mostly beneath the surface of the water, is a wily animal, capturing its prey through trickery. Whereas the elephant, the totem animal of the first

2. I do not expect the reader to remember all the details of chakras and dharmas mentioned in parentheses. All individuals must access the six auxiliary chakras and fulfill their corresponding dharmic tasks to a greater or lesser degree in their kundalini journey and their path to the soul. I am including this information in the discussion of each chakra for the sake of completeness, and to make the presentation of each chakra useful for later reference.

chakra, is often depicted in South Asian art as bearing the entire universe on its back, the symbolic meaning of the crocodile, like the snake, ranges from instinct to wisdom.[3] By weight, the human body is three-fourths water, one of the elements in which the crocodile is at home. Ocean tides are governed by the Moon, as are the "emotional tides" of human beings. The Moon plays a great role in the life of the second-chakra person.

The developmental tasks of the second chakra are generativity, which, if not achieved, results in stagnation. In the second chakra, generativity is both creative and procreative. While the attitude of the first chakra is single-minded and linear, fantasy and multi-

3. The elephant reference comes from *The Herder Symbol Dictionary*, Boris Matthews, trans. (Wilmette, IL: Chiron Publications, 1986), p. 68f. Regarding the crocodile, C. G. Jung writes that the snake, "the commonest symbol for the dark, chthonic world of instinct [may frequently] . . . be replaced by an equivalent cold-blooded animal, such as a dragon, crocodile, or fish." He continues: "But the snake is not just a nefarious, chthonic being; it is also . . . a symbol of wisdom, and hence of light, goodness, and healing." (*Aion*, CW9, ii, ¶385). Cf. also "The Psychological Aspects of the Kore," where Jung discusses mythological and dream images of the daughter (Kore) and the mother: "Sometimes the Kore-and mother-figures slither down altogether to the animal kingdom, the favourite representatives then being the cat or the snake or the bear, or else some black monster of the underworld like the crocodile, or other salamander-like, asurian creatures" (CW9, i, ¶311).

plicity now enter the picture. Generativity implies gestating and nurturing one's inner potential, and eventually giving birth to what has been developing inside. In this sense, generativity is the capacity to parent oneself and one's offspring using one's innate potential, talents, and skills.

Second-chakra problems are what Robert (mentioned briefly in chapter 3), one of my patients, brought to therapy.

Robert's Lust

When he began therapy, Robert was dominated by the second (pelvic) chakra, the focus of sensuality and sexuality. Although he was very generative (a function of the second chakra), his generativity served maya—the pleasure (kama) he derived from his sexual exploits and professional success—rather than the dharmic goals of the second chakra. His hard-driving style (when he was not depressed) betrayed that he was stuck in the pingala nadi in his personal and professional life. But behind the manic fire of his pingala focus lurked the devouring crocodile of his depression.

Generativity, the developmental task of the second chakra, can take many forms. The inspiration to create begins in the second chakra. Generativity finds bodily expression in the procreation of children and the founding of a family, both of which involve sexual activity. But generativity is not limited to sexual procreation (or recreation): inspiration, imagination, and fantasy all beget new things, whether of matter or of the mind. The coincidence of high levels of creativity and virile sexuality is well-known.

In the mayic mode, people literalize and concretize their generative drive as procreativity (and sexual activity) to the exclusion of other modes of creativity. In this case, the imbalances in the second chakra can lead to medical and psychiatric conditions that find expression in problems with the sexual organs: promiscuity or impotence, sexually transmitted diseases, endometriosis, or genitourinary system or prostate problems.

THE SECOND-CHAKRA DRAMA

Many people dealing with second-chakra issues are preoccupied with creation of self rather than with true relationships. They recruit the other person as a sexual partner, and that partner then functions as a vehicle for propagating themselves. Their relationships are frequently unsatisfying, shallow, or exploitative, and often end in tumultuous break-ups and acrimonious divorces. The consequence of their behavior (their karma) is pseudo-intimacy and stagnation. This can lead to what is called the exploiter/martyr drama.

When stuck either in the ida (the "cool" channel) or pingala (the "hot" channel) nadi in the second (pelvic) chakra, people identify the conscious part of their psyche either as the exploiter (pingala) or the martyr (ida), and this becomes their primary mayic mode. Identification with either role results in each person in the dyad projecting the complementary role onto some other suitable person in their life. Projection creates a karmic problem. The person in the martyr role feels helpless vis-à-vis the exploiter, while the exploiter feels contempt (but also unconscious guilt) for the exploited.

When the martyr and the exploiter take back their projections, their energy moves into the central channel (sushumna nadi). They can become authentically generative in their endeavors, whether at work, in relationships, or at play. In short, they experience themselves as parent to their inner potential: compassionate but firm (the strength that previously was all in the pingala nadi) and simultaneously often resistant and protesting (what previously was experienced as the victim, whose energy was all in the ida nadi).

If people caught in the mayic mode in the second chakra are to attain pleasure (the various forms of kama, *the* fruit of authentic generativity), they must return to the first chakra and work on their unresolved survival issues. This may involve grounding themselves in basic life skills, establishing trust in place of exploitation as a mode of relating, and ascending to the third chakra of autonomy and self-control. If they can grow in these ways, they gain access to the pursuit of pleasure in its various forms (kama) and begin to actualize who they really are (their svadharma). Both of these accomplishments play useful roles in their contributing to their communities (their varna dharma).

When Robert first came for therapy, the kundalini was stuck at the root (survival) chakra. Robert tried to compensate for his fear of not surviving by attempting to create himself (through compulsive second-chakra activity), but that attempt at generativity served maya rather than his ashrama dharma. This kept him stuck in the exploiter mode with women. His relationship with his present wife and his attachment to me in therapy helped him access and value the heart chakra (fourth). Now he returned to his work with a much higher level of integrity, motivated by service to the "little people" in his community dharma (sixth chakra). His lust became his motivation not to exploit, but rather to serve women and honor the feminine. These higher motives were now his guide, thus helping him access his seventh chakra of spirituality.

In Robert's experience, we can see the illusory aspect of the manifest world, maya. For Robert, maya was indeed "real," but stood for more than it was. Physical survival, sexual desire, emotional and intellectual power—all are facts of human existence and avenues for generativity. But they are also symbols; they point toward another dimension of reality, the soul's reality. They are also energies in the service of dharma, the recognition and actualization of the divine spark, the primordial cosmic energy in all of us.

On his path to the soul, Robert was able to circumambulate (make the circular journey) up and down the seven chakras, generally up the pingala (masculine) channel that led to his manic highs, then down the ida (feminine) channel that took him back to his depressive lows. He reached his heart and value chakra with the guidance of the Goddess Kundalini, was initiated by his kundalini lust, which eventually took him to the peak of his dharmic destiny, the seventh chakra, where his most masculine professional potential, his Shiva energy, did the dance with his tender values of serving the underdog, his Shakti kundalini energy. When Shiva and Shakti did their dance on the karmic stage of his life—when the opposites were married in his psychic and causal space—Robert arrived in the soul place.

Manipura— The Naval Chakra of Autonomy

The third chakra is called *Manipura*, or "Plenitude of Jewels." Its location corresponds with the solar plexus, between the diaphragm and the naval. The totem animal of the third chakra is the ram, the steed of Agni, the fire god.

The ram depicts the nature of the third-chakra person: fiery, headstrong. Individuals dominated by the third chakra strive for personal power and recognition, sometimes at all costs. When they experience shame, they can get into rage states, attempting to defend and protect their sense of self. Doubt, and self-doubt, are shame's twin emotions. The psychological issues of the third chakra are autonomy versus shame and doubt, and holding on (control) versus letting go.

Roger's Loss of "Fire in the Belly"

Roger is a well-established physician suffering from a combination of schizophrenic and depressive symptoms (schizoaffective disorder). Gradually, Roger lost interest in his medical profession and retired from his practice in his early 50s. Although he is a caring man, devoted to his wife and family, he tends to stay in his head and is unable to express his feelings.

Before he lost the "fire in his belly," Roger had been living out of the third chakra (autonomy) as a competent and intelligent, but ambitious and controlling, master. This was true both in his profession and in his marriage. He tended to enslave everybody around him by dazzling them with the fire of his authority and power. As he approached his 50th birthday, however, several serious medical problems slowed his pace, and his devoted wife became depressed from carrying the feelings and emotions (heart chakra) for both of them. Roger was too intellectual to dabble in heart-chakra matters in relationships or elsewhere. The only way he could experience the fire of his third chakra was in his head, as intellectual excitement.

The task of the third chakra is to develop autonomy (another aspect of svadharma). The person who has failed to develop autonomy experiences shame. Since the third chakra is located in the area of the solar plexus in the abdomen, the digestive system is often the focus of medical problems for people who live out of the third chakra. They experience their emotions in their intestinal tract. Problems weigh heavily on the stomach. When third-chakra people are angry (pingala nadi), they get stomach ulcers and need antacid medications; when they are afraid (ida nadi), they may get diarrhea; when they are obstinate (pingala nadi), they become constipated. Such individuals notice emotions and events only when it disturbs their gastrointestinal system. The psychological issues associated with the third chakra are pride, striving for power, domination, and recognition (excessive energy in the pingala nadi), or shame, powerlessness, and subservience (excessive energy in the ida nadi).

In an early session, I asked Roger why he could not continue to practice medicine. In characterizing his problem, he said, "I lost the fire in my belly about pursuing medicine. The fire of passion for medicine is gone." His lifelong pattern of intellectualization had quenched any ardor and feeling he might have had for his work. As with many of our contemporaries who have well-trained minds, but who are disconnected from their emotions and passions, Roger's professional life had grown stale and pointless.

Roger's energy was all in his head chakra, because he had not matured through the chakras of fire (the naval chakra) and feeling (the heart chakra). His energy had remained in a primitive state in his head chakra and manifested as intellectualization rather than insight. That was the primary contributing factor in his psychiatric problem. For him to heal, he had to work to gradually reestablish his ability to feel emotions (develop his heart chakra) that would enable him to value his work emotionally. Only then would he be able to reclaim the capacity to express feelings and have a conscious, felt sense of devotion to his family.

One of the major medical problems that had slowed Roger down was a chronic form of cancer that caused a gradual, progressive limitation of blood flow to the brain. This would eventually obliterate his intellectual powers. (Here we can see how a physical disease developed to rectify a chakra imbalance—in this case, decreasing the activity in the head chakra.) In the sessions, he talked about his delusional and grandiose schemes of making millions of dollars before he died. What he could not talk about, or even be conscious of, was the motivation behind these delusions. I got an inkling about his unconscious motivations only from my own reactions to him in the session.

Roger's psychotherapy was a very moving experience for me. When he talked about his million-dollar schemes, I found myself getting tearful and extremely sad. He reminded me of my own father, who had always wanted somehow to give me a running start in life beyond what was possible. And here was Roger, a disabled physician, afflicted with cancer, unable to practice, with a depressed (but recovering) wife, a son in college and a daughter recently married, spinning his million-dollar schemes in his psychiatrist's office! Then it clicked. He wanted to accumulate money for his family before he died as his last gift and legacy. Since he could not make anymore money in the world of physical maya, he went into his delusional, psychotic world to do it.

THE THIRD-CHAKRA DRAMA

The psychological drama of the naval chakra centers on issues of authority and control—master (pingala nadi) and slave (ida nadi).

Each of these roles is the shadow of the other, and gets projected onto some significant person, creating karmic difficulties for the projection carrier. When caught on the dark side of the maya of the third chakra, people feel a deep sense of shame, either in the master or the slave mode. Once individuals become conscious of their projections, they have the possibility of taking them back. Integrating the projected characteristics into their personality balances the energy so that it flows in the sushumna nadi rather than in either the pingala or the ida. The experience of partnership with significant others, rather than the master/slave drama that plays out in the karmic mode, leads to a sense of autonomy in important relationships, while maintaining a tender and loving connectedness.

In the third-chakra mode, people get into the maya of control in their work and their relationships. This leads to master/slave karma. Since power excludes love, these relationships lack mutuality, causing doubt about the emotional availability of other people. Consequently, third-chakra people often use shame or rage states to control the people around them. This can affect employees, lovers, or children—whoever does not comply with their wishes (which are often unstated or even unconscious). Their sense of autonomy is easily depleted.

Persons dominated by the third chakra need to access the fourth-chakra energy of true mutuality, relationship, and intimacy with others. They can then use their fiery energy in a balanced and generative way to realize their selfhood (svadharma) and express their creative potential as individuals contributing to the well-being of family and community (varna dharma).

To some extent, the depressive component of his schizo-affective disorder put Roger in contact with his deep unconscious love and feelings (heart chakra) for his family that he could not show previously. His wife and I both had to get into our own fourth-chakra mode in order to experience on his behalf his depression and grief about his chronic morbidity and impending mortality. Gradually, Roger has been able to claim his feelings, and now he is returning to his primary third chakra to manage his available resources meaningfully, and to dedicate his remaining time to the service of his selfhood (svadharma). He is doing this informed by his developmental stage in life (the family life dimension of ashrama dharma), which he has reclaimed via his depression and illness with the help of his wife's depression and my countertransference reactions to him.

ANAHATA—
THE HEART CHAKRA OF INTIMACY

The fourth chakra is called *Anahata*, the "Unattackable." It is located at the heart plexus, behind the sternum. The totem animal of the heart chakra is the deer or black antelope, a very sensitive animal, always full of inspiration.

The developmental task of the fourth chakra is intimacy versus isolation. Just as the deer or antelope runs swiftly, often changing direction, the fourth-chakra person's loving emotions can fluctuate. The intimacy of the fourth chakra is based on feelings and the capacity to commit oneself to affiliations and relationships while making the necessary sacrifices. The maya aspects of the fourth chakra are overdependency on relationships for the regulation of self-esteem, at the cost of autonomy and voicing one's needs, values, and beliefs. The karma of the fourth chakra is the fear of isolation and abandonment, or codependency. To counter this danger, fourth-chakra people may

often preemptively isolate themselves and withdraw from relationships. When optimally managed, the fourth chakra leads to an affiliative matrix maintained by the energy of emotions and feelings, and provides the driving force behind the ashrama dharma, inspiring one to fulfill one's responsibility to family and clan.

A Couple's Heart-Chakra Problem

Mary has been married for many years to a man who does not communicate. Marty, her husband, was unable to express any feelings, and was stuck in power and control issues in his profession (third chakra). Mary was a very feeling type of individual, locked in a dependent relationship with her controlling husband. Mary and Marty shared a fourth-chakra problem.

Fourth-chakra issues can manifest medically and psychiatrically as cardiac conditions, depression, difficulty expressing feelings, and codependency disorders. In my clinical work, I have encountered some individuals who get depressed at the prospect of the loss of intimacy and isolation from a loved one. When such individuals preemptively isolate themselves by denial of affiliative and dependency needs, their heart speaks for them. Cardiac problems can then provoke them to reassess their priorities and lifestyle, and to acknowledge their intimacy needs. When such emotionally isolated individuals can't voice their dependency needs, their broken hearts cry out loudly to speak for them. Some depressed individuals have to find their third-chakra energy of autonomy and self-assertion, and later voice it (by developing their fifth chakra of voice). Others have to let their broken hearts reach out for soothing intimacy with a caring other.

This was the case with Mary and Marty. In terms of the kundalini diagnosis, Mary's natural primary chakra was the fourth. Since she was forced to do all the emotional caretaking in the relationship, however, her fourth-chakra pingala nadi was working overtime, while Marty focused all his energy on being the hero in the work world (dominant pingala nadi in the third chakra). This, in turn, relegated Mary to the third-chakra ida nadi. This caused her to project all her drive for autonomy to her professionally successful, but emotionally controlling, husband. This manifested as financial dependency on Marty. In midlife, Mary had completed graduate school, but had been unable to get much support from Marty to launch her long-cherished hope of a professional career. Consequently, she became clinically depressed and needed psychiatric intervention.

Marty lived out of the pingala nadi of his third chakra (his dominant chakra) as a master of his world (his mayic mode). For his part, Marty projected his unlived dependency needs and unexpressed feelings onto his wife, Mary. Mary got caught in the slave role of Marty's master/slave split and suffered the corresponding karma of isolation and depression, while Marty was trapped in the dependent side of the (fourth chakra) caretaker-dependent dynamic, and finally suffered cardiac problems.

THE FOURTH-CHAKRA DRAMA

When the fourth chakra is optimally functioning, the individual can both give and receive emotionally, can experience loving attachment, mutuality, and intimacy. Predominance of either the pingala or the ida nadi leads to the caretaker-codependent dynamic and the fears of emotional isolation or engulfment. For persons dominated by the ida nadi, the mayic experience is helpless dependency. People whose pingala nadi predominates are forced into the role of all-powerful caretaker. Each projects the other, unlived half of the caretaker-dependent dyad, which in turn creates relationship karma with the significant other. Such are the dynamics of the karmic drama of the need for intimacy and the fear of isolation leading to dependency and codependency.

When people integrate the projected other half of the caretaker-dependent dyad into consciousness, they move into the central channel, the sushumna. This shifts their relationships out of the caretaker-dependent pattern. They then feel like lovers, rather than dependent parasites or overburdened caretakers. This shift in energy flow leads to true intimacy in place of the dreaded emotional isolation (as the caretaker or the dependent). Buoyed by the gentle currents of intimacy, persons feel they can truly love themselves, as well as a significant other. The seed of the human drive is to make a life commitment and to mate and beget children, thereby fulfilling another of life's developmental stages (the mate and parent dimension of ashrama dharma). This psychic soil in which this sense of emotional abundance and autonomy takes root.

Of course, there is a dark side to unresolved karma in the fourth chakra. Those dominated by the ida nadi may get stuck in the codependent role. Taking care of an addicted spouse, for example, far exceeds the bounds of self-love or love for another. Conversely, the pingala nadi manifestation of the fourth-chakra problem may be denial of all feelings and relational needs. Men who have achieved a pseudo-autonomy often get caught in such a void of isolating maya. Sometimes, the only way they can reclaim their fourth-chakra balance is by suffering cardiac problems that often force them to depend on others for care and nurturance.

An interesting shift occurs in the fourth-chakra dynamic during the midlife transition in men and women. Men who live primarily in the third chakra (autonomy, mastery, and enterprise) often can only move into the fourth chakra by suffering heart problems that may slow them down and put them into a dependent role with their spouses. It is as if the kundalini had no other choice but to provoke a medical crisis to force such men to consult their heart chakras and establish mutuality and intimacy in a relational matrix.

In her midlife transition, a woman who is stuck in the fourth chakra of feelings often gets overburdened by taking care of the frog that never becomes a prince. This leads to disappointment and depression. Her marriage may run into the dead-end of irreconcilable differences. A woman in this situation has to return to the third chakra to claim her own authority and autonomy, after which she can return to the relationship, not assuming a dependent role, but informed by her own authority and potential. If the relationship can be revived, it will now rest on the much more solid ground of mutuality, rather than on dependency or care-taking. The enterprise these women undertake in the second life[4] is often very soulful, since it is a manifestation, not only of the svadharma aspect of their third chakra (autonomy and enterprise), but also of the ashrama dharma aspect of their fourth chakra (mate and parent stage of life). The businesses or enterprises they start not only serve as venues for actualizing more of their selfhood (svadharma), but also contribute to their families and communities.

My wife, Usha, started an Indian restaurant in her second life. While it was the realization of a long-cherished dream and the opportunity to live her autonomy and selfhood in a very successful endeavor, it also became a base from which to launch her partner, our daughter Ami, who will perhaps explore and master many new frontiers in her life thanks to her mother's initiative and courage.

A Couple's Heart-Chakra Problem (continued)

Initially, the precarious chakra balance between Mary and Marty worked out well when both were able to live in the mayic mode. Marty projected his feelings and emotional dependency needs onto Mary; Mary vicariously lived her potential for autonomy and enterprise by projecting it onto Marty. Marty needed to be the hero and warrior in the outer world, and Mary needed to be the materially dependent, but emotionally providing, spouse at home, taking care of their children and everybody's feelings. However, in the midlife transition, trouble developed in their paradise.

Mary and Marty had created considerable karma between them. Mary resented Marty's control, and he unconsciously resented having Mary chronically dependent on him. This led to

4. The expression "second life," as I have said earler, refers to the phase of life after an individual has recognized the reality of maya and karma, i.e., that the everyday world that so very much occupies our attention early in life is but a limited portion of reality, and that our actions carry consequences (karma). Moving from the "first life" to the "second life" is a shift from a mayic consciousness to a karmic consciousness.

mutual unconscious resentment, although, consciously and to all outward appearances, the marriage was "conventionally successful." When Mary started to claim her autonomy after finishing graduate school in midlife, she was unable to get much support from Marty to try her wings in the world outside the home. She was depressed and became a patient on behalf of both of them. Even as her depression deepened, she continued to do the emotional work for herself and for him.

Actually, in the unconscious arrangement between Mary and Marty, she had always carried Marty's sad and dark feelings, especially when he was faced with the inevitable reverses in his second life as he was pushed to the bottom of the pyramid in the rubble of the corporate waste heap. When he no longer could live completely out of his third chakra of autonomy and control, as he lost his powerful grip on his corporate milieu and could no longer unconsciously depend on Mary for emotional support, he became more and more disgruntled (and unconsciously depressed). So Mary carried the depression for both of them (in her fourth chakra of feelings).

However, their precarious balancing act broke down when Marty's mother died at age 80. Marty was unable to grieve his mother's death (and his professional reverses) as something to be expected. He expressed no emotions. Mary felt the grief for both of them, becoming more depressed and even suicidal.

This vicious cycle finally broke when Marty had a massive heart attack. He could no longer continue with business as usual. His heart attack forced him to let go of the illusion that he could control all the professional and personal events in his life (with his dominant third-chakra pingala nadi). It "broke his heart" when he was unable to halt his professional decline and personal loss. Marty needed to reassess his life and his marriage.

Finally, forced to attend to his fourth (heart) chakra, Marty began to experience his emotions, and started to verbalize his grief over his mother's death and the hurt and disappointment about his professional reverses. As he permitted himself to depend on Mary for love, nurturance, and emotional support, he withdrew some of the energy from his third-chakra pingala nadi (of master in control) and was able to strengthen the ida nadi of his fourth chakra, telling Mary what he needed (his dependency needs). This began to retire his master/slave karma with Mary. At long last, Mary and Marty were becoming true partners and lovers.

For her part, Mary was now able to move out of her third-chakra ida nadi into her third-chakra sushumna nadi of mastery and appropriate control. She began to shape her personal destiny and assert her autonomy in her relationship with Marty and in her professional ambitions. For his part, Marty permitted himself the luxury of letting Mary take care of him in a new way as he expressed his fears and feelings about reverses and losses in his life. He has claimed access to the feeling capacity of his fourth chakra. He is recovering well from his heart problems and mellowing his aggressive pursuit of professional success. Moreover, he is able to support Mary's quest for autonomy. Mary has found a good position in her chosen profession and is claiming her third chakra of autonomy and mastery in her work and marriage.

Vishudha—
The Throat Chakra of Initiative

The fifth chakra is called the *Vishudha*, or "Purification" chakra, and is situated in the throat, at the pharyngeal plexus. The fifth chakra is the beginning of the realm of abstract ideas and psychic, rather than physical, reality. This is that aspect of our mental life where we start to see all events occurring, not only in physical reality, but in the subtle planes.

The animal associated with the fifth chakra is the elephant, but this elephant has only one trunk. (The elephant of the first chakra had seven trunks.) The fifth-chakra elephant stands for knowledge of nature and the environment, and teaches patience, memory, and self-confidence.

Memory, ready wit, intuition, and improvisation are all related to the fifth chakra. A fifth-chakra person will seek only that knowledge that is timeless, true beyond the limitations of maya, culture, and conditioning. The main problem encountered in the fifth chakra is negative intellect, which occurs when the individual

is cut off from the heart and forehead chakra (governing integrity and leadership).

Angie Finds her Voice

One of my women patients, Angie, suffered a fifth-chakra disorder. In a recent psychotherapy session, Angie said, "I feel that my voice is not heard." The next week, she had a dream in which she was Anne Frank, writing in her dairy in a dark, desolate room. Angie felt alone, isolated, unheard by significant people in her life. The dream image accurately depicted her present life circumstances.

Angie is a successful professional in midlife. Her grandparents immigrated to America prior to the World War II. Many of her uncles and aunts perished in the concentration camps in Nazi Germany. Her own childhood was turbulent. The family struggled to be assimilated into American culture. Her father was overburdened at work and her mother was depressed and overwhelmed by the chores of parenting her family. Angie's parents grossly underplayed their rich ethnic roots in order to fit into what Angie calls the gentile majority culture.

As the oldest child, Angie assumed the bulk of the parenting responsibilities. Although she had a great potential to become a leader (her fifth chakra was the natural dominant), it was her maya to be stuck in the ida nadi of the fifth chakra as a silent caretaker. Consequently, she could not give voice to the emotions in her heart and exercise the initiative to pursue her own path.

She projected her strivings for initiative and leadership onto her ex-husband and present husband while she became the silent follower. This created karmic problems with both her ex-husband and her present husband when she attempted to express her own views about life and her faith, and to take the initiative to realize her life goals.

Urged on by chronic depressive symptoms and guided by her dreams, Angie gradually shifted energy to the sushumna nadi of her fifth chakra and was able to take the initiative on her own behalf. This has led to her becoming able to voice her values and priorities, to come out of hiding as a "Closet Jew" and openly claim her spiritual beliefs and worldview. As Angie communicates her true values and beliefs, she is actualizing the svadharma of her fifth chakra, appropriately tempered by the qualities of her well-developed fourth chakra. She is a source of inspiration for others who find peace, calm, and understanding in her presence. Angie is no longer locked in the role of a voiceless caretaker of others.

Like Anne Frank, Angie is a courageous young woman. Anne Frank perished in the Nazi Holocaust. No one listened to her during her lifetime, yet her dairy became her voice and the immortal voice of oppressed peoples the world over. Anne Frank is a living symbol for my patient to reconnect with her spiritual roots and reclaim her rich heritage.

THE FIFTH-CHAKRA DRAMA

People in whom the fifth chakra is optimally developed are both intuitively perceptive, even clairvoyant, and able to communicate both verbally and nonverbally. They possess a voice and can take the initiative to express and live according to their own values, priorities, belief systems, and philosophies of life. The voice of fifth-chakra people penetrates to the heart of the listener.

Having resolved the tension between initiative and guilt, the energy of fifth-chakra people flows in the sushumna nadi, enabling them to comprehend accurately, communicate clearly, and lead effectively. The drama of the fifth chakra plays out between the those who intimidate (dominance of the pingala nadi) and those who are intimidated and silent (dominance of the ida nadi).

In the fifth (throat or pharyngeal) chakra, the drama of the intimidated and the intimidator is played out in a mutual unconscious projection system of both the silent and the intimidated types. The vocal intimidators are in the mayic mode and project their opposite, unlived half onto their counterparts. In the resulting karma, the intimidator carries the torch of initiative and the intimidated carries the guilt of self-denial.

When the silent ones and the intimidators take back their mutual projections, they (and their relationship) moves to the sushumna nadi (central channel), where either can take the initiative and neither need feel guilt. Both individuals are now able to communicate in their own voice about their views, values, and beliefs. This move to the sushumna nadi leads to a renewed sense of initiative and actualizes svadharma in the realm of optimal self-expression and advocacy.

The maya trap for the intimidator in the fifth chakra is the pleasure that excessive intrusiveness, attack, and conquest appears to promise when he or she catches the other in the web of sophistry, attractiveness, and endearment. For the intimidated, the maya trap entails feeling guilty and hysterically denying one's true voice and views when subjected to the intrusiveness and aggression (initiative gone awry) of the intimidator. For the intimidator, the karma of the fifth chakra is negative intellect, using knowledge unwisely, self-advertisement, and exaggerated self-proclamations leading to isolation from others. For the intimidated, the karma manifests as a diminished sense of self arising from the suppression or denial of one's initiative and authentic voice.

Medical and psychological problems of the fifth chakra manifest in the throat area. Somatically, I have observed people with throat and thyroid problems secondary to energy disturbance in the throat chakra. Men may overadvertize themselves, presenting narcissistic personality disorders, and women may lose their authentic voice, expressing themselves only via their anxiety symptoms or fears of taking a personal or individual stand on an issue.

Women and minority men often present to their doctors with problems of the throat, thyroid illness, and other diseases of the neck. It is a manifestation of their throat chakra heating up, urging them to speak out, to find their own voice. Such minority or politically disfranchised groups may delegate their voice to their partners, leaders, and other sundry loud intimidators, to the detriment of that aspect of their svadharma related to actualizing their potential to take initiative.

AJNA—THE EYE CHAKRA OF INTEGRITY AND LEADERSHIP

The sixth chakra is called the *Ajna*, or "Place of Command." It is located between the eyebrows. The sixth chakra looks like the third eye, or a winged seed. This is the chakra where the inner vision of the psyche originates. It is here that we can see our inner, psychological world, as well as the transcendent or dharmic world beyond the outer, physical reality perceived by our two eyes. No animal form is associated with the sixth chakra, since the activity here is perception of the nonmanifest dimension of reality.

PSYCHOLOGICAL AND DHARMIC ISSUES OF THE SIXTH CHAKRA

The psychological issues of the sixth chakra are ego integrity versus despair. We achieve ego integrity when we have adapted to the trials, tribulations, and triumphs of our unique life journey, and have adequately fulfilled this chakra's dharmic task, which is to discover where and how our particular existence meaningfully fulfills varna dharma, our relationship to our fellow human beings.

Erik Erikson calls this stage of development "post-narcissistic self-love," for we accept our life journey just the way it has been in order to fulfill our svadharma. The labyrinthine, serpentine course of individual lives and the trials and triumphs then make sense and have meaning in the bigger picture of community and place. Ego integrity leads to emotional and spiritual integration, permits meaningful and informed participation in the community and fellowship of men and women, and enables us to assume leadership if called upon to do so.

Jody:
The Woman Who Lived with a Statue

When she initially consulted me about her symptoms of depression, frequent headaches, and lack of intimacy with her hus-band, who had been inattentive for several years, Jody was in her 50s. Her emotionally distant father, a successful, hard-working businessman, had died the year before she started therapy, and Jody was still grieving his death. Consciously, Jody had seen him as a man devoted to his family. Unconsciously, however (as we found out), she knew he had seldom been present for her and her siblings.

In one session, she said that being with me felt like being with a statue as her father had been. I was startled. I had always thought that my comfortable consultation room and my attentive listening put my patients at ease. She said she felt oppressed by my blank-screen demeanor. Jody wanted us to address each other by our first names, rather than the more formal Ms. and Dr. that had been my custom. As I listened to Jody talk about her father and her husband, I realized she had a valid point: I did tend to hide behind my psychiatrist's persona in my immaculate, but formal, consulting room.

As I got to know Jody better, I saw that she tried to appear cheerful, accepting, and understanding of her situation. She worked hard at being a good mother and wife, but that actually meant she did all the emotional work for everybody in her family. Underneath, however, I sensed a scared, dependent little girl, afraid of men, as well as a powerful woman who could hold her own with anybody. Jody was carrying a lot of unlived life. I wondered what was causing her to be depressed and to have headaches.

Her depression was her stuckness in the fourth chakra where she carried the feelings of everyone in her family—especially the men—while her headaches were the call of her sixth chakra, trying to relocate her kundalini energy into the sixth chakra, the locus of insight. Let us now explore the sixth chakra. (I'll return to Jody's story later.)

THE SIXTH-CHAKRA DRAMA

Sixth-chakra people see the world beyond the physical realm just as clearly as they perceive outer reality with physical eyes, and recognize that individual existence is relative, part of a much larger mosaic of higher consciousness. Sixth-chakra people realize that we don't live life; rather, the larger design of nature lives us. They recognize that they are not the subject and the world the object, but rather the world and higher consciousness is the subject and we its mere objects and instruments. Individuals in the sixth chakra become aware that they are personally insignificant, yet tremendously important as the vehicles through which higher consciousness incarnates and actualizes its ends. They see their fragile, transient personal lives as one precious little piece in the divine, cosmic rhythm of life. Sixth-chakra people are most readily able the ride the contours of destiny.

Integrity, one of the attributes of the sixth chakra, carries the connotations of conscience, incorruptibility, soundness, completeness, and honesty. Ajna, the sixth chakra, is also associated with clairvoyance, vision of the inner workings and connections not visible to the "naked eye." In the ida-nadi mode, perception without action is passive. The ability to perceive and visualize, however, also confers the power to establish those thought forms that manifest in the outer or inner worlds. Hence the dark side of the sixth chakra involves the visualization of possibilities not in accord with dharma. This can come about, for example, when individuals in the sixth chakra confuse and interchange the realm of personal insignificance and collective value. They are caught in mayic mode.

The karmic task of people misusing the powers of the sixth chakra is to recognize personal transience and insignificance. If they over-identify personally with the collective issues that must live through them, they become inflated as narcissistic individuals. Then they resemble the bank teller who confuses the huge sums of money for which he has responsibility with personal wealth. The inability to maintain ego integrity while holding such collective responsibility leads to despair, deep demoralization, and fragmentation of self—in short, to existential depression. Existential depression is the despair and depletion that comes from not knowing one's place or role on the stage of life and in the world.

The maya of the sixth chakra may be excessive involvement in community at expense of the true role one must play in the bigger picture of the community. These self-defeating personality disorders befall people who sacrifice authentic selfhood in service of a pseudo-affiliation with community. They then need to access the energy source of the fifth chakra to find their authentic voice (their svadharma) and to visit the realm of the seventh chakra to get a sense of their connection with the higher divine order (reta dharma) and find their true place in the life of the community.

In the sixth chakra, the mayic drama of leader (in the "hot" pingala nadi) and the follower (in the "cold" ida nadi) plays out in the mutual unconscious projection system linking them. The follower and the leader both get caught in their respective maya and project their leader-follower tendencies onto the others around them. This sets up a society of few leaders and many followers, and when the leaders can't deliver on their promises, these societies are plunged into despair.

Sooner or later, the person locked compulsively in the leadership role (through the dominance of the pingala nadi) falls from grace because of the impossibility of fulfilling all the expectations of the followers. This is inevitably the lot of false prophets and self-appointed gurus. Conversely, those who deny their potential for leadership, regardless of how great or limited it may be, set themselves up to resent the chosen or self-appointed leaders.

The karmic debt of the follower's denial of leadership potential, and the leader's lack of humility in surrendering leadership when they should follow, create imbalance in families, organizations, societies, nations, and international relations. When such leader and follower types move into the sushumna nadi, they enter the realm of true participation in the affairs of families, community, nation, and the world. Participation of this sort moves them from a sense of despair that fallen leaders and resentful followers feel, to the state of being empowered that comes from informed, insightful participation. Their sense of integrity develops, and they are able to claim their rightful place in the community and their varna dharma.

Jody's depression and headaches were related to two chakras. Like many women in American society, Jody had been groomed to do all the emotional work for the significant others in her life. This overworked her fourth (heart) chakra. When first meeting women like Jody, people often get the impression that the warmth, caring, and understanding are expressions of a dominant heart chakra. Sometimes this impression is correct, but often the heart-chakra energy these women express, while genuine, turns out to be a social adaptation, a fulfillment of society's expectations, and not the authentic dominant chakra.

For Jody, living from the heart chakra had become a burden. She had to carry not only her own feelings, but the unlived emotional life of her late father and her emotionally unavailable husband. Telling me that I was like a statue (like her father and her husband) was Jody's way of protesting my emotional distance and unavailability to her. Her headaches were not just a symptom to be cured, but the protest of her sixth (head) chakra telling her that she was not seeing the inner meaning of her overworked heart chakra and the depression that it caused. As Jody and I worked on her compulsion to bring her "statues" to life, her depression abated, but her headaches continued. This was puzzling. Then, a series of seemingly chance events caught our attention.

Jody was very active in her church. For some time, there had been talk of establishing a sister-church relationship with another congregation, but it had amounted to nothing more than well-intentioned talk. From time to time, Jody had told me her congregation's inaction frustrated her, but we had not paid much attention to the possible sister-church issue, because it didn't seem to bear significantly on her depression, her headaches, or her suffering from her husband's emotional unavailability. In one session, however, Jody again mentioned the sister-church issue, and it occurred to me that, perhaps, there was more there than we had thought.

As I explored Jody's thoughts and feelings about a sister-church in subsequent sessions, she brightened up. We were on to something. Jody realized that she really wanted her congregation to do something about this, not just talk about it. Jody offered to chair a committee to explore the needs of several inner-city churches and the possibilities for cooperation. As her committee got to work, Jody suffered headaches less often. When she did experience a headache, we discovered it started after Jody had felt frustrated in her leadership role.

Jody has tremendous leadership qualities. Her selfhood (svadharma) is blossoming. As a leader in her church and community, Jody's actions (karma) serve the common good (varna dharma), rather than egotistical ends. She is realizing her dharmic potential.

When Jody first consulted me, she had been in a state of despair. Closer analysis revealed that her despair was related to leading a muted and unauthentic life. Her life was also unauthetic in that she had not been living out her true leaderhip and dharmic potential, but rather was experiencing it via the men in her life.

As she claimed her own self (svadharma) and community (varna) dharma, her inner life "got together" and she felt a coming together with her own soul and dharma.

This is how we feel when we live from the center of our life passions rather than on the fringes This is the stage of ego integrity in which our outer life is connected with our soul strivings. When the ego and the soul work together, our actions (karma) serve dharma. We live with integrity when our outer and inner lives cooperate, when our mayic cravings become the stepping-stones on our dharmic path, when karma serves dharma and ego serves the soul.

Leaders who have navigated the path to the soul reach the realm of the sixth chakra of insight and leadership. When they are in the sushumna nadi of the sixth chakra, their leadership does not serve self-interest, but carries out God's work.

SAHASRARA—THE CROWN CHAKRA OF SPIRITUALITY AND MOKSHA

The seventh chakra is called *Sahasrara* and is located above the crown of the head. This is the place of Nirvana—freedom from opposites—and is considered to be the realm where the individual soul and the Universal Soul are One. This is the realm of the total union of Shiva and Shakti, of all opposite and conflicting tendencies within oneself and between self and the cosmos. In the realm of the seventh chakra, the individual is at one with nature, the collective psyche, and with God. This unity, however, has no experience of self as separate from God and nature. This is reverse of the maya of the first chakra, where there may be little awareness of nature as anything but an appendage of self.

When people in the seventh chakra are in the mayic mode, they are so lost in the collective psyche and the broader and deeper issues of life that they are divorced from outer reality. Such individuals, stuck in the maya of the seventh chakra, may present symptoms such as schizophrenia, schizoid, or schizotypal personality disorders. While they may have profound insight into the deepest questions and mysteries of human life, their insight is unusable for pragmatic purposes and disconnects them from

human encounters. The karma of people lost in the seventh chakra is to reconnect with outer reality and the mundane issues of daily existence. For this human contact, they have to consult and honor the first chakra (survival and security). When they balance the schizoid, autistic withdrawal of the seventh chakra with the karmic task of reconnecting with basic concerns and relationships, such individuals can fulfill reta dharma. They can then become authentic gurus, teachers, and mentors, and guide others on the path of highest consciousness. They help the rest of us get a glimpse of the timeless mystery of our existence in the greater plan of nature.

ATTAINMENT OF RETA DHARMA IN THE SEVENTH CHAKRA

The crown, or head, chakra addresses the issues of reta dharma, the issues of the interface between the human and the divine. The dharma of the individual in the seventh chakra is the struggle with experiencing the meaning of existence in the larger mystery of the cosmos. People with strong seventh chakras are attracted to metapsychological and theological pursuits.

Unfortunately, there is a mayic danger in the seventh chakra, just as there is in the other six chakras. When people are caught in the maya of the seventh chakra, they may get so lost in the transcendent realm that they loose connection with the first chakra of survival. In my clinical practice, people caught in the maya of the seventh chakra often present with schizophrenia, or schizoid and schizotypal personality disorders.

When their seventh-chakra abode is informed and tempered by the first chakra (grounding in reality) and the sixth chakra (meaningful contact with community), they can live their seventh chakra authentically, as the meaningful reta dharma of spiritual pursuit grounded in reality and in service of the community. They have the potential to help humanity find itself and its place in the divine order of the cosmos. Gandhi, Christ, Buddha, priests with integrity, and spiritual guides are examples of this type.

Individuals in the seventh chakra are considered to be old souls in their spiritual journey, souls who have the potential to achieve moksha, liberation from entanglement in maya and karma, and they experience oneness with cosmic energy as the pinnacle of reta dharma.

The Priest Lost in the Seventh Chakra

One of my patients, Martin, a priest with a deep sense of transcendence and of the mystery of life who could hardly function in the world, illustrates one of the dangers of getting lost in the seventh chakra.

When I first met Martin, I was awestruck: he seemed like my mentors and gurus, highly impressive, up on the mountaintop, with a deep sense of connection with God. But he was totally disengaged from the outer world and from people, to the extent that, in spite of a deep spiritual presence, he was unable to guide his flock. His superior had gotten very concerned about his well-being and referred him to me for consultation and evaluation.

Once I had worked through my idealization of him, I started to understand Martin's problem. It was clear that he suffered a kind of schizophrenia, and was totally isolated from his peers and parishioners. It was also apparent that Martin resided in the seventh chakra, where he experienced a deep sense of transcendence and the mystery of life. However, he was so preoccupied with these "higher" pursuits that he had started to ignore his basic survival needs. He sometimes remained deep in thought, not eating or leaving his quarters, for days. In his ethereal realm, he had little connection with the basics of survival or engagement in relationships.

His dwelling in the ethereal realm of the seventh chakra became a sterile connection with his thoughts about God. The experience of this higher reality was not embodied in any tangible manner, and his spiritual inflation cut him off from God's world. My psychotherapy with him focused on two major interventions. First, he had to ground in the first chakra of survival and reconnect with Earth. With my guidance and prompting, he established a simple structure to deal with his daily survival needs. This included attention to meals, exercise, and contact with his mother and a friend. Later, after he was more grounded in basic outer reality, Martin and I explored issues of the sixth chakra: the impact of his withdrawal on his community (his neglect of his varna dharma).

For a while, Martin needed medications to ground him in his outer reality. Gradually, as he integrated the preliminary aspects of first chakra (survival) and sixth chakra (community responsibility) issues, he began to reclaim his seventh chakra "home," now tempered and enriched by connection to his community of priests and parishioners and by respect for survival needs.

THE SEVENTH-CHAKRA DRAMA

The drama of the seventh chakra plays out pathologically between two personality styles: the remote, withdrawn, seemingly other-worldly ascetic, and the narcissistic, self-agrandizing, self-promoting person who claims to have a direct and exclusive connection to God. Locked in their respective mayic modes, the withdrawn, emotionally inaccessible individual is stuck in the (cold) ida nadi, while the narcissist is locked in the (hot) pingala nadi. Each unconsciously projects the unlived other half onto the opposite, who contains it and vicariously lives it out for them.

All too often, we have seen "spiritual leaders" and Eastern "gurus" fall from their pedestals as their clay feet have crumbled. These fallen idols have not been able to balance the energies in the pingala and the sushumna nadis. Had they been able to balance their focus on the highest spiritual enlightenment, while maintaining compassion for fellow human beings, they could have occupied the revered place of guru, teacher, mentor, or guide for those around them. Individuals in the sushumna nadi of the seventh chakra have the potential to be the bridge between humanity and the highest spiritual realm. To be a true bridge, however, they must be connected to both sides: to mortals and to the forces of the cosmos.

Promise and Perils of Kundalini

In the preceding discussion of the seven chakras, we have seen how men and women have been able to change their lives for the better when they corrected imbalances in the various chakras, often by accessing and strengthening a balanced-energy economy in an auxiliary chakra that then enabled them to correct the imbalance in the problematic chakra. As I have pointed out, the kundalini chakras provide a paradigm that usefully links physical, psychological, developmental, and spiritual dimensions so that both my patients and I have been better able to understand what is going on with them and to take steps to reconfigure their energy flow. While the kundalini experience I have described is generally a renewing pilgrimage, it is not without its hazards.

As with all change, we must dismantle old structures before we can erect new ones. We must courageously confront the chaos that change entails on the journey through the dark night of the soul to reach the dawn of new consciousness. While we are going through the awakening and realignment of the kundalini within the psyche, we can feel very disoriented and sometimes devastated.

The focus of my presentation has been on the use of the individual's life events, medical or psychiatric symptoms, relationship strengths and problems, and life goals and aspirations as a diagnostic guide. These variables may help to ascertain the individual's dominant and auxiliary chakras. This approach differs from the use of Hatha Yoga or Tantric exercises intended to activate the dormant kundalini and raise it through the seven chakras. These techniques have a long tradition carried by teachers and adepts who have both the experience and the ability to guide the student through the complicated steps involved. I have encountered individuals who have prematurely activated one or another kundalini chakra without the corresponding mental preparation and psychic apparatus to understand and honor the forces they have unleashed. This has resulted in undesirable medical, psychiatric, and relationship consequences. The approach I am presenting here, however, is no more dangerous than any conventional attempt to remedy a medical, psychiatric, psychological, or spiritual dis-ease. This approach does not arbitrarily interfere with the inherent kundalini configuration of the individual. Rather, it *honors* the inherent kundalini predisposition and balances it in the context of the somatic, psychological, developmental, and spiritual needs of the person.

As we have seen, the kundalini chakras are focal points where physical, emotional, developmental, and spiritual forces intersect. The drama of maya, karma, and dharma plays out in one or more of the chakras. In addition to the matrix defined by the chakras, we must also consider the "functional unit" in which our emotional experiences are encoded. These "functional units" are charged clusters of emotions, memories, behaviors, and expectations that have a strong tendency to lead a life of their own. They are the karmic complexes that we will explore in the next chapter.

POINTS TO PONDER

1. What are your dominant and auxiliary chakras?
2. As you do your life-course chart of important events, illnesses, problems, relationships, goals, and pursuits to date, can you identify the chakras you have traveled through in your life? What did each of these chakra visits tell you about yourself?

3. In which anatomical chakra location do you usually get medical or emotional symptoms (for example, headaches for the seventh chakra, eye problems for the sixth chakra, throat problems in the fifth chakra, heart problems and depression for the fourth chakra, stomach problems for the third chakra, bladder and genital-system problems for the second chakra, and rectal, perineal, and emotional-security problems for the first chakra)?
4. In your significant relationships, which chakra system is dominant (for example, the victim/aggressor-mother system in the first chakra, the martyr/exploiter-parent system in second chakra, the master/slave-partner system in the third chakra, the dependent/caretaker-lover system in the fourth chakra, the silent/intimidator-communicator system in the fifth chakra, the leader/follower-participant system in the sixth chakra, the autistic/narcissistic-guide system in the seventh chakra)?
5. What aspect of your life has activated your kundalini experience: your present life role, your medical or psychiatric illness, life goals, your relationship problems, or some other aspect of your life experience?
6. Based on your kundalini understanding so far, what is the dharmic level you have achieved: artha, wealth and security pursued in the first chakra; kama, pleasure and generativity pursued in the second chakra; svadharma, self-actualization pursued in the third chakra; ashrama dharma, responsibility to family, pursued in the fourth chakra; svadharma informed by varna dharma, authentic expression of self in service of community, in the fifth chakra; varna dharma, responsibility to our fellow human beings, in the sixth chakra; or reta or spiritual dharma in the seventh chakra?
7. Based on the foregoing discussion and some of the definitions from the ancient text of Bhagavad Gita

quoted in this chapter, what is your closest experience of moksha or liberation from human entanglements and connection with the Primal Soul? What crisis or experiences have given you the opportunities for renunciation and detached action?

chapter six

Karmic Complexes As a Path to the Soul

We may say that our complexes are the cards that fate has dealt us; with these cards and with no others we either win or lose the game. . . .

—E. C. Whitmont[1]

The concepts of maya, karma, and dharma explain, in general, how medical and psychiatric symptoms lead us on the path to the soul. Maya is the school in which karma—the necessary consequences of our actions—teaches us the lessons of the four faces of dharma: our individual nature, the reality of the stages of life we all must experience, our relationship to our fellow creatures, and the spiritual laws governing all creation. By localizing the maya-karma-dharma cycle in one or more of the seven chakras, the kundalini template provides a definitive understanding of why we have the physical, behavioral, or developmental symptoms we do. Karmic complexes, the third element in the maya-karma-dharma kundalini matrix, are the psychic or somatic units into which our emotional experience is organized. Karmic complexes are, as it were, the organs that make up the body of our emotional expectations, sensitivities, and reactions. They are the functional units localized in the chakras that have arisen through the interplay of maya, karma, and dharma.

Most people know the term "complex." Complexes have probably always been a feature of the human psyche. In times past,

---

1. E. C. Whitmont, *The Symbolic Quest* (Princeton: Princeton University Press, 1969), p. 72.

what we call complexes were often referred to as spirits, demons, or devils. After many years of clinical experience and much effort to integrate Western analytic concepts and Eastern Hindu spiritual concepts, I have observed that complexes and karma share fundamental similarities. As I discussed earlier, karma arises as a result of the choices we make and the actions we take based on our perceptions. Complexes develop as we are affected by (and react to) what we perceive and experience, and to the meaning we attach to those perceptions of our experience. Further, our actions and reactions bear necessary and predictable consequences that may be desirable or undesirable. This holds true for both karma and complexes. Karma and complexes share a cause-effect-consequence structural pattern. This convergence has led me to speak of "karmic complexes."

Jung called complexes "splinter psyches."[2] The reality of complexes and their tendency toward autonomy and independence is vividly exhibited in another phenomenon that has attracted public and professional attention in recent years—multiple personality. In this condition, various complexes, each having its distinctive characteristics, become autonomous at different times. They usurp consciousness and behavior from the central ego complex, which later reports having "lost time." In multiple personality disorder—now called dissociative personality disorder—the ego complex has been deposed (that is, incapacitated), resulting in an emotional and behavioral free-for-all.

For most people most of the time, intense complexes typically behave and appear in several ways: personified as other people who "get under our skin," or as moods and emotions that take us over to some extent, so that we "aren't quite ourselves" and "don't know what got into us." Although flesh and blood people can trigger our complexes by their resemblance to them, complexes are, at best, "part personalities," "imaginary people with half a face and part of the body missing."[3] Moreover, I have

---

2. C. G. Jung, "A Review of the Complex Theory," CW8, ¶203.
3. I am indebted to Dennis Getto for this graphic image of the complex.

come to the conclusion that some of our complexes carry over from a previous life, as mini-reincarnations of some karma that we still need to resolve. If we are to fulfill our dharma as fully as possible, we must retire not only our "new," but also our "old" unfinished business: the complexes that have developed in this life, as well as those from the past.[4]

The Discovery of Complexes

It is worthwhile to review the history of the discovery of the feeling-toned complexes so that we can better understand them and the role they play in psychic life. While working at Burghölzi Hospital in Zürich, Jung discovered the feeling-toned complexes as an anomoly in a test procedure he was using for another purpose. The test consisted in presenting a series of stimulus words, one at a time, and asking the test subject to react to each word with the first word or image that came to mind. The reaction times varied, and Jung noticed that the responses of his subjects were disturbed in typical ways. From this Jung inferred that the stimulus word had touched something in the psyche over which the subject did not have conscious control. Somehow, the critical stimulus word referred to a personal matter of a distressing nature, often in a symbolic way or as an allusion. Jung eventually called the element that disturbed the conscious response a "feeling-toned complex."

Complex Indicators

Jung summarized a number of responses that he called "complex indicators:"[5]

1. Longer-than-average reaction time;
2. Repetition of the stimulus word;

---

4. Our propensity to form complexes is part of the way the psyche organizes experience. All people form certain complexes, for example around the image of mother and father. However, the positioning of planets in the various houses and signs in the astrological birth chart reveals those areas of life in which the individual is constitutionally likely to develop more troublesome complexes.

5. C. G. Jung, "On the Psychological Diagnosis of Evidence," CW2, ¶1363–1364.

3. Misunderstanding of the stimulus word;
4. Expressive movements (such as laughing);
5. Reacting with more than one word;
6. Reacting in a striking manner (with, for example, a sound or mechanically);
7. Meaningless or nonsense reactions;
8. Failure to react at all;
9. Repetition of the same word in responding to the next stimulus word;
10. Slips of the tongue;
11. Use of foreign words.

Part of Jung's procedure involved his repeating the list of stimulus words. When the subject was not able to respond during the second pass through the list with the same response word as in the first trial, Jung called this a "defective reproduction." This further supported his hypothesis that something was going on in the psyche that was *not* under the control of the conscious mind.

HOW COMPLEXES DEVELOP

Complexes usually develop over time around a typical theme as we experience the same or similar life events. Emotions hold the experienced data together. Fear, dread, humiliation, embarrassment, shame, anger, but also the positive emotions of joy, pleasure, and happiness function as binding forces in complexes. If, for example, we have been chided or ridiculed often enough or by significant people for exhibiting certain behaviors or expressing certain ideas, opinions, or interests, *and* if we have become sensitive to these responses, it is very likely a complex has taken shape. Our corresponding complex can be triggered and the central emotion evoked by any element associated with this cluster of experience: by the thought or sight of the people originally involved; by reference to the behavior, idea, opinion, or interest; or by the mention of the situations or places where the complex or its constituent elements were experienced. A child repeatedly subjected to a fault-finding female caretaker may develop a negative mother complex and respond inappropriately to women. A child consistently nurtured by a supportive female caretaker may develop a positive mother complex and be able to respond appropriately to women and/or opportunities to mature.

Keep in mind that, although a complex always has a history, it can be activated, appropriately or inappropriately, in the present. When a complex is touched in the here and now, we feel its emotion to some degree, and whether or not the immediate or current situation warrants it, the complex's emotion influences our expectations, perception, and judgment of the present circumstances, as well as our behavior, in characteristic ways.

The feeling-toned complexes are not fundamentally bad. They are typical and normal features of the psyche. They operate in the same way that the mind does in cross-referencing experiences in memory. Complexes can be positive as well as negative, pleasant as well as distressing. Nevertheless, when activated, they skew the conscious attitude and behavior. In this way, they can compromise our fulfilling any one (or more) of the four dharmas.

Our karmic complexes can either lead us into more karmic entanglements or serve as stepping-stones toward dharma. It's up to us which path we tread.

How Karmic Complexes Lead to More Karma or to Dharma

A person can have any number of karmic complexes. Some current life event activates a complex, releasing a burst of emotion that can manifest in medical and/or psychiatric symptoms—in relationship problems, dreams, or synchronistic events (meaningful coincidences). We can either react or respond. If we *react* without reflecting, we will probably create consequences we do not savor—that is, we may create primary karma through the discharge of the emotional energy in our karmic complexes. When we do this, we keep getting into the same old messes again and again, and we typically blame our problems in life on others. Complex discharge fails to take dharma into account, because we direct our efforts toward the pleasures and rewards of "this world" (maya, the limited or provisional reality). If we are conscious enough, however, we can chose how we *respond*, and thereby have some influence over the effects of our actions (creating secondary karma). The route of primary karma leads us back into maya. The path of secondary karma leads toward the soul and realizes our dharma.

When we don't let our karmic complexes burst forth unchecked, we contain their emotion and chose *how* and *where* we will respond to the trigger that activated our complex. First, we go into ourselves to explore what in us is so vulnerable, so explosive. Rather than blame others for our troubles, we search our own souls. We deal with the beam in our own eye before we berate our neighbor for the splinter in his or her eye. We learn to see other people as they are, not as they appear to us through the distorted lenses of our own be-complexed perception. We ask ourselves *the* crucial question: What lesson can my complex teach me? In other words, we turn from the pursuit of the temptations of maya to the rewards of dharma. To shift our awareness from primary to secondary karma, however, we must be able to recognize karmic complexes when they appear.

KARMIC COMPLEXES, THE EGO COMPLEX, AND PROJECTION

It is usually easy to recognize when a person is in the grip of a complex. Consider, for example, the "inferiority" complex, which refers to the way a person can feel, relate to others, and think about him- or herself. Those suffering from this complex may be apologetic and timid, seeing others as powerful authorities (secretly both admired and hated). Often their feelings of inferiority make them unsure of themselves, so that they blunder and make mistakes when they are in situations where they feel someone else is more self-confident, more knowledgeable, or more adept.

Opposite those whose inferiority complex has them in its steely grip are those with a superiority complex. These people have no doubts about themselves (or so it seems). They lord it over everyone. Insecurity seems foreign to them. Sometimes you don't even have to ask. (Secretly, the superiority they present to the outside world may be a mask hiding their inner vulnerability.)

Our language provides a rich vocabulary that depicts in vivid metaphors what happens when a complex gets activated. We say, for example, that we "lost it," "flew off the handle," "went ballistic"—all images of uncontrollable emotion. Another group of descriptors refers to embarrassment or shame: we "could have died on the spot" or "wished the floor would have opened up and swallowed us." Sometimes we image disgust by saying that something is "enough to make us puke." Some frightening event makes us "jump out of our skin." All of these images refer to trigger events that set loose intense emotions in us. Those intense emotions are part of the complex that has been activated.

Not all complexes are bad. One central complex I must mention is the ego complex, without which we would be lost. The ego complex—the sense or feeling of "I-ness," of being "oneself"—is grounded in both psyche and soma. It is through the ego complex that we actualize all four aspects of our dharma. The actualization of our svadharma in the ego complex is what creates our unique patterns of response to the various situations life presents. As we have seen, when other complexes are activated, they affect the ego complex. Without a strong, functional ego complex, we would be pulled in all directions by any other complex(es) that are triggered from time to time.

In addition to the ego complex, other karmic complexes take shape as life events cluster around the karmic seeds from a past life or around the currently activated dharmic pattern. The personality comes to resemble a committee or a parliament—or an unruly mob—composed of a variety of members (complexes) with differing views, needs, histories, sensitivities, and agendas. When the ego complex is able to carry on a viable dialogue with the other complexes and integrate them over time, a rich personality emerges. That personality experiences what life presents without distorting it, and consequently grows in scope and depth.

When the internal dialogue among the ego and the other complexes turns into a shouting match in a conflict of interests and commitments, or when the ego complex is unable to choose among alternatives, we are at war with ourselves. In neurosis, one or more of the karmic complexes temporarily influences, or even prevails over, the ego complex. In psychosis, karmic complexes permanently overpower the ego complex. This leads to a loss of the sense of reality, to a failure to distinguish between ego complex and other complexes. Then we are unable to function in the world.

When important relationship and emotional patterns (complexes) repeatedly get projected (that is, when they overlay "what's really out there"), they become our karmic debts. If we choose to acknowledge, honor, and work on retiring these karmic debts, we address the complex of emotions, expectations, attitudes, and behaviors associated with our remembered and felt images of the people involved in the karmic pattern in question. Resolving the complex by withdrawing the projection contributes to our spiritual growth, first by releasing us from our emotional attachment to the specifics of our past actions and reactions, and then by removing the obstacles hindering us from fulfilling our dharma. If we ignore complexes and the attendant karma, however, we do so at our own peril, since they become roadblocks and psychological obstacles, cycling us back into maya and primary karma again and again.

Arthur's Karmic Grandfather Complex

Not all complexes are troublesome. Although we don't often think about it, each of us can probably identify some "good" complexes. Arthur's grandfather/wise-old-man complex is a revealing example and involves a specific object.

All of us have objects that carry meaning. Perhaps we possess something with a long family history, a gift from a special person, a souvenir brought back from a trip, or a memento of some significant event or occasion. One such object is a very impractical walking stick that one of Arthur's grandfathers had made from a piece of wild grapevine. It wouldn't support anybody if he were crippled, but that is not important to Arthur. When Arthur pauses and thinks of the walking stick or catches sight of it, he feels a pleasant nostalgia. Vivid images related to his grandfather come to mind: the smile on his face when his grandfather saw him, the way his grandfather said his name, the sound of his playing the fiddle, and the memory of his giving Arthur permission to enter and use his shop, showing Arthur where the key was kept.

A second circle of memories also arises for Arthur: his grandmother chiding his grandfather for telling Arthur off-color stories. (Arthur can still hear the sound of her voice saying grandfather's name with disapproval.) Then the focus can subtly drift to Arthur's grandmother: the smell of the wood fire in her stove and the heat of her kitchen, the sight of her limping about as she walked. That can also lead to a third circle of memories: summer day trips with her and his mother to visit relatives or to pick berries. When Arthur lets the associations flow, his awareness is soon filled with feelings and images of his mother, while images of grandfather and grandmother are left behind. Arthur's network of associations can expand in yet another direction to include, for example, his boyhood friend, with whom he worked in his grandfather's shop, and then on to other exploits with his friend.

One result of Arthur's grandfather/wise-old-man complex has been his mostly automatic and largely unconscious "loving grandfather" expectation of older men. For example, his experience of his grandfather has played a central role in his attraction and response to a senior colleague early in his professional training, to men whom he wanted to be like when he "grew up."

Another result is the impulse in Arthur to behave in a loving, grandfatherly way toward children and young people (and very junior colleagues). Often, he has seen himself relating to them as he remembers being treated by his grandfather and by his admired and idealized senior colleagues. As you can see, "one thing leads to another." This illustrates the way complexes ramify, tying together seemingly unrelated memories and experiences.

The Structure of Karmic Complexes

Karmic complexes are natural and typical elements of psychic life that may develop along positive or negative lines. These emotionally colored memory clusters and patterns of attitude and behavior share common elements that form interconnections bridging different, but related, groupings of memories. They are indeed "complexes": they are complex in that they are composed of many elements; they can be activated by reference to any one or more of their component elements; when they are activated, we experience the feeling-tone associated with those memory elements. Actually, a complex can consist of all sorts of "contents" that are held together by the shared feeling-tone. The pleasant, positive complexes and the disturbing, troublesome ones are identical structurally, but differ in emotional tone.

The core around which a karmic complex takes shape is a typical human situation, an inherent, *archetypal pattern* ready to organize our perceptions, our emotions, our imagery, and our behavior in a typically human way.[6] Karmic complexes are archetypes in their structured, incarnated form. The archetypal patterns informing karmic complexes organize behavior, perception, representation, and emotion. These four dimensions are interrelated.

We could think of archetypes as high-level sets of "instructions." When an archetype is activated, the instructions in it organize what we see, how we feel, the way we depict it, and what we do. This process creates a perceptual-emotional-representational-behavioral mini-program that can operate in our psyche pretty much independently of conscious choice, and—if we are unaware of it operating in the background—assimilate ever more material to itself.

The complex can be activated by anything closely resembling one or more of its various constituent parts. Then the complex's ruling emotion assimilates a person's consciousness to a lesser or greater extent and leads to corresponding attitudes, feelings, imagery, and behaviors. We first become aware of a

---

6. The archetypes are, so to speak, "dynamic skeletons" that structure the "flesh" of our expectations and our experiences. Archetypal patterns are subsets of the four aspects of dharma as well as adharma, the shadow aspect of dharma. To put it another way, dharma and adharma actualize in typical (archetypal) ways that we can observe in life, in literature, mythology, and history—that is, in any human activity.

karmic complex operating outside of our awareness when we have intense emotional reactions to other people. Our emotional reaction arises because we are seeing a reflection of something in ourselves that we otherwise could not see. The complex is, as we say, projected.

Projection

When an activated complex overlays a present situation or person, we speak of projection. Projection differs from blaming: when we blame, we do so intentionally. We do not deliberately project. Projections happen to us when someone or some situation resembles another person or experience around which a karmic complex has formed, and we do not recognize the difference between what we are seeing now and what we saw and experienced in the past. Jung said, incisively, that we all know we have complexes; what we don't realize is that complexes "can *have us*."[7] When they do get us, we deal with the current experience as we dealt with its historically similar look-alike. Sometimes, the projection works, for the present situation (or person), and the pattern and content of our constellated and projected complex appear congruent. Almost always, however, the fit is imperfect, disappointing us to some degree sooner or later. But what makes a complex karmic?

What's Karmic about a Complex?

Earlier, I discussed primary and secondary karma. Primary karma refers to actions that cycle us back into maya; secondary karma refers to actions that lead us toward fulfilling our dharma. We are acting in the realm of secondary karma when we awaken to the realization that we will have to deal with the effects of our actions, *and*, consequently, we will take action informed by our understanding of our dharma. In Arthur's grandfather complex, we can clearly distinguish primary and secondary karmic aspects.

---

7. C. G. Jung, "Review of the Complex Theory," CW8, ¶200 (Jung's italics).

At first sight, Arthur's grandfather complex may seem quite benign, but it, too, has primary and secondary karmic aspects. In fact, there are two karmic elements in this complex: his "loving grandfather" expectation of older men, and his impulse to behave in a loving, grandfatherly way toward children and young people (and very junior colleagues). When Arthur's grandfather/wise-old-man complex gets constellated, he can follow the path of primary or secondary karma. The direction of primary karma holds two possibilities, depending on whether he perceives a grandfatherly type of person, or is perceived as and hence put into the role of the grandfatherly person.

This calls for a brief clarification. A great many karmic complexes are dyadic. In Arthur's case, one actor is the wise old man, the other the young, immature person looking for kindly wisdom. If Arthur is cast in the junior role, his accurate perception and judgment of the other person may well be obscured and influenced in the direction of the complex. The constellated complex may obscure traits or behaviors in the other that contradict Arthur's emotional expectations (i.e., that the other is a loving grandfather). Sooner or later, this will surely lead to disappointment that may awaken Arthur to the fact that (unconsciously) his grandfather complex has projected itself onto another, fallible human being.

In the second scenario, the other person's emotional expectation of meeting a kindly grandfather may trigger Arthur's grandfather complex. Then Arthur may be (unconsciously) coerced into playing out the grandfather role, but in the limited way the complex dictates. Since "benign" and "kindly" are two of the compelling traits of the complex, Arthur probably will not find it easy or even possible to temper the "kindly" traits with firmness, when firmness, limit-setting, and maintenance of generally accepted standards may be called for—traits necessary if a personality is to be balanced and not one-sided. (You can see why Jung referred to complexes as "splinter psyches.")

Arthur has indeed suffered from the shadow side of his grandfather complex: being "too nice a guy," and compromising when he should have calmly stood firm. This shadow side offers Arthur an opportunity to chose the dharmic path of secondary karma.

What's Dharmic about a Complex?

What, then, would Arthur's unfinished grandfather/wise-old-man business be? For some past-life "reason," part of Arthur's task in this life is to work through his grandfather karma. First, as he strips the complex of its autonomy, it will skew his feelings and judgment progressively less, and he will become able to honor worthy older men realistically. Second, Arthur will no longer be coerced by his complex to relate to younger people *only* as a kindly grandfather. Retiring the karma of this complex comes about as Arthur has more choices in how to relate to older men or junior colleagues. By diminishing the power of the complex, Arthur will have greater freedom to actualize aspects of his dharma that otherwise would be blocked by the complex.

When Arthur no longer looks for a grandfather in the outer world, but *experiences* his grandfather as an inner presence, he will have retired much of the power of the complex. As the archetype becomes a functioning figure in his psyche, the projection to carriers in the world will diminish, yet the vivifying emotion—the fond memories and the loving counsel—will still be present. Arthur will then have taken a major step toward retiring this particular piece of karma and claiming his dharma.

Fortunately, Arthur is moderating his automatic "benign grandfatherly" behaviors. He is clearer with himself and with others about his expectations; he is learning to insist that people fulfill their agreements with him; he speaks up much sooner when something does not suit him. Through all of this, Arthur is learning that he can still be kind and understanding, but it need not be at a great emotional and financial cost to himself. By moderating his automatic kind and understanding attitude and behavior, Arthur is developing a side of his personality that appropriately complements his basically good qualities.

Arthur's example illustrates how complexes initially compromise our lives by altering our conscious abilities. When we begin to recognize the discrepancy between what we believe is happening and what is actually happening, we have the possibility of choice: we can blame others, circumstances, the gods, history, or fate, *or* we can retire this karma and start to claim its dharmic potential.

DHARMA AND THE KARMIC COMPLEX

Earlier, I discussed the four dharmas: ashrama dharma, varna dharma, svadharma, and reta dharma. Reta dharma refers to the physico-chemical "laws," as well as to the transpersonal or "spiritual laws" of energy patterning. Varna dharma embraces the laws of the various species, the "laws of one's own kind." Hence, owls act like owls and human beings like human beings. Ashrama dharma encompasses the stages of life with their various bio-psychic, developmental, social, and cultural patterns with which we must deal. Finally, svadharma refers to the inherent, individual potential and possibilities in each human being, "the law of one's own nature." Each of us must live in accordance with each of these dharmas, fulfilling their demands to the best of our ability, if we are not to get waylaid on the path to the soul—the sense of fulfillment and completion.

Of course, circumstances and opportunities play a significant role in how we fulfill our four dharmas. For example, the members of a Hispanic family experience and live their varna dharma differently than an Anglo-American or Hindu family. The varying emphasis on individuality shapes a Caucasian American's realization of svadharma much differently than does the importance attached to group consciousness and identity of a native Japanese. Cultural, social, and familial factors condition the ways and means through which individuals fulfill their four dharmas.

It is important to remember that the four dharmas are not essentially products of convention, although encrustations of convention and custom certainly vary from culture to culture. Rather, the four dharmas are "lawful," or "impersonal," or "objective." By this, I mean that each of them refers to a given set of patterns that calls for adequate satisfaction in each person's life. When a person has not, for whatever reasons, been able to satisfy a dharmic condition, he or she must make conscious peace with that dharmic deficit.

Another example of a feeling-toned complex in action illustrates the effects of a troublesome karmic complex. The experience of Nancy, one of my patients, illustrates the way in which a karmic complex can interfere with realization of dharma.

Nancy's Stepmother Complex

Nancy is a congenial woman in her mid-50s. Nancy's mother died when she was 18 months old, and her father remarried soon after. Nancy became her stepmother's Cinderella: forced to do the housework, and sent to her room as soon as chores were done. Fortunately, Nancy's two grandmothers lived nearby and, when she entered high school, Nancy lived with one of them every weekend, spending the week in the home of her father and stepmother. Although her father loved Nancy, he did nothing to protect her from her stepmother's harsh treatment.

Nancy entered therapy with me when her husband started to work with another therapist. At first, Nancy didn't think she had any issues to deal with; it was her husband who was suffering, and she wanted to understand as much as she could about his condition. Although I saw only Nancy's distress about her husband and her marriage, I encouraged her to watch her dreams; they might very well tell us something important about her. Nancy complied.

One day, Nancy brought to her session a "little dream," in which *an old college classmate approached her, telling her he was available again and would like to be with her. Nancy told him her stepmother would be very upset when she brought him home for the holidays.* In fact, Nancy had never spent the holidays during her college years with her father and stepmother, and bringing a fellow home would have been totally unthinkable.

This dream gave me the clue that Nancy's stepmother was alive and well in her psyche as a karmic complex, even though Nancy believed her only troubles were due to the stress in her marriage arising from her husband's therapeutic issues. Nancy's dream showed us that she was going to do something "unthinkable" that would challenge her stepmother. Nancy's dream suggested that she had the opportunity to retrieve a potential (symbolized in her male friend) and make it a part of her life in defiance of her stepmother complex (imaged as her stepmother).

Nancy's dream has opened a new vista in her life. She is seeing the workings of the stepmother complex that has hindered her fuller realization of her essence (one of the aspects of dharma): feeling intimidated, taken for granted, exploited. No longer is she her husband's compliant servant, taking sole responsibility for maintaining the home, for rearing the children, and for their social life. She is rediscovering interests she shelved long ago. Now Nancy works for a cultural organization in the city, planning exhibitions and trips. She is developing a circle of friends separate from her husband.

Some remnants of Nancy's karmic stepmother complex will always be with her. Now, however, she knows what to watch out for, as well as how to deal with it. Nancy is no longer a Cinderella.

John's Karmic Raccoon Complex

Another patient of mine, whom I will call John, had a complex related to his experience with his father. Although John was an extremely successful businessman who appeared to be Mr. Important and created the impression of someone with a big ego, underneath he experienced depression and abused habit-forming substances. John was one of the middle children in a large "sibship" of successful professionals, but John's oldest brother was his father's favorite. Although his brothers had completed college and graduate studies, John had dropped out of college. He got scant attention from his father, except for his ability to play soccer, which he continued to do, even when his knee was injured and he needed painkillers. John started a business with a loan cosigned by his father, and, while the business was wildly successful, his father paid no attention. A dream of John's tipped me off to the complex that dominated his consciousness.

In his dream, *John was camping. A raccoon tried to sneak in to steal leftover food.* As we talked about this dream, John's associations led him to recognize that the raccoon was a significant, emotionally charged figure. Whereas John consciously presented himself as Mr. Ego, unconsciously he felt like a raccoon, feeding on his father's leftovers. As we worked through his raccoon complex, his feelings about himself and about his father gradually changed. More and more, he was able to honor his true competence and claim his success as his own.

The karmic element in John's raccoon complex developed in relationship to his father. His raccoon complex usurped his sense of self, which he masked with an outer appearance of success, of being Mr. Important. However, John needed his drugs to keep his Mr. Important image inflated, because his raccoon complex was continually making him feel that he was stealing scraps and leftovers to survive emotionally.

In psychotherapy, John experienced me alternately as the dominating, devouring father, or the supportive, admiring father he had always looked for. In other words, when his raccoon complex was activated, I looked to him like the father he had grown up with. At other times, the unfulfilled aspect of the father archetype—in John's case, his lifelong search for the supportive father—prevailed, and he experienced me as caring. John's experiences of me were both instances of projection: first, the projection of the father half of the "father-raccoon-son" complex, and then, the archetypal projection as the good father.

In the course of therapy, John and I worked through the projections. Now John can relate to me man to man, without the excesses of emotion that accompanied both projections. Although his father has not changed, John no longer feels he has to steal scraps from him to survive. John has retired the karma with his father, and has been able to develop trust. This internal sense of emotional and material security is the task and goal of the first chakra.

Maggie's Karmic Rapunzel Complex

My next example involves both parents. Maggie is a successful professional woman who has struggled with lack of intimacy in her marriage. Though married to a caring and devoted man, she continues to feel an invisible wall between them in their relationship. Maggie is also success-phobic, having sabotaged her professional achievement at the very last stage of her endeavor.

Maggie was born in Europe. When she was 4, her father was drafted into the army of their native country. Her last memory of her father is of kissing him on his cheek as he left for the war. Later, he was reported missing in action and presumed dead. (Maggie's mother had died a year earlier from complications of an abdominal ailment, because wartime conditions made it impossible to get timely medical attention.) Maggie's uncle and aunt took her in and reared her. In her early 20s she met her husband, an American soldier, while he was stationed in her country. They later settled in the Midwest.

In her marriage, as in her therapy, Maggie felt as if something were missing. She felt a lack of deep attachment and connection, and a chronic sense of anger and resentment toward me and toward her husband. These deeply disguised emotions were concealed, however, under a very pleasant veneer. Then, in one session, she reported a dream in which she was Rapunzel, the princess in the well-known fairy tale.

Once upon a time, begins the tale of Rapunzel, there were a husband and wife who had long wished for a child and who finally believed their wish might be granted. One day, as the wife looked out her little window at a garden surrounded by a high wall behind her house, she spied some corn salad or lamb's lettuce, known as rapunzel. She craved the rapunzel, but no one dared enter the garden, because it belonged to a witch whose power everyone feared.

Nevertheless, the wife's craving grew more urgent each day. She began to waste away as she feared she would never get any rapunzel. Finally, her husband, worried that she might die, stole into the garden at night to get her a handful of rapunzel. The next day, the wife's craving increased threefold, and, that night, her husband returned to the garden. This time, however, the witch saw him. He pleaded for his life, saying that he had trespassed into the witch's garden only because he feared his wife would die without some rapunzel.

Hearing this, the witch agreed to let him have all the rapunzel he wished, on the condition that he give her their child when it was born. The frightened husband agreed, and, when the baby was born, the witch named her Rapunzel and took her away.

Rapunzel grew to be the loveliest child under the sun. When she was 12, the witch took her deep into the forest and locked her in a tower that had no door and only a little window at the top. In the evening, the witch would come to visit, calling out, "Rapunzel, Rapunzel, let down your hair for me." Rapunzel would lean out the little window and let down her golden hair, and the witch would climb up to visit her.

One day, a prince riding through the forest heard Rapunzel singing in her loneliness. Enchanted, he looked for a door into the tower, but could find none. He rode away, yet his heart had been touched, and he returned every day to listen. Once, as he stood behind a tree, he saw the witch come to the tower and call out, "Rapunzel, Rapunzel, let down your hair for me." Now he knew the secret.

The next day, he went to the tower and called, "Rapunzel, Rapunzel, let down your hair for me." Rapunzel let her hair down to the ground, and the prince climbed up. When she first saw him, Rapunzel was frightened, for she had never seen a man. He calmed her, saying he had been touched by her singing. He then asked her if she would marry him, and she agreed, thinking the prince would love her more than her godmother, the witch. In the course of their conjugal visits, Rapunzel made a plan whereby the prince was to bring skeins of silk every day, and she would weave a ladder to escape.

One day, Rapunzel said to the witch, "Tell me, Godmother, how is it that you're so much harder to pull up than the young prince?" The witch was furious at the betrayal. She cut off Rapunzel's hair and sent her to the desert to live in misery. When the prince returned and called out to Rapunzel, the witch let down the hair and the prince climbed up. The angry witch threatened to scratch out his eyes as she told him Rapunzel had gone. In despair, the prince leapt from the tower. As he fell, the brambles scratched his eyes and blinded him.

For several years, the prince wandered through the forest, weeping over the loss of his wife. Eventually, he came to the desert where Rapunzel was living with the twins she had borne, a boy and a girl. She took the prince in her arms and, as her tears fell into his eyes, he could see again. The prince then took his family to his kingdom, where they lived happily ever after.

The story of Rapunzel formed the script for Maggie's life. Maggie felt betrayed by her parents, who "sold her off to the witch," her adoptive aunt. She felt deep rage at her parents' betrayal and abandonment of her to her aunt, who, in classic fairy-tale fashion, had criticized and humiliated her throughout her childhood and considered her a burden.

Maggie saw her husband as a kindly wimp—certainly no prince. For his part, he had been ineffective in rescuing Maggie from her sense of emotional depletion and the lack of self-esteem she felt. Her own heroic potential (the second chakra of generativity), which could have shown her the path to success and empowered her efforts, was thus blinded and robbed of its power. She felt imprisoned in her tower and lost in America.

As she worked through her anger and disappointment, Maggie gradually reclaimed her initiative and heroic perseverance from the witch (a form of the negative mother complex), which not only led to increased intimacy with her husband, but also established her authority at work.

As she retired her Rapunzel karma, Maggie was able to fulfill various levels of dharma. She is claiming her ashrama dharma in the areas of intimacy with her spouse and her professional accomplishment. Her professional achievement is very soulful, considerably benefiting her community and contributing to fulfilling her varna dharma. As she comes more and more into the fullness of her being, she is further realizing her svadharma.

Arthur's Karmic Homecoming Complex

Arthur was in therapy while he was a student attending college away from home. For nearly two years, whenever Arthur returned to the family farm on weekends, he suffered a painful surprise: his stepfather hardly noticed him, certainly did not appear happy to see him, and immediately had work for him to do. His mother helplessly wrung her hands and went off to the kitchen with tears in her eyes. He often returned home on weekends at the urging of his parents. Arthur had not had a comfortable relationship with his stepfather for some time. His mother, feeling caught between her son and her husband, could only wring her hands in anguish. Arthur did not feel that his mother supported him, although he knew she recognized the tensions between him and his father. Whenever she plaintively urged Arthur to go work in the fields with his father, "because it means so much to Dad," Arthur felt both furious and betrayed. The family farm was not a Norman Rockwell picture of the idyllic rural home.

Although Arthur was not consciously aware of having expectations about how he would spend the time with his parents, he consistently felt jolted and bitterly disappointed by the actions and attitudes of both father and mother when he returned home.

After several months of repeating this painful experience, Arthur began consciously to remember that each visit had been an emotional disaster, yet the pattern of surprise and disappointment did not change. Something in Arthur continued to expect the welcome and emotional warmth he never got. What was going on?

The personal experiences, held together by an emotion, that make up a complex take shape around typical—that is, "archetypal"—situations, experiences, and relationships. Further, archetypal patterns "program" people to expect specific emotions as well as behaviors. In the example of Arthur's weekends on the family farm, we have identified his emotional core—the expectation of a warm welcome, followed by disappointment and anger when that expectation was regularly thwarted. We have also identified the behaviors of mother, father, and Arthur—Mother wringing her hands, Dad essentially ignoring Arthur while expecting him to change clothes and get to work, and Arthur feeling surprised, hurt, angry, and not wanting to visit on weekends.

Contrary to his experience, Arthur continued to *expect* his parents to receive him with affection, acceptance, interest, and warmth. For a long time, Arthur's actual experience of his parents did nothing to alter this automatic, autonomous expectation, *even when he consciously knew what to expect*—namely, a cold, unloving, unwelcoming reception. The core of his parental complex "prescribed" that his parents receive him with open arms.

The core structure of a complex is not personally acquired, but is considered as part of our endowment. Since this idea is perhaps difficult to grasp or accept, I want to illustrate it with several examples.

Anyone who has observed infants and children will readily recognize a variety of behavioral and emotional patterns. For example, an infant first forms a bond with the caretaking person, usually the mother. For a period of time, the baby does not notice anyone other than the mother. At a certain stage of development, however, the growing child becomes aware that Mother is not the only person in the world. "Strangers" exist, whom the infant views with suspicion. After learning to walk, however, the toddler changes its view of the world: the urge to exercise the new power of mobility and to explore has replaced the stranger anxiety. The toddler hurries off, but after a sortie comes running back to Mom or Dad or Grandma to refuel for another venture into the world.

These steps and stages in development follow an inborn timetable or program that cannot be accelerated by parental ambition or manipulation. When parents are able to adapt to their baby's developmental timetable and fulfill their role in the program, the baby develops normally: the growing child acquires mobility, but also the trust that the world is safe enough to explore, and that love, comfort, encouragement, admiration, and safety are in the background in the persons of mother and father when the baby needs to replenish (i.e., baby develops positive mother and father complexes). These experiences, in turn, contribute to the child's *internal* sense of safety, competence, self-worth, and lovability. These positive feelings gradually depend less on immediate parental input. Fulfillment of the demands of the inherent pattern lead to physical and emotional maturation.

We have all seen children who do not possess the security and trust that result from a satisfactory actualization of the inherent developmental program. Children who are chronically anxious, fearful, distrustful, needy, and clingy suffer from deficits in the fulfillment of their innate developmental programs, whether because of parental inability or unavailability, medical conditions that interfered with the child's ability to develop or interact with the parents, or the death of a parent, abandonment by a parent, or placement for adoption.

Returning to Arthur, it was apparent that his expectation of a warm welcome from his stepfather was never fulfilled. Instead, his grandfather became the source of emotional and spiritual nurturance. His father complex was so barren and unfulfilling that his soul took him to the realm of the grandfather for needed emotional supplies. In his early adult life, Arthur lived out the template of his grandfather complex. He became a nurturing and soulful mentor and grandfather figure to his patients, friends, and students. However, it also got him stuck in a caretaker role, at times neglecting his own personal needs and ambitions.

In kundalini terms, Arthur was stuck in the first-chakra realm. Since he lacked love and nurturance from his stepfather, he would depend on apparently nurturing women to compensate for this emotional void. He also became the first-chakra support for others in his life, like his grandfather was. This precluded his capacity to fully honor his third chakra of ambition and enterprise.

In therapy, Arthur was able to confront the constellation of his various karmic complexes, understand how they got hold of him in his earlier life experiences, and examine the impact they had on postponinng his dharmic life. Gradually he moved from the first to the third chakra, and started to assert his own talents, ambitions, and potential. This was apparent in his continuing success in his creative and profesisonal enterprise. Now he is able to attend to his dharma. In his svadharma, he is more in touch with his own life passion as a creative writer; in his ashrama dharma he is more successfully attending to his marriage; in his varna dharma, he is a great service to his community as a teacher and guide; in his reta dharma mode, he is an important bridge, doing God's work by integrating transcultural concepts in his writing, thus furthering spiritual and religious tolerance and mutual respect between peoples.

Clearing the Minefield of Karmic Complexes

Each of the people I have described faced the challenge of retiring their karmic complexes. They recognized their karmic patterns when they realized they were caught in repetitive loops, going nowhere. Many of these loops were repetitions of patterns of expectation, reaction, and behavior they experienced with a parent. At some time in the past, the behaviors they developed were the best they could manage. Those behavioral patterns had, or promised, survival value, but later they no longer served them well. After identifying the expectations that set them up to cycle through the old paths, each person was able to risk questioning those deeply rooted and emotionally insistent survival stratagems by experimenting with different reactions and behaviors, and then comparing the new outcomes with the old. To identify constellated karmic complexes, they had to learn to recognize four telltale emotional and behavioral clues.

Regression: A complex that has been touched usually urges us to react in a more primitive manner than we normally would. Colloquial language has a multitude of images that vividly capture the moment when a complex takes over: we "lose our grip," "fly off the handle," and "go ballistic." (Of course, if the complex only tugs at us, we may not actually "lose our grip," but only feel it slipping.) Complexes do not absolutely have to be nuclear blasts. Nevertheless, a constellated complex inclines us to regress to a more primitive level of personality and social development. *Regression*, then, is one of the four clues.

Emotionality: We must remember that a feeling-toned complex involves emotion. In fact, emotionality is one of its most distinctive clues. When our reaction to a situation is disproportionate to the stimulus or triggering event, we are well-advised to look for a complex that has contributed its emotional charge. One of the most reliable psychological rules of thumb is that, the more emotional we become, the less appropriately we adapt to the current situation. That is, we tend to regress. So the second clue is *emotionality*.

Projection: We often look for someone to blame. Again, colloquial language is psychologically astute: "They made me do it"; "It's their fault"; "They should have known better than to say that to me"; "You'd think people would be more considerate"; "If only . . . " Blaming of this sort is an example of the classic notion of projection, seeing the source "out there," rather than "in here." Pogo got it right: We see the enemy, and he is us. *Projection*, therefore, is our third clue.

Persistence: The last clue is another we have all experienced. Colloquial language identifies it in phrases such as: "It spoiled my whole day"; "I couldn't get it out of my mind"; "I thought it would never go away"; "I chewed on it forever." When we cannot get rid of a nagging thought, emotion, or image, we speak of *persistence*, our fourth clue that a feeling-toned complex has got us.

I could add more to these four clues. As you recall, C. G. Jung identified thirteen indicators of complex, but these four will do: *regression*, *emotionality*, *projection*, and *persistence*—REPP.

While karmic complexes can sometimes explode with a bang, they often exert only a pervasive, subtle influence, as in Arthur's grandfather complex. Both the subtle and the raucous complexes, however, show us where we are stuck. We cannot go very far on the path to the soul when we ignore them. They are actually whispers of the soul, showing us where our tasks lie.

When complexes get in the way of appropriate behavior, we need to recognize and act on the answers to several questions:

- What emotions am I feeling?
- How are these emotions rooted in my experience and history?
- Do these emotions suit the present situation?
- Who or what stirred up these emotions? (This is the mayic aspect of the complex.)
- How do these emotions lead me to imprudent or inappropriate choices? (This is the karmic consequence of the complex.)

Once we understand these emotions and their origin, how do they free us to pursue our dharmic path?

Redirecting a Karmic Complex from Maya to Dharma

Primary karma consists of actions that cycle us back into maya. Secondary karma consists of actions that move us toward realizing dharma. In order to move from primary to secondary karma, we must learn to recognize the patterns of emotion and behavior typical of our karmic complexes. (Sometimes we need the help of other people who see us better than we see ourselves.) We also need courage, the courage to question the seeming self-evident truth of the intense reactions we feel when a complex is activated. We have to ask where our karmic complexes are taking us, as well as where we would arrive if we did not let them have their way with us. Answering these questions opens up the possibilities for redirecting our actions toward dharmic goals. In this way, our karmic complexes can serve us as stepping-stones on the path to the soul.

On the path to the soul, we work through our karmic complexes by reconfiguring their trajectory from maya toward dharma. Some of our complexes are an unwanted legacy from our ancestors. In a sense, we were born into them, and have to retire them if we are to continue on our journey. They are our clan karma, the subject of the next chapter.

POINTS TO PONDER

1. How would you define a karmic complex?
2. List the important karmic complexes in your life. What emotions does each of these complexes provoke, sad, glad, mad, afraid?
3. What happens in your body when a karmic complex is activated?
4. When a karmic complex is triggered, which person gets routinely implicated in having messed up your day or plans?
5. Identify each important person (or event) in your life who contributed to this karmic complex: father, mother, grandparent, immigration, school, illness, etc.
6. Describe the impact each of these karmic complexes has had on your life in both past and present.
7. What individuals, events, and circumstances activate your karmic complexes?

8. How do you retire karmic complexes? That is, how do you 1) recognize the complex; 2) challenge old behaviors and assumptions about yourself, the world, and the future; 3) experiment with new behaviors; 4) and be open to receiving help from friends, family, therapists, or others?

chapter seven

Clan Karma

. . . the father's faults [are punished]
in the sons and in the grandsons
to the third and fourth generation.
—Exodus 34:7[1]

We are the authors of some, but not all, of the karma with which we must deal. I have seen countless patients who contend with karma that appears to be unrelated to their own life experience. On closer assessment, I discovered that they were grappling with their ancestors' or their parents' karmic complexes.

Each one of us must retire not only the karma we have created, but also the karma we have inherited before we can fully live our own lives and actualize our own essence (svadharma). On our path to the soul, the legacy of our ancestors lights our way. Yet, ancestral curses often entrap us in futile struggles with which we must contend. In healing the wounds of our ancestors we not only retire their karmic debt, but, in the process, also claim our own dharmic goals. Thus we leave the world more complete and healed than we found it. While it is our hope that Mother Earth will nurture us, often we must heal the Great Mother by accomplishing our dharmic quests.

1. Jerusalem Bible, Exodus 34:7.

In clinical work with numerous individuals, I have encountered their complexes, which on closer examination have turned out to be a legacy from their parents or forebears. When individuals retire their clan's or family's complexes, not only do they heal the soul of their ancestors, they also claim instruments that are necessary to fulfill their own dharmic goals and tasks. Their lives become more grounded in their own dharmic soil. New and rich possibilities open up that had been obscured by carrying the burden of clan karma. The following examples illustrate the crucial task of recognizing, retiring, and growing via the process of retiring clan karma.

Professor Lehrer's Clan Karma

Professor Lehrer is an academician in his early 60s who consulted me about problems in his relationship with his wife and two daughters, his concern about a creativity block in his work, and a continuing conflict with his female peers who hold a feminist philosophy. His presenting problems were at odds with what he defined as his authentic inner ground: his very liberal philosophy of life, and his championing of the rights of women and minorities. I was puzzled by the apparent contradiction. On closer analysis, Professor Lehrer and I discovered that he was burdened with the task of retiring clan karma: a pattern of men who dominated others and of women who resentfully submitted to them.

He and his mother had a loving relationship, and yet she unconsciously kept sabotaging him with her criticism and lack of affirmation. His mother, like other women in his family, had had a despotic and dominating father who had treated his wife and daughters as lowly creatures. While Professor Lehrer's grandmother tolerated this, his mother protested and developed subtle but powerful ways of disempowering the men in her life.

Without realizing it, Professor Lehrer's mother treated her son, Professor Lehrer, with the same mixture of love and contempt she felt toward her tyrannical father. Unconsciously, this forced Professor Lehrer to behave like his grandfather! Although he is a liberal man, extremely respectful of women, Professor Lehrer continued to subtly and unconsciously behave contemptuously toward women, just as his grandfather had done. This set up contentious relationships with important women in his life: his wife, his daughters, his female colleagues and students.

In psychotherapy, Professor Lehrer has recognized his ambivalence toward women. As he and I explore it, he is changing his ways of relating, and, by doing so, retiring his karmic legacy. Professor Lehrer's attitude toward women is becoming authentically respectful. His relationships with all the women in his life are much more comfortable, and he is making good progress on a book that, for years, he has wanted to write.

In my years of practice as a psychotherapist and psychiatrist, I have been amazed at the number of patients who continue to struggle with problems and issues that have little to do with their own lives, but that appear to arise from sources beyond their personal histories. It seems as though they are retiring some invisible karmic debt. On closer review, I have discovered that most of these people are really caught in the karma of *their* parents, trying to work it out and retire it, as if to complete an unfinished chapter in the parents' journeys. It seems that, until most of these individuals had retired their parents' or ancestors' karma, they could not claim their own life paths, growth and individuation, and selfhood.

Retiring our individual karma and claiming the potentialities of our ashrama, varna, sva, and reta dharma is not just an individual, esoteric, and spiritual pursuit. It is also our responsibility to our children and grandchildren so that we will not burden them with unretired karmic debts that may encumber their journey and thwart their individuation.

Sally's Story

Sally, a student in her mid-20s, consulted me for symptoms of depression, difficulty in sustaining relationships with men, and problems with math in her college courses. When she was 10, her father was transferred to Milwaukee from the state where she was born. Her parents' marriage was skating along on thin ice before the move, as her mother had started a relationship with another man.

Sally was aware that her mother clung to the marriage for the sake of the children, even though the relationship with her husband was emotionally bankrupt. Subsequent to the move, when her mother became depressed and resorted to alcohol, Sally became very attached to her math teacher, who became her mentor and emotional support during her painful transition to a new community amidst parental turmoil.

In college, Sally met a young man on whom she soon became dependent (like her mother had depended on her father). In her senior year, her fears of abandonment intensified as the time approached for her to think seriously about graduate school and career, because that might mean a separation from her boyfriend.

Sally entered therapy and hesitantly began to explore her abandonment fears and her dependency. Gradually she came to depend on herself, and in the course of therapy, was able to make the difficult choice to enroll in a good graduate program in another state although that temporarily disrupted her relationship with her boyfriend.

Initially, Sally repeated her mother's clan karma of anxious and crippling dependency on a man. Yet she was ultimately able to break through her mother's karmic pattern because she came to trust that her relationship with her boyfriend was strong enough to survive a temporary separation, and she now had the freedom to pursue her path and goals as a separate, but related, individual.

THE ROOTS OF CLAN KARMA

Jung made a similar observation about intergenerational emotional patterns in his research. My concept of clan karma extends Jung's idea of the family constellation, his term for unconscious similarities in emotional reaction patterns in the nuclear family discovered through his word association experiments.[2] The word association experiment consists of a list of common words (for example, mother, father, home, school, food, fear, happiness),

2. C. G. Jung, "The Family Constellation," CW2, ¶999–1014.

which, one at a time, are read to the subject, who responds to each with the first word that comes to mind. The subject's reaction time is noted for each response. When the reaction time to a stimulus word falls below or above that subject's average reaction time, it indicates the presence of a complex—that is, an emotionally charged group of associations and experiences that interfere with consciousness. Jung's associate, Dr. Emma Fürst, administered the word association experiment to twenty-four families. Altogether, they numbered one hundred subjects. Analyzing the data revealed several typical emotional reaction patterns, or types. The reaction types of the children in each family came nearer to their mothers' reaction types than to those of the fathers. Dr. Fürst additionally noted that people related to each other showed a tendency to agree in reaction type, indicating a similarity in the nature of their emotional sensitivities and psychological problems—what Jung would call the emotionally toned complexes. From these observations, Jung postulated that a family's conscious and unconscious emotional background had a determining influence on the individual's destiny.

Based on these experiments and observations, Jung's prescription for counteracting parental or clan karma was "education to free the growing child from unconscious attachment to the influences of his early environment, in such a way that he may keep what is valuable in it and reject whatever is not."[3]

Adult Children of Addicted Parents

The issue of clan and family karma is well-illustrated in the psychodynamics of the adult children of alcoholics. These adult children continue trying to retire the negative karma of their parents' addictions by a variety of adaptive strategies that impede their own life paths and compromise the achievement of their dharmic journeys. Often, it takes them a lifetime to undo the impact of their clan karma, let alone achieve their own dharmic potential and selfhood.

3. C. G. Jung, "The Family Constellation," CW2, ¶1013.

The research literature suggests that children of alcoholics are at increased risk for the development of emotional and psychosocial problems. Black and associates[4] studied adult children of alcoholics and found that 37 percent described themselves as alcoholics, compared with 9.5 percent of control subjects. These subjects also married alcoholics more often (20 percent versus 12.9 percent). These adult children of alcoholics continued to have interpersonal difficulties in adult life, such as problems in trusting others, dependency, responsibilities, expressing feelings, family disruption (including divorce and death), verbal arguments, physical violence and abuse, and feeling responsible for parental conflict. Belestgis and Brown[5] found that adult children of alcoholics exhibit poor communication skills, difficulty in expressing feelings, role and identity confusion, and an excessive sense of responsibility. Sons are at higher risk for problem drinking; daughters are at increased risk for depression; both are at higher risk for divorce than are controls.[6]

Wegschieder[7] relates family role to birth order in adult children of alcoholics. The eldest is often the *family hero*, a compliant overachiever whose function is to provide self-worth to the family system. The hero feels inadequate and angry inside, but responsible for the family's distress. Frequently, the eldest child must function as a responsible "parental child," becoming intensively involved with the nonalcoholic parent. Wegscheider sees the second or middle child typically as the *scapegoat*, whose role as troublemaker provides distraction from conflict and focuses the

---

4. C. Black, S. F. Bucky, and S. Wilder-Padilla, "The Interpersonal and Emotional Consequences of Being an Adult Child of an Alcoholic," *International Journal of Addictions*, 21(2) (1986): pp. 213–231.

5. S. Belestgis, and S. Brown, "A Developmental Framework for Understanding the Adult Children of Alcoholics," *Focus: Women's Journal of Addiction and Health*, 2 (1981): pp. 197–203.

6. D. A. Parker, and T. C. Harford, "Alcohol-Related Problems, Marital Disruption and Depressive Symptoms among Adult Children of Alcohol Abusers in the United States," *Journal of Studies on Alcohol*, 49(4) (1988): pp. 306–313.

7. S. Wegscheider, *Another Chance: Hope and Health for Alcoholic Families* (Palo Alto: Science and Behavior Books, 1981).

family system onto him- or herself and away from family issues. The scapegoat often withdraws and acts out in a destructive and irresponsible manner the anger, loneliness, and rejection he or she feels inside. The *lost child*, who is often the third-born, functions to offer relief to the family system by withdrawing emotionally and physically, not wanting to cause additional problems or make demands. Consequently, this child receives little attention or nurturing, appearing aloof and independent. Yet inside, he or she feels hurt, lonely, and inadequate. The youngest child is often the *family mascot*, with the role of providing fun and humor to relieve the pain experienced in the family system. The mascot diverts attention by entertaining. This child remains immature and experiences insecurity, confusion, and loneliness underneath the external clowning.

You may recognize yourself in one of these children. Regardless of children's place in the birth order, they have to retire the karma of parental alcoholism and addiction. They have to work through the clan-defined karmic identities of hero, scapegoat, lost one, and mascot to discover their own relationships to maya and karma, and eventually achieve their dharmic potential.

Now let us return to Professor Lehrer and to Sally, and explore the clan karma with which they were struggling.

Professor Lehrer's Clan Karma: Living Out Mother's Anger at Men

From my closer observation of Professor Lehrer in therapy, and through his own meditation, active imagination exercises, and analysis of his dreams, a clearer picture emerged that explained his predicament. All his life, Professor Lehrer had been carrying the clan karma on behalf of his mother and her father, and he had been trying unconsciously to retire his mother's karma in relation to the men important in her life, as well as his grandfather's karma in relation to women.

The grandfather had been ineffective with women, but compensated for it by dominating them and acting impatiently with them, especially in rearing his daughter, Professor Lehrer's mother. The experience of a dominating, impatient tyrant informed the conscious part of her father complex; but her father's actual ineffectiveness shaped the unconscious part of her father complex. Thus, her father complex had both domineering and weak aspects. Both sides of a complex—conscious and unconscious—can emotionally influence, even coerce, other people, who, in turn, may respond (consciously or unconsciously) to the influence, either by complying or by resisting. The stage was set for Professor Lehrer's troubles.

What Professor Lehrer's mother consciously knew and felt about her father, and consequently about men who could potentially have power over her, comprised the conscious part of her father complex. If someone had asked her what she thought of her father, she probably would have told them that she saw him as a dictator. What she did not consciously recognize—that her father had actually been ineffective and weak for all his bluster—nevertheless influenced her view of men. Not wanting a husband like her father, Professor Lehrer's mother compensated for the dominant part of her father complex by choosing two husbands, both weak and ineffective men. This choice protected her from feeling overrun by a man, as she had felt overrun by her father.

A dominating father usually impairs his children's development of the dynamic masculine potential inherent in both girl and boy children. Consequently, Professor Lehrer's mother was not able to cultivate and live that side of human potential that openly takes initiative and strives toward the realization of goals, since youthful enterprise potentially threatens the existing order maintained by the representatives of the status quo (in her case, her dominating father). Unable to adequately and openly express the dynamic potential in herself, she lived it vicariously through her only child, Professor Lehrer

His mother's vicarious ambition did not make Professor Lehrer an effective man, because his mother still needed the safety she found with weak men. Hence, even though not consciously taught to fail, Professor Lehrer "knew" unconsciously that he must not succeed in being strong. Why, then, did he continually get into conflicts with his wife, two daughters, and women colleagues? The answer is to be found in his weak father's and stepfather's shadow: their unlived assertiveness. Professor Lehrer had not only to live out his mother's father complex, he also had to live the shadow of his mother's two husbands.

The shadow is not bad per se, but it is primitive, undeveloped, not yet civilized and housebroken. Unless we become aware of what is trying to live through us—another person's karma, for example—we will find ourselves behaving and feeling in ways that puzzle us, that confound our conscious intentions. Professor Lehrer carried a double burden of projection, and that was the source of the discrepancy I discerned in him.

Professor Lehrer is a caring, fair man who acted in a dominating, but ineffective, manner with important women in his life, including his wife, his daughters, and his female peers. This dominating behavior toward women had a compulsive quality about it and lacked authenticity. All his life, he had contained the clan karma created by the dominating and ineffective manner with which the men in his family behaved toward women. This pattern was easily traced back to his maternal grandfather. My guess is that it could be traced back several generations earlier.

Professor Lehrer also had to carry the burden projected on to him of being the champion of oppressed women. Hence, the conflict and contradiction that he experienced was uncovered, and it presented him with several challenges. He had to recognize and retire this clan karma by reclaiming his own nondominating, effective relational potential with women. He also had to unblock his creativity and develop new ways to express initiative. Success in meeting these challenges would alleviate his chronic depression, because he would be freed from the burden of the past to lead his—not someone else's—life.

Sally's Clan Karma: The Ghostly Lover

As an adult, Sally is very close to her mother. Time and again in her therapy, it has become apparent that she functions as the container for her mother's unresolved relationship struggles.

Although Sally is emotionally warm and relational, she sabotages her relationships with men when intimacy or commitment starts to become an issue. Committing to a man would be tantamount to abandoning her mother, just as her mother's committing to her lover would have meant disrupting the family. Part of Sally's journey has involved her emancipating from the karma of her mother's relationship difficulties. Her present problems with math have dynamically emerged as a wish to reincarnate a mentor and friend akin to her supportive math teacher in the past.

Alice's Clan Karma: Daughters Who Marry Their Fathers

Alice first approached me for therapy when her husband, Dustin, was in residency training. Alice and Dustin married shortly after graduating from college and before Dustin entered medical school. Alice was a hard worker, and had taken a job to help Dustin while he pursued his medical studies. All went fairly well until Alice got pregnant with their first child in Dustin's first year of residency. Alice felt overwhelmed. Dustin had not been as available as she had wanted since their college days, but they had managed. But now with the baby and her job, it was too much.

In therapy, Alice told me about her family. Her maternal grandfather had been a successful physician. Alice's mother, Martha, always wanted to be close to her father, but he had always been rather formal and distant with his family. In college Martha met the man who she believed was the love of her life, Alice's father, who, after medical school, joined Martha's father's practice. But like Martha's father, her husband became singularly devoted to his work, with little time for Alice or her mother. Martha's health gradually deteriorated over the years; she had become a ghost of the vital young woman she had been in her 20s.

Like mother, like daughter. Both women married successful but emotionally unavailable doctors. Dustin had become inattentive and lived only for his work. In therapy, Alice realized that her marriage was a repetition of her mother's marriage karma. Alice had to confront this vicious cycle of clan karma and break it. She challenged Dustin to pay more attention to her and their child. They struggled for several months: Alice gaining more and more insight into the similarities between her and her mother's choices; Dustin protesting that he had to work as hard as he was. She realized that her marriage was headed in the same direction as her mother's. Finally Alice gave the ultimatum. She told Dustin she was contemplating divorce. That was a shock for him. Didn't she know what life with a doctor was like? That, she told him, was exactly what she did know. She wasn't going to live out her life as her mother had. When Alice said she was contemplating divorce, Dustin heard the wakeup call. He realized he didn't want to lose Alice and his child. He asked Alice to give him some time to negotiate his workload, to which she agreed. Three months later, Alice was pregnant with their second baby, and Dustin had cleared regular times in his busy schedule to be with Alice. Alice had broken the cycle of clan karma.

Clan Karma in Greek Mythology: The House of Thebes

The ancient myths of various cultures are rife with examples of clan karma. For the present discussion, I have chosen the myth of the royal house of Thebes, its founder Cadmus, and his great-grandson Oedipus as illustrative of the tragic aspects of the theme of clan karma.[8]

The myth begins when Zeus, disguised as a bull, abducts Europa. Europa's father sends her brothers to search for her, bidding them not to return until they find her. One of them, Cadmus, goes to Delphi to ask Apollo where she is. The god tells him not to trouble further about her whereabouts or his father's command, but to found a city of his own. Cadmus founds the glorious city of Thebes. Later, he marries Harmonia and they have four daughters and one son. Through their children's

8. E. Hamilton, *Mythology* (New York: Little Brown & Company, 1940), pp. 254–267.

misfortunes, they learn that the wind of the gods' favor never blows steadily.

After a period of great prosperity, Cadmus and Harmonia, in their old age, experience great sorrow. Their son dies and their daughters either go mad, die, or witness their own sons killed. Daughter Agave, driven mad by Dionysus, tears her son apart with her own hands.

After this tragedy, Cadmus and Harmonia flee Thebes, as if trying to flee misfortune, but misfortune follows them. When they reach distant Illyria, the gods turn them into serpents, but not as a punishment for wrongdoing.

With the reign of Laius, third in descent from Cadmus, Apollo's oracle at Delphi begins to play a leading part in the family's misfortunes. At the birth of King Laius's son, Oedipus, it is prophesied that he will kill his father and marry his mother. In an effort to avert fate—which of course fails, as do all such efforts in Greek mythology—the king gives the infant to a shepherd, who is told to expose him on a nearby mountain. Moved by pity, the shepherd cannot bear to let the infant die, but instead arranges for him to be adopted by the childless king and queen of Corinth, who raise him as their son.

When Oedipus reaches adulthood, the oracle of Delphi repeats the same prophecy: Oedipus will kill his father and marry his mother. Horrified, the young man runs away from Corinth and from the parents he believes are his own. In his wanderings, he returns to Thebes. On the way, he quarrels with a stranger and slays him. The stranger is none other than King Laius, Oedipus's birth father. Unknown to Oedipus, the first part of the prophecy is fulfilled.

When Oedipus succeeds in ridding Thebes of the dreaded Sphinx by answering her riddle, the grateful populace gives him the hand of King Laius's widow, Jocasta, and makes him king of Thebes. The second part of the prophecy is thereby accomplished. They learn their marriage is incestuous only after Jocasta bears him four children. She hangs herself on discovering the truth; Oedipus puts out his eyes and becomes a wanderer again.

Troubles continue to plague the family. A power struggle for the throne erupts in a war between two of Oedipus's sons, resulting in the death of one of them, Polyneices. A daughter, Antigone, defies an order that her brother shall not be buried, and, for her disobedience, she is sentenced to death. For Thebes's dishonor to the dead, the city is eventually conquered by neighboring Athens and destroyed.

This Greek myth is a classic example of clan karma. As is apparent from the multiple tragedies, it is as though Cadmus, his children, and his grandchildren are retiring a negative family karma. Beginning with Cadmus's dishonoring his father's wishes, he and his lineage had to retire the consequences of his choice through their own tragic fates. In particular, the sons in this lineage were destroyed for disobeying their fathers, a vicious cycle that continued to repeat itself until the entire clan, and the Theban civilization itself, was annihilated.

Psychotherapy and the Web of Clan Karma

Such repetitious karmic loops engulf many individuals caught in the web of their ancestral clan karma. Children of abusers, for example, often abuse their own children or their partners. Children of divorce frequently repeat the pattern of divorce. Unless the karmic pattern is recognized and interrupted, it wreaks havoc on the lives of individuals, families, cultures, and even nations. Present-day Germany is still struggling to retire the national karma of its Nazi past. Present-day India may be attempting to retire centuries of national karma for her unjust treatment of the so-called untouchable class and her repression of the rights of women. America struggles to retire the karma of having enslaved its black citizens and is perhaps beginning to suffer the consequences of raping the environment.

In the psychotherapy of individuals, it is necessary to differentiate personal karma from clan karma. Clan karma is more difficult to diagnose, because it emanates from outside the individual and often dates back several generations. Genealogical assessment of family dynamics is essential to accurately assess and retire clan karma. Doing so can free the individual to pursue her or his own journey, selfhood, individuation, and dharma. Individual and clan karma are our teachers in the school of maya. This is one of the most exciting aspects of discovering this concept of therapy, for we, as individuals, can heal ourselves and thereby help heal the many generations of family dysfunction that the present generation carries.

POINTS TO PONDER

1. What is your favorite (painful or joyful) family story? How do you fit into that story?
2. What would best describe your family of origin in a word or sentence?
3. What best characterizes your role in your family of origin (that is, troublemaker, hero, peacemaker, comforter)?
4. In what ways are you still playing that role in your life at work or at home?
5. Which problems in your life are a consequence of the problems of your parents or your family of origin?
6. What are significant problems in your life that may have considerable impact on the lives of your children (that is, depression, addiction, relationship problems)?
7. In what ways are you still continuing to live the script of your family of origin? How are you attempting to script your own life drama now?

chapter eight

Attending to the Soul

And so individuation can only take place if you first return to the body, to your earth, only then does it become true.

—C. G. Jung[1]

How can we attend to our souls and their connection to the Primal Soul in the hustle and bustle of everyday life? Short of seeking professional help (which is often a good way to start), can we honor the whispers of the soul day by day? How do we make our lives into vessels that can contain the sacred and transform the profane—the lead of routine, the dross of old habits, the scars of old wounds—into the gold of the soul?

As the examples mentioned earlier have illustrated, the intense heat of karma transforms our mayic consciousness into dharmic consciousness. When our actions and their consequences cause us enough distress that we begin to question our ways, we have taken the first step toward the necessary transformation. That is the point at which we begin to attend more closely to our individual soul.

The individual soul, the atman in Hindu terminology, is a fractal of the Primal Soul, the Brahman. The individual soul, moreover, is capable of spiritual and physical experience. It is both

1. C. G. Jung, *The Visions Seminars* (Zürich: Spring Publications, 1976), p. 473.

our window to the Primal Soul and the "organ" that registers the quality of our lives. When our individual souls are afflicted, as I have discussed throughout the preceding chapters, we suffer in the various ways I have elaborated. Moreover, our connection to the Primal Soul is obscured, sometimes to the point that we need to be vividly reminded that there is any such thing as a soul connection, as we saw in Michael's airplane dream in the chapter 1.

In the preceding chapters, I have presented the clinical, analytical, and spiritual aspects of the individual soul and its relationship to the Primal Soul. The examples have illustrated the Hindu and psychological concepts I use with my patients, but have not elaborated on the various ways of attending to the soul. In this chapter, which you may find useful as a guidebook, I discuss a number of practices and techniques that have been of value to me and my patients, and can be of use to you in attending to your soul.

THE STARTING POINT

The prerequisites for attending to the individual soul are three: be in the present, notice the whispers of the soul, and make time to reflect.

The human mind chatters. There's always something going on in our minds. It's like a busy street corner in a metropolis: all kinds of emotionally toned thoughts, hopes, fears, and memories crisscross and bump into each other, tugging on our attention and distracting us from our focus. In order to stay in the present, we must do two things simultaneously: pay some attention to the chatter, and maintain some degree of detachment.

We have to pay some attention to the chatter because it contains signals from the soul. Each of the memories, fears, hopes, regrets, or fantasies that scurries about has some degree of emotional charge. The emotional coloration and intensity tell us the significance of the specific content of consciousness, and the content often identifies or symbolizes the area of life concerned. (I will return to this point later.)

We also have to maintain a degree of distance, an "observing ego," as it is called. "Feelingless objectivity" is *not* the appropriate degree of distance. Total disconnection from the emotion leaves only our rational minds on the job. Feeling is a function of the incarnated individual soul, and we must be aware of our feelings if we are to attend to our souls! Only when we are able to both observe and feel do we have the possibility of understanding the messages of the soul. When we let the heavy traffic that sometimes fills our minds run us down and carry us away, we lose the necessary degree of detachment.

The second necessary element for attending to our individual souls is noticing the whispers of the soul. We must take time to reflect actively on what is going on in our lives—outer and inner. We must also make space in our busy lives for active reflection. It's as important as regularly brushing our teeth. Actively reflecting is a habit we need to form. It requires that we stop, look, and listen *before* the alarm goes off, *before* a complex erupts, *before* a relationship goes sour, *before* we fall ill.

I have already mentioned the importance of paying attention to our emotions and to the traffic in the mind that disrupts our tranquillity. As I will discuss below in detail, our complexes, our relationship fascinations and antipathies, our dreams and fantasies, synchronistic events, and medical and psychiatric symptoms are all important messages from the soul that offer us information on the condition of the soul. It is important that we *actively reflect* on these messages the soul sends us.

The third necessity for attending to our souls is time. We have to take time to notice what is going on. We have to take time to reflect on what we notice. When an emotionally colored thought or image or experience of whatever degree of intensity completely fills our consciousness, we do not have the degree of detachment necessary to reflect on it. Setting aside time to reflect, safe from intrusion and distraction, creates the space in which we can ponder the whispers of the soul, and explore their meaning for our lives.

Maintaining these three prerequisites—being in the present, noticing the whispers of the soul, and making time to reflect—is an ongoing challenge. We don't get it perfect the first time. All three elements demand patience and discipline. With practice, we can steadily improve our skills and increase our harvest of insight. Let's now very briefly review specific whispers of the soul and consider some techniques for working with them.

FASCINATIONS AND ANTIPATHIES

Whenever we experience fascination or antipathy, we are reacting to a reflection of some part of ourselves that is not adequately integrated into the conscious personality. Attraction tells us that we want what we see; repulsion tells us the opposite. Either way, the soul is reacting to a reflection of its unlived potential. For one reason or another, this unlived potential of the soul has not been ennobled in our lived life. A fascination or antipathy is a signal from the soul that the present situation offers optimal conditions for the incarnation of this potential. We do not fully control this fascination or antipathy, this attraction or repulsion, since it emanates from the depths of the soul rather than from the waking consciousness. The response can be to another person, an idea, a possible experience, or a memory—the list is nearly inexhaustible.

How to Work with Fascinations and Antipathies

1. Carefully note the content of the emotions you experience. Every detail may be significant, so don't edit or elaborate (yet). Get the facts.
2. Systematically review the content and emotion. For each image in the content, and for each emotion, write what spontaneously comes to mind.
3. Does the image remind you of someone or something? Where or with whom have you felt these emotions?
4. What was or is the significance of the image or emotion? What role did the image or emotion play in your life in the past?
5. What role does the image or emotion play now?
6. If you are exploring a fascination, what is it in the content of the fascination that you want as a part of yourself? How would

incorporating the content of the fascination change your life now?

7. If you are exploring an antipathy, what is it in the content of the antipathy that you want to disown? How would eliminating the content of the antipathy change your life now?
8. List and prioritize the steps you can take to effect the changes you have identified.
9. Chart your progress.

Dan's Story

Dan is a physician in his 40s, a surgeon, who consulted me for depression in the midst of his divorce. He reported that he was a very unartistic, left-brain individual with little interest in art, literature, and the "lighter" side of life. He was very disturbed that he found himself aimlessly wandering in the evenings, and invariably ending up at a jewelry shop, gazing in the window with no conscious interest in jewelry. He was concerned that this interest in women's jewelry was some kind of perversion. I invited him to honor the fascination, rather than being critical of it. I inquired how he might see the jewelry fitting into his lifestyle. He said that was the last thing he wanted. He was unconsciously fascinated and consciously antipathetic to this jewelry.

I proposed that perhaps this was precisely what he needed to do, to honor his interest in jewelry in some way, perhaps by taking some classes at the local university in jewelry making or appreciation. Dan undertook this enterprise, mostly to get me off his back. I am glad to report that he is now an adept jewelry maker, using a specialized enameling technique, and has received considerable acclaim for his blossoming talent. The jewelry he makes reflects the unlived, but now embodied, feeling and aesthetic aspects of his soul. Additionally, by getting in touch with these finer aspects of his soulfulness, he has been able to repair his marriage.

RELATIONSHIPS AND PROJECTIONS

Relationships are an important area in which we can attend to the soul. More focused than fascinations and antipathies, close relationships bring out the best and worst in us. Close relationships can be a crucible in which the fire of our intense emotions transforms us.

The old saying, "opposites attract," is often true. Frequently, we are attracted to somebody who seems to us to be our "other, missing half." When this is indeed the case, the half we are missing is usually difficult to develop, and often at odds with a more developed facet of our personality, so that, after the initial phase (the "honeymoon" of the relationship), we experience disappointment and "disillusionment." We discover that the other is not all we had at first experienced: "You're not the person I thought you were." This realization tells us that we were seeing only part of the other person, the part that was our own, unknown face reflected to us, and that made us feel complete when we were with the other.

An overwhelming attraction is pretty good evidence that we are experiencing the other person as an opposite to ourselves. Although we don't recognize it at the time, the "overwhelming attraction" is a measure of the gulf between us and the other, but also between our conscious view of ourselves and our unlived soul, as well as the amount of energy needed to bridge that gulf. If we can learn how to deal with the difficult and attractive aspects of relationship, we have the opportunity to access and make our own a facet of our soul that has always been carried by some other person.

How to Work with Relationships and Projections

1. Take careful note of the thoughts, fantasies, and emotions you have about the other.
2. Identify the qualities, characteristics, and habits in the other that you desire, like, or love; then identify those you dislike or hate.
3. Who, in your earlier life, have you desired, liked, or loved with feelings similar to those you have for the other in your present relationship? How did that person (from your past)

respond to your desire, liking, or love? How did that person (from the past) respond to your dislike or hate?

4. What developed qualities in you does the other person in your present relationship enhance?
5. Which of your underdeveloped (inferior) qualities or skills does the other person alert you to or criticize you for?
6. Work out a plan of action to develop those inferior skills and abilities hitherto carried by your partner.
7. Monitor your progress. How much of what was carried by the other do you now manage, using your own skills and potentials?

Rachel and Steve's Story

For example, Rachel and Steve have been married for two years. Steve is a quiet, caring, devoted husband—an engineer by trade. Rachel is a vivacious, beautiful, attention-seeking hysteric. When they go to a bar, she socializes effervescently with other men, often drinks too much, and wants to stay there till the wee hours of the morning, while Steve is tired and insists on leaving in a timely manner to be prepared for work the following day.

Rachel's father abandoned her mother when the mother was still pregnant. She has never met her father, nor has she ever seen his picture. Consciously, she finds strength and security in Steve's rock-solid personality. Unconsciously, however, she keeps provoking him. On closer exploration of their relationship, it was apparent that she had a hostile-dependent attachment to Steve. Through him, she attempted to reincarnate the missing father, provoking him to set limits on her as if he were her parent, and simultaneously behaving in a provocative and contemptuous manner to metabolize her rage at the father who abandoned her.

In a session, I invited Rachel to explore what she would do if Steve, after offering to take her home, left and agreed to come and pick her up from the bar when she was ready. She commented that she would be enraged and get drunk just to get even with him. I deepened this image. She reported that she would get drunk several times and be there till six in the morning, hoping that Steve would call and come looking for her. "What if he didn't?" I inquired. "Then reluctantly, I'd call my friend Mary to come pick me up," she said. "So finally you would take care of yourself!?" I exclaimed. Rachel was amused and amazed that she could parent herself, and did not need to project this need for a father onto her loving husband all the time. This vignette is from a multitude of such interventions. Gradually Rachel recognized that she was seeking (in her marriage) a father who would take care of her, and a father who made her angry because he abandoned her. Gradually, she has learned to parent herself. The marriage was unburdened of this dynamic of hostile dependency. Her capacity to be her own good parent and a loving wife was reincarnated in the sacred vessel of the marriage.

KARMIC COMPLEXES

Karmic complexes are a normal part of our psychic makeup. Not all complexes are troublesome, but the troublesome complexes are the ones that we most often notice. Complexes represent emotionally vulnerable spots. We "go ballistic" or "fly off the handle" when somebody triggers a volatile complex by word or deed.

Karmic complexes take shape around typical experiences—birth, death, marriage, transitions, parents, siblings. The core pattern of the complex is archetypal (that is, typically human, and not a personal acquisition). The specific content, or shell, however, derives from our life experience. Together, core and shell constitute the whole complex.

Complexes manifest in several ways, perhaps most frequently in our relationships (as fascinations, antipathies, and other strong emotional reactions), in "spontaneous" floods and (sometimes) discharges of strong emotion, and in dreams and fantasies (that I will discuss below).

When a karmic complex is activated, our behavior changes in four ways: our adaptation regresses to that of an earlier developmental level; we become (much) more emotional; we blame the other for "making" us react; and our emotions tend to rumble about in us for a long time. Learning to understand the soul's message sent in the form of activated complexes offers us a stepping-stone to fuller actualization of our dharma.

How to Work with Karmic Complexes

1. Recognize when you have become unusually emotional.
2. Identify the current trigger event that activated your emotions (in case it isn't obvious).
3. Identify and write down: a) your emotions; b) your fantasies; c) your memories of similar experiences (people, places, events).
4. What unresolved issue or undeveloped potential does the complex represent?
5. How effective is your usual way of dealing with the activated complex?
6. Work out a sequence of different behaviors (in increasing order of difficulty) to address the core issue in the complex.
7. Chart your progress by noting contra-habit and contra-your-own-nature behaviors to situations and individuals that activate your complex: increased lead time; more rapid recovery from complex discharge; less frequent activation.

Trudy's Story

For example, Trudy, a midlevel executive, was referred by her employer because of relationship problems with her peers. In her first session, Trudy took control and spoke incessantly, not giving me a window to get in on the conversation. When this pattern continued for a few sessions, I confronted her. She broke down in remorse and tears, followed by a long silence. I invited her to share the image in her mind. She recalled an incident on Christmas Eve when she was 8. She was the second youngest of ten children. Her father was drunk and watching sports on TV; her mother was depressed and had retreated to her bedroom; the oldest two siblings were trying to manage the household; the younger children were in chaos. Trudy remembered darting first to her father, then to her mother's room, chattering incessantly, trying to revive them from their alcoholic and depressive stupors, striving to be heard above the din of the chaotic family. Trudy had learned this anxious, excited, talkative method in order to resuscitate her emotionally dead parents. This became an intrusive, overbearing caretaker complex that regularly got activated in her staff meetings. We worked on the dynamic roots of this complex. Trudy learned to honor and hold her anxiety, and to hear others out. Paradoxically, people now seek out her views and opinions with respect and reverence for her creativity. She has been steadily climbing the corporate ladder and has made substantial contributions to the success of her enterprise.

DREAMS

Dreams show us how the soul views our lives. As a general rule, a dream supplies the information that consciousness either does not have, or does not adequately perceive or value. The following very general rules of thumb will help you orient yourself to your dream.

Typically, dreams have a recognizable *dramatic structure:* setting, development, turning point, and resolution. Sometimes, one or more of these elements is missing, in which case we have an unfinished dream. (Don't worry; from time to time we all get dreams that are or seem incomplete. We can still work with what we have.)

When *known people and places* appear in your dream, they refer either to the actual people and places, or—more probably—to something in you that resembles those people and places. For example, when your mother or father appears in your dream, the message may be about the mothering or fathering capacity in yourself. When a known person or place appears in your dream, but differs from reality in some way (age, looks, actions, attitude), you can be pretty sure that the dream is talking about a part of your psyche that functions like that person or place.

Dreams do not tell us what to do; rather, they provide a different view that may augment, modify, correct, complete, or contradict our conscious position. As a rule, when a dream presents an extreme view of a situation, it is counterbalancing an equal, but opposite, conscious position. In other words, the truth lies somewhere in the middle.

Working with your own dreams is challenging, because the dream presents the view that you do not consciously see. In other words, the dream fills in what your blind spot misses. (Often, it is expedient to work individually or in a group with a therapist or analyst skilled in dream work.)

Your dreams can tell you a lot more than you know. Other people will often see meaning in your dream, where you see nothing but the images themselves. Take care that the people with whom you share your dreams are trustworthy and bear you no ill. In telling your dream, you are exposing sides of yourself that even you don't see.

Working on your own dreams is about the process of dream work, not its outcome. It's amazing. The "product" you end up with may not look like much, but the process you have engaged in works on you, and will subtly deepen your consciousness and inform it of the intentions of your soul. Here are the basic elements of dream work that you need to know. With practice you can acquire the fundamental skills.

How to Work with Dreams

To catch your dreams:

1. Keep your dream notebook and pen or pencil next to your bed.
2. When you go to bed, suggest to yourself that you will recall a dream *and* write it down.
3. Write down your dream as soon as you wake.

To work with your dreams:

1. Review the dream you want to work on. Revisualize the images; feel the emotions again; reexperience the dream. This brings it back to life.
2. Consider the structure of your dream. What is the setting? How does the action develop? Is there a turning point? What conclusion does the dream reach? (Often, dreams end before

the turning point or the conclusion, which implies that the development cannot go further at that time.)

3. Contemplate each image. Note the feelings, memories, and impressions that arise when you reexperience each image, situation, or person in the dream. *Stay with the image; circle around it; don't let your associations lead you far afield.*
4. What does the dream appear to be commenting on in your life? Your relationships? How you get around in the world? The (emotional and mental) space you inhabit? What is opposing you or assisting you?
5. Compare the current dream with other dreams where the same or similar people, places, themes, and images have appeared. What changes do you notice? How is your presence in the dream now different than it was in the past?
6. After working on your dream, note how your emotional state has changed in the course of your dream work.
7. Honor your dream by carrying out some action or ritual in your waking life that honors the images and intent of the dream.

For example, if a long-forgotten friend appears in your dream, first understand what aspect or quality of this friend that you need to activate in your life to deal with a present situation. Additionally, pick up the phone and call your friend. If you honor your dream and its images by some sacred ritual, the dreams will honor and reward you by continuing to send helpful, guiding messages. This establishes a positive feedback loop.

In one of my recent dreams, *there was a huge, gray garbage truck that I was using to deliver food for my wife's catering business. I inquired of her why we needed such a big truck, suggesting that a small, cute, yellow delivery van with her restaurant's logo on it would be more practical and functional. My friend and mentor, Dr. Terrence Lear, was visiting us from England. Terry and I took this garbage truck for a ride. To my amazement, he said that he had a one-day lesson in how to use this garbage truck as an amphibious vessel, so we sailed off to a small island on Lake Michigan with our families, and spent a day picnicking on the beach of this island. We had a small condo for the day that had a magnificent view of the Milwaukee skyline. I realized that this was no ordinary truck, and I just needed some brief instruction to explore its amphibian wonders.*

Consciously, I had been trying to simplify my life (like the elegant little yellow delivery van), but it always got complicated and burdensome (like the large gray garbage truck). I decided to accept the cumbersome complexities of my life, including accepting my wife's restaurant business that obviously encumbered my conscious life. This, in turn, deepened my soulfulness. I am honoring my dharma by accepting that I must navigate this truck onto the waters of my unconscious and get a view of life from the outside in, from island to mainland, and relinquish my wish to be mainland and mainstream. Paradoxically, by accepting my karma of complexity, I have actually started to make my life simpler. To honor the dream, I went to a toy store and bought a cute yellow delivery van and a huge gray garbage truck. They now sit side by side in my study.

SYNCHRONISTIC EVENTS

Synchronistic events are those meaningful coincidences that we notice—for example, dreaming about somebody you haven't seen or talked to in months, and then getting a postcard or letter from that person the same day; or different people in different places having similar or identical thoughts, ideas, or dreams at the same time. Neither can be explained by causality. Synchronistic events are evidence of a close connection between two or more parties or things. They are a kind of "heads up" urging us to pay attention.

The soul arranges synchronistic events to draw our attention to a constellation of energies, events, people, and circumstances in such a way that some aspect of our soul potential can be embodied in our life at that moment. It is a mysterious and sacred moment when cosmic forces, our soul energy, and events and people in outer life are in optimal alignment for some invisible aspect of our soul to become visible. We need only acknowledge it, attend to it, and act upon it in a conscious manner.

For example, a colleague and I decided to meet to discuss a possible research idea. With our busy schedules, we both decided to have a brown-bag meeting. To our amazement, we found that we both had, independently, brown-bagged a grilled chicken sandwich on whole wheat bread, with a dill pickle and the same size bag of potato chips. Immediately, I knew that our souls had spoken, and that the outcome of our cooperation would be numinous. We coauthored an excellent little article that was published in a reputable journal, received broad acclaim, and made a small, but significant, contribution to improving a certain treatment method.

MEDICAL AND PSYCHIATRIC SYMPTOMS

Medical and psychiatric symptoms, as I discussed in chapter 3, are the soul's most urgent distress call. If you are experiencing physical symptoms (shortness of breath, or difficulty breathing, dizziness, chest pains, chronic headaches, blood in your urine or stool), or recurrent bouts of depression, anxiety, hallucinations, loss of time, or severe relationship difficulties, you should consult your primary physician and ask for treatment or referral.

Once your symptoms have been professionally diagnosed and the appropriate treatment regimen begun, it may be worthwhile to review the chapters on medical and psychiatric symptoms and the two chapters on the kundalini chakra system as an adjunct to your primary treatment. In those chapters, I have discussed the effect of habitual lifestyle on physical and emotional health.

It is important to inform your primary caregiver of your habitual lifestyle, because the way you live significantly influences not only the quality of your life, but the length of your life as well. Medical and psychiatric symptoms are a final distress call from the soul to alert you to the danger of suffocating, alienating, or losing your soul. On the other hand, if you respond to this call, you have one last opportunity to cross the bridge that leads you back to the soul. A hard-driving, controlling, logic-driven, outcome-oriented, emotionally distant executive gets chest pains as a prelude to an impending heart attack. Symbolically this may be a call from his soul to address and honor his heart chakra, the feeling realm, before he loses his soul—and perhaps his life.

We must honor the whispers of the soul, attend to its message, and implement its intent to establish healing in our wounded lives and wholeness in our incomplete existences. Our lives then become sacred temples for the soul, and all aspects of our being acquire the potential to manifest and enhance our lives in countless ways. More importantly, we have the opportunity to live out the meaning and mystery of our own unique dharma on the stage of our life, while bringing something to the community as well.

More Ways to Listen for the Soul's Whispers

We can respond to the soul's whispers by working on dreams, dealing with complexes, attending to relationships, and noticing synchronistic events. There are also several other approaches that are of value: silence, meditation, spontaneous writing, journaling, active imagination, and divination. I will briefly discuss each.

SOLITUDE

Philosophers have aptly noted that solitude is the food of the soul. I have found that the capacity to invoke and honor solitude is crucial. When we regularly maintain some amount of solitude in our lives, we create the indispensable precondition for opening consciousness to the invisible unconscious background, the ocean whose invisible currents carry the ego and inform our individual soul.

In the hustle and bustle of modern materialistic society, it is not easy to cultivate a daily period of solitude. If we recognize our need for solitude and protect it, however, it can become a bridge connecting us to our individual soul and, further, to the Primal Soul. For example, you can devote some regular daily time to retreating within yourself—time when you do nothing but sit quietly and see what emerges into your consciousness. Later, after this period of solitude, record what emerged in your journal and reflect on it to get in touch with the deeper feelings and images that arose.

On occasions when you cannot create the space of solitude, improvise. I have often counseled individuals who, when commuting to and from work, instead of turning on the radio should maintain quiet and silence, converting the commute time into a time for solitude, silence, and communion with their souls.

SILENCE: THE MAUN WRATHA

In many of the great spiritual and cultural traditions of the East and the West, the importance of silence and solitude have regularly been emphasized. Examples include the Roman Catholic tradition of retreat, daily silence, solitude, prayer, and meditation; the great Buddhist tradition in which monks maintain silence and solitude to experience the inner spiritual ground; and the Zen practice of sitting in silence.

Mahatma Gandhi, the great Indian spiritual leader, followed a ritual of maintaining total silence one day each week. He participated in all activities of life, but remained essentially nonverbal and quiet. This was a day when he allowed the outside world and his inner spiritual world to affect him, without mediation or verbal intervention on his own behalf.

This mode of ritual silence is referred to in Indian holy scriptures as the *maun wratha*, the silence ritual. It is often fascinating to see what emerges when we do not interact verbally with the world around or within us, but rather watch what unfolds on the stage of life. When we do not try to modify what is going on through speech, we gain a unique opportunity to palpate the pulse of our inner and outer environments.

Language and speech, among the higher achievements of evolution, not only express, but also limit, consciousness. Because our intuitive images come from the deepest source of Being, language often cannot translate them into any known concept. When we become too earthbound by conditioned consciousness and by the use of language for self-expression and communication with others, we limit what we can experience and perceive to the bounds set by the spoken word. So, when we maintain total silence for a period of time, we temporarily abandon language and free ourselves to explore the territory of our inner and outer worlds, unfettered by linguistic maps.

When we combine solitude and silence, we shut out the external world, as well as our linguistic interaction with it and our filtering of it. We then have the opportunity to perceive and experience inner images and riches, because we are not trying to force them to fit the procrustean bed of our vocabulary.

MEDITATION

There are essentially two forms of meditation: directed meditation that focuses on a *mantra* (a sound, syllable, word, or phrase, usually drawn from scripture or the sayings of a teacher), and undirected meditation that observes whatever floats through consciousness without holding it in focus. Both forms are valuable. Focused meditation disciplines the mind to attend to only the object of choice, ignoring all distractions. Undirected meditation disciplines the mind to detach, to let go.

A variation of directed meditation (useful in dream work) involves circumambulating an image. Choose an image (from a dream or a fantasy), focus on it, and note what comes to mind, always maintaining the chosen image as the center point around which your associations gather. The challenge of circumambulatory meditation is to keep returning to the chosen image and not follow your associations away from the image to which you chose to associate.

STUDIO TIME

Studio time is that part of our lives that we devote exclusively to expressing and getting in touch with the creative flow. It is time we regularly set aside every week when we exclude all other agendas, responsibilities, and distractions, and place our skills of expression exclusively in the service of the creative spirit. For example, I devote three hours every Sunday morning to recording my ideas and concepts on tape (as I am doing this morning), without any agenda other than a broad idea of what I might say.

This morning, I decided I would dictate something about the creative process without making any outline ahead of time. Of course, once I capture the ideas in whatever order they occur to me, I then subject them to the academic process of restructuring, rearranging, and adding references, life experiences, case examples, and other materials.

Working on what comes to me spontaneously establishes an appropriate partnership between the creative source and my conditioned consciousness. Their dance will become apparent in the ultimate outcome of my creative endeavor, which I hope will be an intelligent, well-written essay that respects both the unconscious source of the ideas and my accumulated knowledge, experience, and judgment on the subject.

To make optimal use of studio time, try to set aside the same time every week, or several times a week. It should be a quiet time without intrusions, as studio time is spent in solitude. You also need to have the tools and materials for your mode of expression. If you are a painter, you are in your studio where you have your canvas and your paints. Choose a quiet time when you can draw from inner inspiration, images, and ideas.

Because I am interested in writing, I set up my tape recorder Saturday night so that on Sunday morning I am ready in my studio time to start dictating some of my ideas on whatever subject I have chosen beforehand.

Occasionally, no inspiration emerges. You should honor that, too, because the unconscious may be incubating some particular idea of which you are not aware at the time. Nevertheless, it is essential to set aside the studio time on a regular basis to give the unconscious and the ego consciousness an opportunity to enter a partnership that may bring forth something unexpected.

The value of this exercise in studio time is to "let nature speak." People who give themselves studio time have discovered that this exercise, when regularly practiced, opens the floodgates of creativity.

JOURNALING

Journaling is more structured than spontaneous writing or painting, or whatever your medium of expression may be. Perhaps the best-known journal format is that developed by Ira Progroff. You can, of course, create your own journal format. For example, you may have sections on daily life, dreams, meaningful personal encounters, synchronistic events, or activated complexes. As you work the various parts of your journal, look for recurring patterns (between dreams and daily events, or meaningful encounters and activated complexes). When, for example, a dream figure reappears several times, try to discover more about that figure by practicing the next exercise, active imagination.

ADVANCED TECHNIQUES AND PRACTICES

There are three additional ways of opening yourself to the whispers of the soul that I want to mention. These are advanced practices that you should engage in only under the guidance of a competent practitioner.

I Ching: The ancient Chinese classic of change, the I Ching, has been a cornerstone of Chinese culture for several thousand years. The I Ching (pronounced "yee jing") consists of 64 six-line figures and a number of attached commentaries. The six-line figures, called hexagrams, represent the momentary interaction of the two primal forces in the universe *(yang and yin)* as those forces relate to the question you ask. Since the commentaries on the hexagram, itself, and on the individual lines are usually in the form of images rather than explicit statements (*not* "Do this" or "Do that"), it takes considerable skill and practice to accurately understand the I Ching's response to your question.

Therefore, it is wise to have an experienced guide.

Tarot: Another valuable tool through which the soul can speak is the tarot. Traditionally, the tarot consists of a deck of cards, the twenty-two cards of the major arcana, and the four fourteen-card suits of the minor arcana. The tarot cards, like the hexagrams of the I Ching, represent archetypal situations and processes in pictures. The correspondence between the cards in a tarot spread and our question is not based on causality. Rather, like the hexagrams in the I Ching, the connecting link is not "magic," but shared meaning: the cards we draw and our life situation have the same structure and pattern of meaning.[2]

Sand Trays: This method accesses the inner child. When you are invited to create a diorama in a sandbox using the miniature toys provided by the therapist—or yourself—the soul speaks through the created image and informs your consciousness of its

2. J. Sharman-Burke, and L. Greene, *The Mythic Tarot* (New York: Simon & Schuster, 1986), p. 12.

depths. Serial images created over the duration of therapy are like a serial X ray of the soul and its state of spiritual development and incarnation in outer life.

Active Imagination: This approach differs from the I Ching and the tarot in that you actively engage in a dialogue with the figures and situations the soul presents in imagination. Active imagination is a technique that C. G. Jung developed. In active imagination, you chose an image or a figure from a dream (for example), and engage it in a dialogue, just as we would a flesh-and-blood person. This interior dialogue can move very rapidly, so it is important to keep a written record as you proceed. Otherwise it is too easy to forget the exchange; and since the other in us often tells us things we would never listen to from another person, our "ocular evidence" counteracts our tendency to deceive ourselves that nothing important took place..It is well worth the effort to come to terms with the other in us, because in this way we get to know facets of our personality we otherwise might never confront.[3]

As with the I Ching and the tarot, the value of a guide when doing active imagination lies in having someone who can help you meaningfully relate the vivid images to the realities of your current life. It is very easy to make too much or too little of a picture; either extreme overshoots the mark, and you can lose the message in the exaggeration.

CONCLUSION

The various approaches I have discussed here can be of great value on your journey, and I encourage you to try them and discover for yourself what works best for you. Gaining insight into the complex nature of your personality—your soul—and its relation to the Primal Soul is what the path to the soul is all about.

The techniques I have discussed are important. Traditionally, the East has been obsessed with respect for the spiritual dimen-

3. C. G. Jung, *Mysterium Coniunctionis*, CW14, ¶706.

sion of life to the exclusion of the material realm and methodology. Typically, the West has focused on the outer world and rational consciousness, often being seduced by the *methods* of soul work to the detriment of the soul work being undertaken. Method is useful only when it produces results.

It is my hope that you will find a balance between the *intent* and the *content* of your spiritual path. If you cannot deal with the personal content of your life, you have nothing *real* to deal with. Unless you deal with that personal content in spiritual terms, however, you cannot touch its driving power and *meaning*, nor can you reach that which is to be transformed.[4]

One of the dangers Westerners face is that of getting swept away by spiritual ideas. If that happens, we lose our ground. We're no longer in the body. It is too easy to be swept away by great ideas and powerful symbols, but nothing comes of these "trips" unless we ground them in our day-to-day life. In other words, to make spiritual ideas real, we have to return to the body, and this means feeling their import in our flesh. No matter how inspiring our experiences, we must find a way to relate them to the earth, our place and condition in life.[5]

Individuals, nations, and cultures have lived for generations in one or another of the chakras. For centuries, the East has lived in its dominant sixth and seventh chakras of rarefied spirituality. Now people of the East are beginning to attend to their first three chakras to honor the material aspect of existence that grounds us here and now.

It is the task of the informed seekers in the West to attend more to the sixth and seventh chakras. Paradoxically, the task of the West is to investigate and actualize the spiritual principles of the Eastern traditions, and lead human consciousness, including that of the East, into a grounded spiritual consciousness of the sixth and seventh chakras. The torch has passed to the West, and

---

4. Paraphrase of E. C. Whitmont, *The Symbolic Quest* (Princeton: Princeton University Press, 1969), p. 69.
5. C. G. Jung, *The Visions Seminars*, p. 473.

people of the West have an opportunity—and an obligation—to carry the spiritual light of consciousness for humanity into the future.

POINTS TO PONDER

There are three important prerequisites for attending to the soul: be in the present, attend to the whispers of the soul, and make time to reflect. How can you address these three aspects of soul work?

1. List your most significant fascinations and antipathies. Using the guidelines mentioned in this chapter, compose a worksheet to explore how the soul speaks via your fascinations or antipathies.
2. Identify your most significant relationship. What aspect of your soul incarnates via this relationship?
3. Reflect on your major hang-ups or karmic complexes. What do they suggest about the potential for your soul to manifest your dharma?
4. Identify some of the synchronistic events (meaningful coincidences) in your life. What opportunity for soulful living did these open up for you?
5. Note your significant medical or emotional symptoms or illness. How do these bridge you to your dharma and your soul?
6. We all need to create a sacred space and conditions in our life to attend to our soul and honor its whispers. What provisions have you made to implement this space? How do you make room for silence, solitude, studio time, and journaling?
7. What system do you have for actively dialoguing with your soul? How do the methods of active imagination, I Ching, sand tray, or tarot work for you?

chapter nine

ON THE PATH

One's own dharma,
even when not done perfectly,
is better than someone else's dharma,
even though well performed. . . .
—Bhagavad Gita[1]

In the preceding chapters, I have discussed in detail several major points: maya, karma, and dharma; karmic complexes; clan karma; medical and psychiatric conditions; and the kundalini chakras. Taken together, they constitute a detailed map of the path to the soul. Let me now come full circle and review how the basic ideas discussed in this book lead us on the path to the soul.

Svadharma, one of the four dimensions of dharma, refers, to the constitutional disposition of the individual. Svadharma includes physical characteristics, emotional makeup, latent talents, mental capacities, and the legacy of past karma. In a sense, our svadharma is the vehicle we must use in this lifetime, as well the medium through which we retire karma and realize the other dharmas. Ashrama dharma refers to the stages of life—our developmental sequence from infancy through adolescence and maturity to old age and death. In each stage of life, we face challenges, growth opportunities, and necessities. No person is an

---

1. *Bhagavad Gita*, Antonio de Nicolás, trans. (York Beach, ME: Nicolas-Hays, 1990), chapter 3, verse 35, p. 45.

island. We are interdependent and have to live together on our small planet. Varna dharma addresses the social aspect of our existence: family, community, nation. To fulfill varna dharma, we have to recognize and live in accordance with our fellow creatures. Reta dharma, cosmic order, the rule of the infinite intelligence, the Primal Soul, is the all-embracing first principle. The arena in which we work on actualizing the various aspects of dharma is the created, time-space world.

The time-space world into which we are born includes not only physical reality, but also our emotional, mental, and spiritual realms. This is maya, the whole of manifest existence. Maya is the context in which our spark of divinity—our individual soul—attempts to realize itself through svadharma, ashrama dharma, and varna dharma on its way back to the universal Primal Soul. In the process of actualizing the divine spark entrusted to each of us, we make choices and take action that sets in motion a chain of reaction and further action. This is karma. As we progress in recognizing the ways our perceptions and actions further or hinder our realizing, here and now, the divine spark in each of us, we develop spiritually. We tread the path to the soul. Let's now review each of these facets of journey to the soul in more depth.

Maya is experienced as a hunger for material success, for mastery in the realm of the physical, social, and relational world. For some people this may seem to be the dark side of existence, but maya is the essential ground on which we exist as physical, social creatures. It provides the soil in which the seed of soul consciousness takes root and blossoms. Those who attempt to bypass the realm of maya continually trip over it, so to speak. Each of us must embody and ground our existence and our experience in material reality. Individuals who live overly spiritualized lives, without the experience of the mundane and the profane, must, at some time and in some manner, honor the mayic realm. Otherwise, their journey is delayed until they honor maya and give it due recognition.

Experiencing maya is crucial for each one of us. Having once experienced maya, however, we must detach from it without condemning it moralistically. This is what Jesus meant when he said, "What gain, then, is it for a man to have won the whole world and to have lost or ruined his very self?" (Luke 9:24) If we cannot caringly detach from maya, we get stuck, and our journey on the path to the soul is suspended until our awareness of karma awakens and we extricate ourselves.

In the realm of maya, we live out the various facets of ashrama dharma, life's developmental stages. As we realize and fulfill our ashrama dharma, we learn to manage the developmental challenges of our life cycle. Such challenges include all our transitions in our progress from infancy to old age. Traditional Hinduism recognizes four life stages—student, householder, mentor, and religious solitary. Hinduism identifies the age of 12 to 24 as the student stage. Western psychology has added to the Hindu stage the period of infancy to age 12, and has studied the period from birth to young adulthood in great detail.

Developmental psychologists such as Erik Erikson, Daniel J. Levinson, Margaret Mahler, and many others have done a monumental job of delineating ashrama dharma from the developmental perspective of Western psychology.[2] We experience the phase of bonding between infant and parent in which growing mastery leads to the infant's gradual separating and becoming more of an individual, returning to "refuel" when the world gets too scary. Another phase has been called the "family romance," in which the little girl is going to marry Daddy when she grows up, and the little boy will marry Mommy. When children go to school, their new challenge is to learn to adapt and relate to a wider community outside the nuclear family. This contributes to further cognitive, emotional, and social development. Puberty plunges the growing individual into profound biological, psychological, and social changes, pointing the adolescent girl or boy toward sexual maturity and intimate involvement with a partner.

---

2. E. H. Erikson, *Childhood and Society* (New York: W. W. Norton Company, 1950); D. Levinson, *The Seasons of a Man's Life* (New York: Ballantine Books, 1978); and M. Mahler et al., *The Psychological Birth of the Human Infant* (New York: Basic Books, 1975).

The quarter century from the mid-20s to about age 50 is the householder stage. Marrying, supporting and rearing a family, and caring for the elderly occupy much of this phase of life. For many, the householder phase is also the time of worldly accomplishment and the accumulation of wealth, honor, fame, and power. It is also a period of inner challenges. The first occurs around age 28, when many individuals begin to examine their life's direction, accomplishment, and meaning, and often set out on a chosen path of endeavor with greater dedication. Again, in the early 40s, we are visited by what we have come to know as the "midlife transition" or "midlife crisis." Unfortunately, many people use this opportunity for self-reflection and self-examination only after they have acted in ways that create much pain for themselves and for others (karma!).

Although during this period of life we are very busy with the outer world and with our midlife transition, a subtle shift in awareness is often underway. In the first half of life, up into our 40s, we have often (even if not often enough!) acted reflectively as our karmic consciousness has developed. On the cusp of 50, many people sense a subtle, but distinct, change in consciousness, a kind of reversal, or a shift of emphasis from acting reflectively to reflecting actively. In the first half of life, consciousness is predominantly mayic, although we begin to develop some karmic consciousness. In the second half of life, it is important to shift our emphasis from pursuing the rewards of maya to acting in ways that retire karma and further dharma. Reflecting actively becomes, therefore, the watchword for the second half of life. Gradually, over the next quarter century, our interests shift away from engaging with life's immediate challenges and responsibilities toward sharing our experience by advising and guiding younger generations. Little by little, we develop into mentors. In the last stage of life, we retire even more and reflect more intensely, often detaching from the world almost completely, devoting our remaining energies only to those tasks and activities that carry the deepest meaning we have discovered on our journey through life.

If we have lived and reflected well, seen through maya to the universal patterns informing the phenomenal world and karma, we ripen into wise old men and women, wisdom carriers, aware that our tiny existences are but small segments of the great fabric of Being, individual droplets in the ocean of Primal Soul. On our journey through the various stages of ashrama dharma, we are called upon to act and to sacrifice. We must act if we are to deal with the developmental challenges of studenthood, parenting, grandparenting and mentoring of the younger generations, and devotion to spiritual life. We must sacrifice to balance the reality of our svadharma against the imperatives of our own growth and the demands of the relevant aspects of our life in community, our varna dharma.

In each phase of life, we exist in relationship to some community: nuclear family, extended family, friends, neighborhood, school, business or professional association, or city. Varna dharma addresses the social side of our nature. Although some of the demands of varna dharma are culturally determined, the foundation of varna dharma is archetypal—that is, inherent—a given in our human nature. At this stage, we fulfill the archetypal, cultural, and social expectations, and also often extend ourselves in altruistic ways, such as through community volunteerism and social activism to further the greater good of our society. We start retiring our debt to the community by contributing to our community. This stage of our journey to the soul calls for action and devotion.

Varna consciousness is evolving in the world today, led primarily by the American people, with their admirable emphasis on volunteerism, altruism, and philanthropy. President Jimmy Carter's Habitat for Humanity is one well-known example of pioneer work in varna dharma, but you don't have to be famous to be altruistic. I will let two examples serve for many.

Every day, many teachers in inner-city schools work in an atmosphere of racial tension and violence. Often, the school facilities and supplies are inadequate. Frequently, their students come from broken or single-parent homes in impoverished, drug-infested, and crime-ridden neighborhoods. Despite these formidable handicaps, many inner-city schoolteachers instruct, comfort, and nurture the children in their classes, day in and day out. Their devotion goes far beyond the call of duty. Work provides one setting in which we can fulfill varna dharma. Voluntary service is another venue that offers rich opportunities for contributing to the community.

Many organizations offer opportunities for voluntary service in which people fulfill their varna dharma. A glance at the Yellow Pages under "Organizations" lists many types of groups that provide formal opportunities for fulfilling one's varna dharma, from animal protection services to youth centers. Many people are unsung heroes and heroines of varna dharma.

We move through the various developmental stages and strike a satisfactory balance between our responsibilities to our unique nature and those to the archetypal and cultural necessities of the social side of our human nature. When we can do this without getting stranded in maya, our consciousness begins to develop in a new direction. We see more and more clearly that our actions bear consequences. Our karmic consciousness starts to develop when the fruits of our actions begin to concern us.

RELATIONSHIPS, MAYA, KARMA, AND DHARMA

We taste karma in our choices of occupation, places to live, and ways we spend our time, energy, and money. Karma also follows us in our relational entanglements with parents, spouse, children, and the other important people in our lives. Our relationships with significant individuals in our lives also play out in our relationship with our soul. In others, we glimpse our unseen face, that side of our soul that we can see in no other way, and we fall in love with it or hate it. The karma of emotional relationships—our actions and what follows from them—is a preparatory outer voyage. In the fascinating Other, we discover outside what we must sooner or later seek within, yet without devaluing the real, flesh-and-blood other person who has been the mirror of a part of our soul.

Relationships are complex and often treacherous. We need to live and honor them. If we attempt to possess the other person, however, we are trying to own the mirror rather than embrace the reflection. To detach from an intense relationship is not necessarily to discard it. Rather, we no longer clutch at the Other with cramped fingers and white knuckles, but hold the Other in our open palms, like an offering to the Higher Power. Because most people only look at the psychological dynamics of relationships and miss the finer and greater aspect, this point of view offers us an opportunity to examine our relationships in a spiritual context.

If you ask why we must encounter the murky karma of relationships on our path to the soul, I answer that, in the crucible of relationships, we have an opportunity to separate the gold of our essence from the dross of illusion. The Other reflects to us that side of our potential personality that we do not otherwise see. To possess what fascinates and terrifies us in the Other, however, we must discover it in ourselves. After we have made our discoveries, we must cultivate what is desirable and compost what we experience as our garbage, turning it into the fertile nutrients for our further spiritual growth. In the intensity of honest encounter, we develop integrity and courage. We separate the reflection of ourselves from the reality of the Other.

Integrity in relationships is a preparation for integrity and courage on the inner path to our more direct encounter with our soul. In a relationship, we get to know two people: the Other as he or she really is, and ourselves. Those who attempt to avoid the vicissitudes of outer relationships risk the peril of experiencing these same challenges as overwhelming inner forces and figures. For example, the schizophrenic individual avoids involvement with flesh-and-blood people, but ends up struggling with inner figures in the form of voices, visions, demons, and gods. Since schizophrenics do not have much practice dealing with people, and lack practice relating to and negotiating with others, they encounter the soul directly and the ego is overwhelmed. When we meet the Other in an important relationship to which we feel some attachment, we see another incarnated facet of the Primal Soul. When we treat that relationship with integrity, we honor another manifestation of the Primal Soul. We must also treat ourselves with dignity and fairness. If the relationship is abusive, toxic, or dysfunctional, we have the opportunity to learn to honor the best interests of our soul in its journey through its dark night with the other person.

The Primal Soul, the Higher Power, transcends the individual, yet each individual embodies a fragment or a reflection of the universal soul. Our human spiritual task is to actualize, as fully as possible, the droplet of the Soul entrusted to us in this life, fulfilling as best we can our svadharma, ashrama dharma, varna dharma, and retiring our accumulated karmas. Our guide—what keeps us balanced on the tightrope—is our sense of soul.

In addition to maya, karma, and dharma there are some principles and patterns that have been implicit in the foregoing chapters that I want to discuss now. The first is the importance of being in the present.

BEING IN THE PRESENT

As I drove to a medical society meeting one afternoon, I turned on the radio and heard the Beatles' song, "Yesterday." A wave of nostalgia swept over me, a yearning for the past, for my carefree student days in India, for my glorious residency training years in Europe, for the carefree lifestyle of simple living and high thinking, of lofty ideals and vibrant energy. Then, it now seems, life was easy, troubles were far away. The memories of many yesterdays flashed past like bright comets in the dark sky of my current life as I drove to my meeting on that cold, snowy, stormy, slushy, blustery, Milwaukee winter afternoon.

I started analyzing why the past seemed so glorious and the present so tedious. I knew there was some distortion there. Actually, I am very happy in the present. My psychiatric practice is thriving; my children are progressing handsomely in their developmental pursuits; my marriage is at an optimal romantic and loving peak; and my academic endeavors are blossoming to my personal satisfaction.

So why do I misperceive the present as being so tedious? Perhaps my present bliss is eclipsed by the shadows of an uncertain future.

Then it dawned on me that the past seduces and entices me so powerfully because it is the only sure thing in my life. We have already lived the past. It is finite, completed, ***known***. The future is uncertain, unlived. It is an abyss into which we peer without seeing its contours. The future is yet to be experienced. The only certainty about the future is death. Although the future may hold promise and potential, it nevertheless remains a mere possibility, at best a probability.

The present is a glorious—or terrible—experience that is constantly receding into the past as we rush toward the inscrutable abyss called the future. The past may be enchanting, romantic, nostalgic, sad, or terrifying, but we have lived through it and believe we have some knowledge of it. The past is one of the faces of maya, a relative reality now experienced through the filter of memory. The present is the future happening to us now: surprise, toil, tedium, pleasure, satisfaction, disappointment—the unknown becoming known. The present is one of the faces of karma, the opportunity to retire the debts of the past, but also the invitation to choose dharma rather than maya.

The past lures us with its illusion of reality; the present burdens us with the immediacy of its karmic toil and dharmic challenge; the future frightens us with its prospect of the unknown. In the future, we can reconnect our individual souls with the Primal Soul, but we can also just as easily drown in maya's murky waters if we do not perceive our dharmic opportunities. As the future becomes present, we tread the round of maya, karma, and dharma again and again, circumambulating that invisible point as we come closer and closer to the dharmic center of existence. To appreciate that we are not just blindly marching into the unknown without guidance, we need to understand two points of view: "How come?" and "What for?"

"How Come?" and "What For?"

The "How Come" point of view looks for the causes that make things happen, what is called the "efficient cause." The tree falls because the woodsman cuts through the trunk. The couple quarrel because each does not feel the other understands. The "What For" viewpoint seeks the purpose, end, or intention that informs action. This is called the "final cause," from the Latin, *finis*, meaning "end." From the "What For?" point of view, the tree falls because the woodsman needs lumber to build a house; the couple quarrel because they want to resolve the differences between them and rectify the hurt each feels the other has inflicted. Both points of view are valid; both are important in reflecting on our lives.

Dharma, in its four aspects (svadharma, ashrama dharma, varna dharma, and reta dharma), is a "final cause," the "What For" that continually tugs and pulls at us to actualize what we inherently are. In psychological terms, this process is called individuation. Just as the acorn develops into an oak tree according to its innate pattern, we develop according to our innate genetic and spiritual pattern into individuated human beings.

INDIVIDUATION AND ADAPTATION

Individuation and adaptation are two aspects of the same process. In a certain sense, the process of individuation is both a tightrope walk and the most natural thing in the world. The various facets of dharma naturally nudge us in the direction of actualizing our potential. We continue to cycle through specific aspects of maya and karma until we learn the intended dharmic lesson. We easily lose sight of the dharmic lesson and goal, and fall off the tightrope, when those aspects of maya to which we are vulnerable again seduce us with their promise of being "the answer."

We walk a tightrope in another sense—between "outer" and "inner" worlds. By "outer," I mean adaptation to the physical-social-work-world in which we exist; by "inner," I mean caring for our souls and keeping track of our demons. We must, of course, adapt to both worlds.

Our individual soul comes ever closer to the Primal Soul, our Higher Power, as we individuate, that is, "undivide" ourselves. In Hindu terms, we speak of actualizing svadharma, retiring past karma, and fulfilling the various dharmas. The psychological term "individuation" refers to the ongoing dialogue between ego and shadow (discussed in chapter 1), that is, between our conscious sense of ourselves and all that we have not developed or that we have attempted to disown. As we individuate over the course of a lifetime, we progressively actualize our unique mix of innate, typically human potentials (svadharma). We also come face to face with our shortcomings and failings as our sense of karma deepens. If we have the courage, we tackle and make peace with those stubborn aspects of our attitudes and behaviors that repeatedly trip us up, those we cannot always control by acts of will.

It is important to note that the notion of individuation differs significantly from the Western, especially American, idea of heroic individualism. In its extreme form, individualism loses touch with the common ground of human nature. Individualism divides people. Individuation differentiates people. Individualism often scorns collective norms; individuation *adapts* as necessary to accepted standards, while actualizing one's svadharma. Hence, we have a twofold task in individuation: adaptation to the world into which we have been born, *and* adaptation to our unique potential.

The journey on the path of the soul embraces adaptation to our outer life and our inner calling. This reminds us of the tension between varna dharma and svadharma. Varna dharma is our nature as interdependent, social creatures, and refers to our obligations and responsibilities within the nation, society, community, class, occupational subgroup and family; svadharma is our individual physical, mental, emotional constitution. When we fulfill varna dharma, we are at peace with the world; when we live in accordance with our svadharma, we are content and at peace with ourselves.

If we fail to adapt to either the outer or the inner world, what we have neglected will make its demands known with ever greater insistence, finally breaking through as a life problem. If we neglect the environment—the climate in which we live, the people with whom we live, or our financial or personal commitments—our negligence will ultimately coerce us into taking notice. Likewise, if we neglect the inner world—needs, impulses, fantasies, and "inner promptings"—the inner world will make its demands known in the irruption of personal elements into the sphere of outer adaptation. This usually takes the form of medical or mental health problems, or disturbances in relationships.

The effect we have on others as we individuate is twofold. As we become more fully what we inherently are, we become more and more differentiated from other people. Our unique blend of typically human traits becomes more distinct, more recognizable. Nobody can mistake us for someone else. At the same time, however, we become "more fully human," better able to understand and relate to all sorts of people, because we have felt and recognized in ourselves the motivations, impulses, and reactions we encounter in others. Individuation is incremental. Little by little, we approach and progressively actualize our dharma, the invisible center point around which all our meanderings relentlessly circle. We have to play the hand that our circumstances and our choices have dealt us, or we have lost the game.

The idea of playing the cards we hold is consistent with the concept of karma as the inevitable lot of human beings, the outcome of the consequences of our choices and actions to date, and with the inscrutable workings of dharma. To live according to dharma, we need to accept our lives as gifts of nature in all their triumphs and tragedies. Embracing our lot and making the most of it is an essential part of the bigger plot of life's drama, in which we all are but actors, and where nature, or the Higher Power, or God is the supreme director whose invisible finger traces our destinies and our karmas.

In our humanness, we often try to second-guess our destinies, try to take short cuts, try to master life, only to find that we keep getting in the way of the larger, deeper, and higher goals that dharma holds for us. We become our own biggest obstacles. We become our own worst saboteurs. Abstinence from willfully interfering in our own lives demands the humility to accept our physical, emotional, intellectual, and spiritual gifts, our limitations, and the consequences of our choices and actions. It also demands the courage to live out the scripts of our lives in the context of the world into which we have been born, as well as to have faith and trust in the higher order of nature, the Primal Soul.

CIRCUMAMBULATING THE LABYRINTH

Circumambulation—the act of circling round a point of reference—defines the boundaries of a sacred space by relating to a center of value, whether by meditating, by performing a sacred ritual, or by following the meanderings of our lives. In the course of life, we gradually recognize that we have "circled around" and thereby identified and protected certain central values many times.

The labyrinth often symbolizes the process of individuation. When we enter a labyrinth, such as the labyrinth on the floor of the Chartres Cathedral (figure 2), we are quickly led toward the center. But soon the path veers, and as we proceed on our way, we turn right and left, switching back and forth, until we are far from the center in some peripheral alley. The early promise of reaching the center seems a hoax. At this point, the temptation may be to give up or turn back. Surrender or defeat, however, guarantees we will never reach the center that first drew us toward it. Only if we retrace our steps out of the blind alley to the

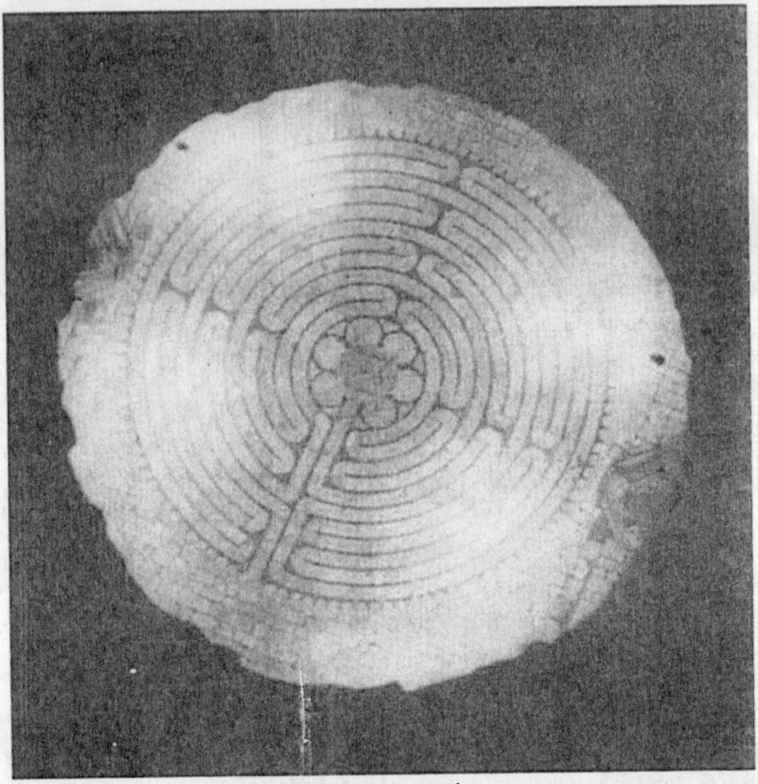

Figure 2. The Labyrinth.

previous fork in the path and follow the other route can we hope to continue our journey. Flight or capitulation defeats the purpose of the whole undertaking.

At one level, our circumambulation is personal, at another, transpersonal. At the personal level, we each create a self: an identifiable, stable personality, part of our sense of who we are, our identity. As C. G. Jung says, "The idea of the *circumambulation* . . . is . . . to find a centre and a container for [one's] whole psyche."[3] At the transpersonal level, we each discover our own relationship to the greater reality, the Higher Power, the Primal Soul. Hence, circumambulating the labyrinth of life is both a psychological process and a spiritual path, the path to the soul.

Looked at in the context of circumambulating the center along a labyrinthine path, our life's journey could be described as balancing inner and outer as we discover the center—the meaning of our individual existence in the bigger picture. As we more fully identify, embrace, and ground our svadharma, it becomes the foundation upon which we fulfill other dharmas. Over the course of a lifetime, a person who faithfully heeds the whispers of the soul and follows the labyrinthine spiral of individuation circumambulates a virtual center point or axis that represents that person's dharma. In circumambulating the center, we repeat cycles of maya and karma, but at progressively "higher" levels of consciousness and development that gradually approximate a realization of our innate, individual potential (the svadharma). Thus we accomplish the developmental tasks that each stage of life demands of us (ashrama dharma). We discover our right relationship to fellow human beings (varna dharma), and ever more fully live in accord with the Primal Soul, the Higher Power (reta dharma).

Our individual soul is the unique gift each of us has from the Primal Soul, the Higher Power. The path to the soul—that psychology calls individuation—is not a "straight and narrow path,"

---

3. C. G. Jung, *The Tavistock Lectures*, CW18, ¶411.

but rather a labyrinthine course. As we traverse it, we gradually circumambulate and thereby define the core of meaning that centers our life. Individuation is a totally personal journey, unique in the details, but typical in its overall pattern. To follow the labyrinth of individuation to the center, we need the courage to look at ourselves, as well as the knowledge to understand what we see.

The Holy Cross: Integrating Maya and Dharma

The structure of the Christian cross symbolizes the relationship between maya and dharma. The vertical axis represents the spiritual dimension (dharma); the horizontal axis represents the physical dimension (maya) (see figure 3). Our task is to find the center at which the axes cross. When we have found the center, the spiritual dimension is the point around which our material existences pivot. When we are centered, we are living a dharmic life here and now. When we go too high up the vertical axis, we flee into ungrounded spirituality; when we descend too far down the vertical axis, we end up in depression or psychosis. At either extreme, we lose the world. If we go too far out on either horizontal axis, we lose the spiritual pivot point. The task at the center is to see *through* the visible world, to perceive the spirit informing the manifest.

Figure 3. The Holy Cross.

The preceding chapters provide the map we need for the journey to the center, to the soul. We have discussed, in general psychological terms, some aspects of the experience of individuation. But what is the *spiritual* dimension of the experience of individuation? What have people said about approaching or being in the center, in the soul? These are the questions we will address in the next chapter.

POINTS TO PONDER

1. What has been the nature of your path to the soul? Has it been a straight line or a maze?
2. What detours, roadblocks, or hazards have you experienced? How have these distracted you from your path or informed you more accurately of the deeper meaning and mystery of your life?
3. How have your medical and psychiatric symptoms informed and deepened your understanding of your path to the soul?
4. Have you been able to identify your dominant and auxiliary kundalini chakras? How has this information clarified your dharmic goals?
5. Do you have some understanding of your hang-ups or complexes?
6. Has your understanding and management of your complexes assisted you to move from mayic karma to dharmic karma? How does this karmic shift manifest in your life? Has this shift from mayic to dharmic karma aligned you more closely to your dharma?
7. Have you been able to identify and retire your clan karma? In what ways has this retirement of clan karma impacted your life, symptoms, and relationships? Has this change permitted you some freedom to live a more soulful, dharmic life?
8. In retrospect, how have some of the major crises, catastrophes, medical and psychiatric illnesses, relationship problems, and family curses been hidden blessings aligning you to your dharma and your soul?

9. In your present life, what is the balance between maya and dharma?
10. In your present life, what is the nature of your karmic choices? Do they lead to more maya, or move you closer to your dharma?
11. To what extent do you feel that you are able to live in the present moment? How often do you feel preoccupied with the past or the future?
12. If you assess your two important life trajectories, with spirituality as a vertical axis and materiality as a horizontal axis, when they intersect, what is the nature of the holy cross you bear? What is the relative strength of the material versus the spiritual axis? Are they balanced? Is your material preoccupation informed and tempered by the spiritual dimension of your life?

chapter ten

In the Soul

These bodies, it is said, come to an end,
(But they belong) to an embodied one who is eternal,
indestructible, immeasurable. Therefore, fight,
O Bhārata!
—Bhagavad Gita[1]

As we become who we potentially are, we actualize our unique mix of qualities and gifts (our svadharma) in the context of our stage in life (ashrama dharma), while fulfilling our responsibilities to our fellow human beings (varna dharma). The four aspects of dharma both guide and seek actualization through our cycles of maya and karma. Little by little, as we get older, we seek to understand where we fit into the sacred order, the great round of being, reta dharma, that guides the entire process. But what is our immediate, day-to-day experience? What are we looking for? What prompts us to take action (karma) in the created, limited world (maya) in which we exist as embodied souls?

The Fourfold Good

The path to the soul is close to the life we live. In chapter 1, I spoke of the "fourfold good," chaturvarga. It refers to the four pursuits of human life: wealth (artha), pleasure (kama), and liberation (moksha), all under the guidance of the four aspects of dharma.

1. *Bhagavad Gita*, Antonio de Nicolás, trans. (York Beach, ME: Nicolas-Hays, 1990), chapter 2, verse 18, p. 33.

The Hindu concept of kama addresses the experiential dimension—pleasure, love, and enjoyment. Earthly love, sexual love, the pleasures of the world, aesthetic and cultural fulfillment, the joys of family and friends, intellectual satisfaction[2]—all have their place in kama. This is foreign to much of the Christian tradition. Hinduism does not make pleasure the highest good, but there is nothing wrong with pleasure and seeking pleasure so long as one obeys the basic rules of morality: don't cheat, steal, lie, or succumb to addictions. Kama also embraces the satisfactions and enjoyment of one's happiness, of one's security, creativity, usefulness, and inspiration—all "nonmaterial" and very personal. Hindu texts do not condemn pleasure; rather, they include instructions for how to enlarge its scope. Pleasure is one aspect of life. For simple people, the texts present a regimen ensuring health and prosperity; for the more sophisticated, they elaborate a sensual aesthetic foreign to the West. If pleasure is what you want, seek it intelligently.[3]

Sooner or later, however, every person comes to the realization—Hinduism would say in this or a subsequent life—that pleasure is not enough, pleasure is not all that one wants. Eventually we recognize, not that pleasure is wicked, but that it is trivial—too limited to arouse our unwavering enthusiasm.[4] Self-centeredness shifts from the pursuit of pleasure to the pursuit of worldly success—artha in its three aspects: power, wealth, and fame, under the guidance of dharma.

Artha, wealth, is a broad concept, including the satisfaction of basic needs (food, shelter, clothing, money). Beyond the material necessities, however, artha embraces wealth in many nonmaterial respects foreign to Western ears: worthy children, good friends, leisure time, the joys of giving, offering hospitality to guests.[5] Clearly, the notion of artha, wealth, is much more broad

---

2. Subramuniyaswami, *Dancing with Siva* (Kappa, HI: Himalayan Academy, 1993), p. 793.
3. Huston Smith, *The World's Religions* (New York: HarperCollins, 1991), p. 14.
4. Huston Smith, *The World's Religions*, p. 14.
5. Subramuniyaswami, *Dancing with Siva*, p. 792.

than the typical Western concept, for artha measures not only monetary riches, but also quality of life at a certain level. As with kama, eventually we come to realize that artha, in its various aspects, is also limited, and lacks something essential. Material riches do not make us wealthy; fame does not warm us when we are lonely; power isolates us. Riches, fame, and power in the outer life do not multiply when we share them, although sharing may deepen our soulfulness.[6] The arthic drive is insatiable; success, power, wealth is never enough. Ultimately worldly accomplishment is transitory.

Kama and artha lie on the "path of desire." Perhaps no group of people more aptly typifies those who have lived the path of desire to the end than the chief executive officers of huge corporations, the CEOs. Wealth, power, fame—they have them all in full measure. For many, however, that all evaporates when they retire. "Chief executives have a great drive to differentiate themselves from others. With retirement, a lifetime of reputation building suddenly dissolves, eroding before their eyes." For them it is "a plunge into the abyss of insignificance."[7]

There is another path, however, the path of detachment. Detachment has two faces: the face of sour grapes, and the face illuminated by the experience that there is more to human existence than being slaves to pleasure, power, wealth, and the successes of the limited reality we call our world. When we discover that we are on a treadmill, running faster and faster for rewards that mean less and less, the question may arise: What are we serving? It may occur to us that the problem stems from the smallness of the life we have been scrambling to serve. What if our concerns were shifted? Might not becoming a part of a larger, more significant whole relieve life of its triviality?

The focus shifts from the personal self and its desires and needs to some larger context of reference, to something outside

---

6. Huston Smith, *The World's Religions*, p. 15.
7. L. Grant, "You've Got the Stock Options, Now Get a Life," *Fortune*, 133,12, (June 24, 1996), p. 60.

or beyond oneself. There are, of course, many levels beyond oneself: family, community, ethnic group, profession, nation, political or social cause, ideal. This shift marks the first step in spiritual development, for with it we awaken to dharma, the third great aim of life in the Hindu outlook.[8]

The spirituality of service and duty (ashrama and varna dharma) yields noble rewards: the satisfaction, for example, of rearing healthy sane children, of caring for older parents and relatives, of contributing to the well-being of one's community, of furthering a worthy cause, of contributing to the dissemination and increase of human knowledge. But all of these, fine as they may be, turn out ultimately to be limited, as well, for death puts an end to our efforts, and our accomplishments will eventually fade into oblivion with the passage of time. Is there nothing more? What is it human beings really want, if not pleasure, wealth, power, and success and fulfillment of life's duties?

What we really want is moksha—liberation: release from the limitations that separate us from the bliss, joy, fulfillment, and peace we taste in those rare and fleeting moments of peak experience.

MOKSHA: LIBERATION

Moksha comes through the fulfillment of artha, kama, and dharma in our current or past lives, so that we are no longer attached to worldly joys or sorrows. As we move from a mayic or karmic consciousness to a dharmic consciousness, the center of gravity of our personality shifts from the ups and downs of outer life to the centering experience of the soul. We do not become callous and indifferent, but detached. The result of this transition, when successful, is that we suffer, as it were, in the lower levels of our personality, but in the upper levels we are singularly liberated, experiencing both suffering and joy with equanimity.[9]

---

8. Huston Smith, *The World's Greatest Religions*, p. 19.

9. Adapted from C. G. Jung, "Commentary on the 'Secret of the Golden Flower'," CW13, ¶67.

Stated very simply, as our sense of something greater than our individual life grows stronger, caring detachment replaces our slavish, anxious attachment to worldly achievement, pleasure, power, and wealth. Gradually we experience more and more liberation, moksha.

In the traditional view, moksha is release from the round of births and deaths that occur after karma has been resolved and the transpersonal self, *Parashiva*, has been attained. To achieve this complete liberation, individuals raise the kundalini energy to the seventh chakra. They have the potential to achieve complete liberation from the enticements of maya and the tangles of karma, and experience full union with the Primal Soul, the Higher Power, Brahman. These individuals are privileged to have the responsibility of bridging between human and Divine Consciousness, of retiring their varna dharma, while at the same time achieving reta dharma. In the Bhagavad Gita Lord Krishna characterizes the person who has achieved complete moksha:

> *Having forsaken the sense of I, might, insolence,*
> *Desire, anger, possession;*
> *Unselfish and at peace,*
> *he is fit to become Brahman*
>
> *Having become Brahman, tranquil in the self,*
> *He neither grieves nor desires;*
> *Regarding all beings as equal,*
> *he attains supreme dedication to me.*[10]
>
> *And I am seated in the hearts of all;*
> *From me are memory, wisdom and their loss.*
>
> . . . .
>
> *I am the one to be known by the Vedas;*
> *The Author of the Vedānta,*
> *I am also the knower of the Vedas*

10. *Bhagavad Gita*, chapter 18, verses 53–54, p. 123.

He who, undeluded, thus knows me,
as the supreme puruṣa (puruṣottama);
He is all-knowing and worships me
with his whole being, O Bhārata.[11]

It is true that individuals in the seventh (crown) chakra are considered to be old souls in their spiritual journey. Having attained complete liberation, such persons are free from the cycles of reincarnation. They are the great spiritual teachers.

Many discussions of the chakras emphasize "raising" kundalini from the root to the crown chakra, usually under the guidance of a guru. From this emphasis, it is easy—but incorrect—to infer that the six "lower" chakras are less important than the seventh, the crown chakra, and that moksha is possible only when the practicant has succeeded in moving his or her consciousness to the crown chakra. This is an unfortunate misunderstanding. Each of the chakras plays a significant and indispensable role in life.

MOKSHA AND THE KUNDALINI CHAKRAS

The seven kundalini chakras in the body are active at all times. Each of the seven produces a specific attitude and focuses our attention and concern on a certain aspect of life (see figure 1, page 87). As you will recall from the extended discussion in chapters 4 and 5, imbalance among chakras causes medical and emotional suffering, while restoring chakra balance restores physical and emotional health.

In each of us, one or perhaps two chakras are more dominant than others, either "naturally" (we were born that way) or "unnaturally" (we were conditioned by early experiences). When we are able to draw on the energies of the seventh chakra (and of our nondominant chakras as needed) to temper the one-sided strength of our primary chakra, we can attain a level of caring detachment—moksha—while continuing to function from our primary (natural) chakra.

---

11. *Bhagavad Gita*, chapter 15, verses 15, 19, p. 107.

For me personally, and in my work with individuals in touch with the kundalini energy of the seventh chakra, the best clinical, empirical, and pragmatic description of moksha is "caring detachment." We can develop caring detachment when we live life to the full, embracing our opportunities and celebrating our victories, as well as suffering our defeats and disappointments. When we do our utmost to actualize our svadharma (that fractal of divinity that constitutes our uniqueness), and actively participate in the affairs of family, community, and spirit (varna dharma), but leave the outcome to reta dharma, the Higher Power, we detach from our endeavors in a caring way. Whatever we undertake in this spirit—our individual life, our work, our involvement with others—then becomes "God's work," the fuller manifestation of the Primal Soul in our world.

Individuals in any chakra have the potential to attain moksha provided that they have been tempered in their life experience by the energy and perspective of the seventh chakra.

Individuation is a process of approximating an ideal state: wholeness. Wholeness implies, first, that we have come to terms with our complexes. This does not necessarily mean that we have mastered or eliminated them; rather, we recognize them, know what triggers them, and have gained the upper hand over them so that they do not run away with us and make us do and say things that we later regret. As we continue to individuate, we come to terms with the suchness of our endowment, and our formative, life-defining influences and experiences. We actualize ever more fully the four aspects of dharma in the proportions innate to us. We accept ourselves as we are, and consequently are better able to accept others as they are. We are detached, but remain caring.

In addition to caring detachment, individuals who have attained some level of moksha have several additional characteristics. Their participation in life is intense. We sense their integrity and their passion for their endeavors. Their involvement in life is like the love and labor of a grandparent: intense and permeated with love, but free from the preoccupation with the outcome of the effort. With such individuals, we feel as though we are in the presence of a silent, deep ocean. In psychological language we speak of their level of individuation.

RETURN TO THE SOUL

In my work with patients, I find again and again that they heal and grow beyond their psychic wounds as they ever more fully realize they are intimately related to a transcendent reality that permeates everything. From time to time we sense the dharmic order of reality and endeavor to incarnate it. Deep down, each of us knows that we are but a droplet of water from the infinite ocean of Being, but we easily forget this truth when maya fills our field of vision.

We can lose our soul in our preoccupation with maya, or the clan karma we inherit, the karmic complexes and karma we create, our physical and emotional suffering, or the imbalance in our chakras. Too often, these troubling areas of personality behave in soul-killing ways directed both toward ourselves and toward others. When we experience these mad areas in us, considerable panic can emerge. We no longer experience being a participant in the Primal Soul. We then need to remember that maya is the school, karma—in all its various forms—is the teacher of the dharmic lesson, and we live in a cosmos with many levels of order.

The soul is capable of spiritual and physical experience. The soul needs the body in order to incarnate dharma. Without a body, the soul remains stranded in empty spirituality (stuck in the seventh chakra, ungrounded). Likewise, the body needs the soul to inform it of the dharmic path. Without the soul, the body is only an organization of natural elements that would quickly decompose without the vital essence the soul imparts. The task of life is to embody Primal Soul and ensoul the body. And this is possible only when we are connected to our individual soul. We split off from our soul when we cannot embrace the seeming obstacles as stepping-stones on the path.

On the path to the soul, we can use courage. We require the courage to face and embrace our challenges. We require the courage to seek the symbolic message in concrete events. Courage allows us to trust the whispers of the soul that we hear in dreams, fantasies, inspirations, creative impulses, memories, relationships, joy, and suffering. We all can have the courage to step with open eyes into the darkness of our unknown selves, as well as the courage to affirm what we know to be the soul's truth. Finally and fundamentally, it takes courage and integrity to honor and cultivate what seems small and insignificant, because often, what we hardly notice, or what doesn't fit well with our "business-as-usual" attitude, turns out to be the very center point, the axis around which our cycles of maya and karma have been circling time and again.

Preponderance of the Small

Most of us have the misconception that the path to the soul and the experience of being in our soul must be a "mega event," a momentous life experience. While on rare occasions this may be the case, in most instances the soul speaks in whispers and manifests in small and apparently inconsequential events in life. We can only encounter the soul in these experiences if we are tuned in to the soul's whispers.

The soul whispers in many ways: through people, events, meaningful coincidences, dreams. These are all golden threads that we can follow to the soul. But it is up to us: if we ignore them, we lose a dharmic opportunity. The golden threads, the whispers of the soul, need our attention. We must deliberately nurture them.

Three great spiritual traditions agree. The Hindu tradition speaks of the relationship between the atman, the individual, as a fractal of Paramatman, absolute reality, the transcendent god within. Christianity teaches that Jesus, the Christ, is the true self, yet, we remember that Jesus was born in a manger and threatened with death by King Herod. The psychological truth of the nativity is that the existing order of consciousness, represented by Herod, seeks to destroy the New King, the Christ. Our responsibility is not to let the Herod in us destroy the golden thread of new life that needs our protection and nurturing. The I Ching, one of the classic Confucian and Taoist wisdom texts, is perhaps the world's oldest book. Hexagram 62 addresses the significance of small things, which form the golden threads leading to the soul.

The Primal Spirit is like a great river. The individual soul is a sample of the waters of the great river which we carry in the a small vessel of our conscious life. We have several choices: We may live a dharmic life and further purify these waters entrusted to us, and return them to the great river. This enhances and amplifies the flow and the quality of the waters of the great river; this is how a well-lived life improves the collective consciousness, enriches it, and carries the work of the spirit forward. Alternatively, a life muddied in complexes, lost in maya, ignorant of its karma, returns the waters entrusted to it more toxic thereby polluting the great river and its spirit. Each one of us, though small and seemingly insignificant in the bigger picture of the spirit has the opportunity to improve its flow or impede its purity. When each one of us retires our individual and clan karma and starts living a dharmic life, then our "small" life becomes the building block of the flow of the Primal Spirit. We may then leave this planet a better or worse place than we found it.

To follow the path to the soul, we must be like water: venturing onward with the flow, conforming to the course, risking falling into the deep, until we reach the bottom, filling, and overcoming the dangers that confront us, only to flow onward again, without reserve. In this way, we hold fast to the center, continuing to grow, fulfilling dharma.

Venturing wholeheartedly does not mean merely swallowing whatever is put in our mouths, but actively, yet humbly, engaging it, adapting to it. Following the path to the soul demands wholehearted venturing into the unknown that is life. Thus we come to know that we participate in the life of the Primal Soul, like a plant thriving in the full light of the Sun.

When we recognize our relationship to the Soul, we find that our task is to help all things prosper. We can let our light shine forth calmly and with strength so that it may augment and enhance all about us. Thus do we pass the light on from one to another in a natural succession. The light we share fertilizes the inner field of the individual soul, whose yielding service in turn spreads prosperity and manifests the Primal Soul.

At first, our progress may be halting. We may encounter difficulties. If we grapple with them, however, they will lead to meaning. We must empty out our willfulness and be still within until we can see the universal principles clearly. Then we can act appropriately. An open mind, informed by dharma, has no regret. Free from worry about loss or gain, we continue on the path of the soul, with good and beneficial results in every way.

Seeing through maya, learning from karma the lessons of dharma, we overcome ourselves. We have emptied our minds. Though we conquer ourselves, however, we remain in the province of striving. We fall, but get up again to walk further on the path. Thunder rises within us as we hear the call of dharma, and impels us to move on. New energies sprout, thrusting up from below. To be in accord with dharma, we must yield to the impulse by accepting the guidance offered.

The True Center

The goal of the world's great spiritual traditions has always been the union of the individual with the transcendent, the individual soul with the Primal Soul, with God, with the Tao, with Parashiva. The human self arises from the inexhaustible, infinite source of being. This hidden center of the individual soul (the atman) is no less than the Primal Soul, the Godhead (Brahman). St. Paul expresses the same idea in Christian terms: "I have been crucified with Christ, and I live now not my own life but with the life of Christ who lives in me" (Galatians 2:20). The story of the rainmaker in chapter 1 expresses this same truth. Zen speaks of chopping wood and carrying water before enlightenment, and after enlightenment still chopping wood and carrying water. In other words, unless we have the courage to live out our spiritual insights in our daily lives, they degenerate into mere rhetoric. Unless we see our life as a unique incarnation of something vast that transcends our individual existence, life will have no dharmic meaning. We do not fully account for our human soul until we recognize that our bodies and personalities are only small fragments of the Primal Soul.[12] The Bhagavad Gita expresses this

---

12. Huston Smith, *The World's Religions*, p. 21.

same idea eloquently: "A fraction of my self, in the world of the living becomes a living self, eternal, and draws into its power the (five) senses and the mind as sixth that come from *prakrti* [nature].[13]

In the Yajur Veda, we read: "A part of Infinite Consciousness becomes our own finite consciousness, with powers of discrimination and definition and with false conceptions. He is, in truth . . . , the Source of all Creation and the Universal in us all. This spirit is consciousness and gives consciousness to the body. He is the driver of the chariot."[14] In other words, a fractal of the Supreme Being, Brahman,[15] incarnates in each of us as the atman, which is the essence of each of us, rather than the physical body, the emotions, or external mind or personality.

In the Kena Upanishad, we read: "By whom willed and directed does the mind fly forth? By whom commanded does the first breath move? Who sends forth the speech we utter here? What god is it that stirs the eye and the ear? The hearing of the ear, the thinking of the mind, the speaking of the speech. . . ? That which speech cannot express, by which speech is expressed . . . which the mind cannot think, by which the mind thinks, know that as Brahman."[16]

A Christian writer of the third century eloquently expressed the relationship between the individual and the higher power, the Primal Soul:

> *Seek him from out thyself, and learn who it is that taketh possession of everything in thee, saying,* my *god,* my *spirit,* my *understanding,* my *soul,* my *body; and learn whence is sorrow and joy, and love and hate, and waking though one would not,*

---

13. *Bhagavad Gita*, chapter 15, verse 7, p. 106.

14. From the *Yajur Veda*, cited by Subramuniyaswami, *Dancing with Siva*, p. 88.

15. Brahm'an, the Supreme Being, from the root *brih*, "to grow, increase, expand," is described in the Vedas as the Transcendent Absolute, the all-pervading energy and the Supreme Lord or Primal Soul. *Yajaur Veda* in Subramuniyaswami, *Dancing with Siva*, p. 696.

16. *The Principal Upanishads*. Ed. with introduction, text, translation and notes by S. Radhakrishnan. London: Allen & Unwin (1953), p. 581ff, cited in C. G. Jung, *Aion*, CW9, ii, ¶348.

and sleeping though one would not. And if thou shouldst closely investigate these things, thou wilt find Him in thyself, the One and the Many, like to that little point . . . , for it is in thee that he hath his origin and his deliverance.[17]

When our individual soul becomes aware of our relationship to the Primal Soul, a profound shift takes place in our experience. Jung captures the essence of this experience:

It is always a difficult thing to express, in intellectual terms, subtle feelings that are nevertheless infinitely important for the individual's life and well-being. It is, in a sense, the feeling that we have been "replaced," but without the connotation of having been "deposed." It is as if the guidance of life had passed over to an invisible centre. . . . Religious [spiritual] language is full of imagery depicting this feeling of free dependence, of calm acceptance.

This remarkable experience seems to me a consequence of the detachment of consciousness, thanks to which the subjective "I live" becomes the objective "It lives me." This state is felt to be higher than the previous one; it is really like a sort of release from the compulsion and impossible responsibility that are the inevitable results of participation mystique.[18]

The compulsion and impossible responsibility of which Jung writes are the allure and power of maya. When we recognize that maya is but a partial reality, and develop our karmic and dharmic consciousness, we have taken important steps that put us in tune with the Primal Soul. Being in harmony with the Primal Soul not only benefits us individually, but has an effect that extends beyond ourselves.

---

17. C. G. Jung, *Aion*, CW9, ii, ¶347, citing from the *Elenchos* of the third-century Greek Christian writer Hippolytus, in the English translation of Francis Legge, *Philosophumena*; or, *The Refutation of All Heresies* (London and New York, 1921), vol. 2, p. 10. The teachings of Monoimos were preserved by Hippolytus whose *Elenchos* was not discovered until the middle of the 19th century on Mont Athos (C. G. Jung, *Mysterium Coniunctionis* CW14, p. 50, note).
18. C. G. Jung, *Alchemical Studies*, CW13, ¶77f. Brackets mine.

Recall the story of the rainmaker from chapter 1. There had been a great drought. Finally the people of that district in China summoned the rainmaker. The rainmaker had to get himself in harmony with the natural order before it began to rain. When we attune ourselves to the Primal Soul, it can work through us. The rainmaker parable is not just a nice story; it illustrates the relationship between the individual, the collective, and the Primal Soul.

THE INDIVIDUAL, THE COLLECTIVE, AND THE PRIMAL SOUL

The idea that individuals—you and I—can be instruments through which the Primal Soul manifests in the world is one of humankind's most important insights into the natural unity of the universe. In the Bhagavad Gita, Lord Vishnu, the preserver and restorer of right order, incarnates as Krishna. Krishna is Arjuna's charioteer and his teacher. Krishna teaches Arjuna many things, but one of the great lessons is that the individual can be the instrument through which the Higher Power works and accomplishes its purposes.

Mystics and seers of all ages have proclaimed the intimate relationship between the Primal Soul, the Higher Power, God, and human beings.

When we attune ourselves to the Primal Soul and become its instruments, we are best able to fulfill the four aspects of dharma. By fulfilling dharma, we set an example for others and leave the world we have passed through just a little bit better for having been here.

Stop, look within, and listen. Discover who you are. Listen to the whispers of the soul. Recognize the created world for what it is: a relative reality. Develop karmic consciousness by learning to foresee the necessary consequences of your actions. Sort out your karmic complexes and your clan karma from your essence. Recognize your primary kundalini chakra, and balance its energy by strengthening the other chakras, so that your energy becomes harmonized and you are able to function in each chakra as necessary.

Your svadharma is different from mine, so become what it is in you to be. If you can do this, then you will fulfill each phase of your ashrama dharma authentically: childhood, adolescence, adulthood, old age. If you can live each phase of your ashrama dharma authentically, you will in turn fulfill varna dharma, your responsibilities to your fellow human beings. As you fulfill these three dharmas, your understanding will gradually grow and deepen, and you will ever more clearly perceive reta dharma, the divine order.

Our very being affects others. We can help heal our people and the planet, or perpetuate the harm and hurt. The choice is ours. The path to the soul is the first step toward leaving the world a little bit better than we found it.

INVITATION

There are many paths to the soul. The path I have charted in these pages has proven useful to me, a Hindu living and working in the West, and to my patients, who come from many spiritual traditions. Whether or not you chose to venture upon the path I have laid out does not matter. What does matter is that you find a path that works for you, and follow it faithfully. By whatever path you and I may go, we will eventually meet at the same destination.

In wishing you well on your journey on the path to the soul, I leave you with a few ancient and wise words from my Hindu tradition, from Lord Krishna's advice to Arjuna, addressing him as Bhārata:

And I am seated in the hearts of all;
From me are memory, wisdom and their loss.
I am the one to be known by the Vedas;
The author of the Vedānta,
I am also the knower of the Vedas.

There are two puruṣas *in the world,*
the perishable and the imperishable;
The perishable is all beings,
the imperishable is called Kūṭastha (the imperishable).

But other than these is the uppermost puruṣas
called the supreme self,
Who, as the imperishable Lord,
Enters the three worlds and sustains them.

Because I surpass the perishable
and even the imperishable,
I am the supreme puruṣa
celebrated in the world and in the Vedas,

He who, undeluded, thus knows me,
as the supreme purus a (purus ottama);
He is all-knowing
and worships me with his whole being, O Bhārata.[19]

You have now visited my ashram, dear Reader, my spiritual workshop, my spiritual home. Thank you for coming on this journey, along this path to the soul. I honor the spirit in you.

Namaste!

POINTS TO PONDER

1. Review the big events in your life that turned out to be a tempest in a teacup. What role did small and seemingly insignificant events have on the course of your life? What meaning did they have in the larger picture?
2. What are the four basic human pursuits (chaturvarga)?
3. What is your assessment of your pursuit of artha, kama, dharma, and moksha in your overall life-picture?
4. What is the nature and your level of connection with your four dharmic goals? Where are you in your alignment with the goals of your svadharma, ashrama dharma, varna dharma, and reta dharma?

19. *Bhagavad Gita*, chapter 15, verses 15–19, p. 107.

5. What are the events, experiences, problems, illnesses, or relationship problems that put you in touch with the energy of your seventh (crown) chakra? How did this deepen your connection with your Higher Power, the spiritual dimension of your life? How did this spiritual connection impact your life?
6. In your life and relationship problems, in your medical and psychiatric problems, in your hang-ups and family problems, in the disappointments and detours of life, in failures and successes, in friends and foes, what reflection of the nature, meaning, and mystery of your soul have you been able to see?
7. In important challenges, do you try to control the events from A to Z, or do you do your personal best and then let be, let go, and let God?
8. Do you try to guide your life, or are you able to let life guide you?
9. Do you tend to see obstacles in your life as roadblocks to be removed at any cost, or are you able to reflect on these obstacles as the wisdom of the soul trying to guide you to ride the contours of your destiny?
10. In your life enterprise, do you regard yourself primarily as the general, or do you see yourself as a soldier and recognize some higher purpose or principle as the general?
11. In major endeavors, are you generally more concerned about the integrity of your effort or the outcome?
12. In retrospect, do you feel that your goals and enterprise have primarily been for self-enhancement or has your life journey also had an impact on the betterment of your family, community, humanity, and service to some higher purpose, as best you understand it?
13. As you review your life story, do you feel that you have made this world a slightly better or worse place than when you found it? What has been your contribution to the enhancement of the world around you?

Glossary

active imagination: A technique developed by C. G. Jung. In active imagination, we chose an image or a figure from a dream (for example), and engage it in a dialogue, just as we would a flesh-and-blood person. The value of a guide, when doing active imagination, lies in having someone who can help us meaningfully relate the vivid images to the realities of our current life. It is very easy to make too much or too little of a picture, but either extreme overshoots the mark, and we lose the message in the exaggeration.

ahimsa: (*a* = lack of, *himsa* = violence): The principle of nonviolence. Gandhi's principles advocate prohibition of physical, emotional, or spiritual violence against self or the adversary. One may confront the dark side of the self or other, but with love, and in awareness of the humanity of self and the other and their underlying goodness.

archetype: Natural laws or "dynamic skeletons" that structure the "flesh" of our expectations and our experiences. Archetypal patterns are subsets of the four aspects of dharma as well of a-dharma, the shadow aspect of dharma. To put it another way, dharma and adharma actualize in typical ways that we can observe in life, in literature, mythology, history—that is, in any human activity. We could also think of archetypes as high level sets of "instructions." When an archetype is activated, the instructions in it organize what we see, how we feel, the way we depict it, and what we do. This process creates a perceptual-emotional-representational-behavioral mini-program that can operate in our psyche pretty much independently of our conscious choice, and—if we are unaware of it operating in the background—assimilate ever more material to itself.

artha: At the most primal level, the pursuit of the wealth and prosperity necessary for security and survival. In the Hindu view, however, wealth—artha—is guided by dharma, but is much more than material possessions. Artha includes the basic needs—food, money, clothing, and shelter—and extends to the wealth required to maintain a comfortable home, raise a family, fulfill a successful career, and realize our spiritual tasks. In its broadest sense, artha embraces the blessings of worthy children, good friends, leisure time, trustworthy colleagues, and the means to support worthy causes.

ashrama dharma: The necessary developmental tasks of each of life's several stages; the calling to fulfill the responsibilities life presents us as we mature. Adolescence transforms the child; marriage and family transform the single young adult into parent and householder. When the children leave home and the nest is empty, we enter another developmental stage that calls us again to change and transform from parenting children to mentoring younger adults, often other people's children, often also younger colleagues and coworkers. As we look forward to our later decades, we become more concerned with the meaning of life and spiritual issues than with the day-to-day affairs of the world.

atman: The individual soul, a fractal of the Primal Soul, the Brahman. The individual soul, moreover, is capable of spiritual and physical experience. It is both our window to the Primal Soul and the "organ" that registers the quality of our lives. When our individual souls are afflicted, we suffer in various ways. Moreover, our connection to the Primal Soul often is obscured, sometimes to the point that we need to be vividly reminded that there is any such thing as a soul-connection.

Brahma: The function of Brahma/Saraswati, the name of the universal force in its aspect as creator, is to bring multiplicity into being in place of the Primal Unity. Thus, it is Brahma that creates maya, the limited or relative realities in which we actually live on Earth, in collaboration with his consort Saraswati, the goddess of knowledge, arts, academic pursuits, and truth. Creative enterprise remains uninformed and ungrounded if Saraswati is not honored.

chakras: The seven chakras in Kundalini Yoga are centers of subtle energy situated along the spine from the tailbone to the crown. Each chakra is associated with specific bodily organs, typical emotions, characteristic attitudes, and levels of spiritual development. A totem animal is associated with the first four chakras. The three nadis, the subtle energy channels discussed earlier, penetrate the chakras like the cords on which beads are strung. The chakras, in other words, are focal points where the physical, emotional, and spiritual dimensions of our life intersect.

circumambulation: Literal or figurative circular motions that express the impulse or intention to define, relate to, approach, or protect the center and what is enclosed in the circle. This practice of encircling is an "archetypal idea," that is, an idea that is ancient, that occurs in many cultures and times, and that has a powerful emotional effect on people. Circumambulation—the act of circling round a point of reference—defines the boundaries of a sacred space by relating to a center of value, whether by meditating, by performing a sacred ritual, or by following the meandering of our lives. In the course of life, we gradually recognize that we have "circled around" and thereby identified and protected certain central values many times.

chaturvarga: "Fourfold good." Hindu ethics recognizes four pursuits that embrace everything a person could desire: pleasure (kama), wealth (artha), freedom (moksha), and a life in harmony with one's inherent nature, developmental stage, station in life, and the higher power and order of the universe (the four aspects of dharma, which is the sure guide for the other three).

complex: "Feeling-toned complex" is the technical name for our emotional hot-spots, our hang-ups. These are not fundamentally bad, but typical and normal features of the psyche. They operate in the same way as the mind when it cross-references experiences in memory. When we have a hang-up—or a complex has us—our normal personality is affected, and we feel its emotion to some degree. Whether or not the immediate or current situation warrants it, the complex's emotion influences our expectations, perceptions, and judgment of the present circumstances, and our behavior in characteristic ways. Typically, we attempt to disown what just came through us, and say, "I wasn't myself;" "I don't know what got into me." These hang-ups get us into difficulties in our relationships and compromise our inner and outer adaptation.

cross: The symbol whose structure symbolizes the relationship between maya and dharma. The vertical axis represents the spiritual dimension, dharma; the horizontal axis represents the physical dimension, maya. Our task is to find the center where the axes cross. When we have found the center, the spiritual dimension is the point around which our material existence pivots. When we are centered, we are living dharmic life here and now. When we go too high up the vertical axis, we flee into ungrounded spirituality; when we descend too far down the vertical axis, we end up in depression or psychosis. At either extreme, we lose the world. If we go too far out on either horizontal axis, we lose the spiritual pivot point. The task at the center is to see through the visible world, to perceive the spirit informing the manifest.

crown chakra: The seventh chakra, called "Sahasrara," governs spirituality and moksha. It is located above the crown of the head. This is the place of Nirvana, the freedom from the opposites, and is considered to be the realm where the individual soul and the Universal Soul are one. This is the realm of the total union of Shiva and Shakti, of all opposite and conflicting tendencies within oneself and between self and the cosmos. In the realm of the seventh chakra, the individual is at one with nature, the collective psyche, and with God. However, one has no experience of self as separate from God and nature. This is reverse of the maya of the first chakra, where there may be little awareness of nature as anything but an appendage of self.

depression: One of the most frequent, painful, and medically treatable of psychiatric disorders. It should be aggressively treated by both medication and psychotherapy. However, therapists and patients alike consistently bypass the soul-healing aspects of depression. Depression is often a messenger of the soul that arrives with a script for reestablishing balance and wholeness in life. Medical and psychiatric conditions are Janus-faced: they look both to the past and to the future.

dharma: The "timeless order of nature," archetypal patterns and natural laws. There are four principal aspects, or archetypal dimensions, to dharma, ranging from the individual to the cosmic: svadharma (the law of one's own being, the individual uniqueness that strives for actualization within the context of one's family, society, place and time in history), ashrama dharma (the stages of life with their various culturally shaped archetypal patterns to fulfill and the attendant responsibilities), varna dharma (the typical patterns of behavior, attitude, and emotion of one's species); and reta dharma (universal spiritual and physical laws). A person's life can be out of dharmic balance: an excess here, a deficit there. When this is the case, the principle governing the organism's adaptation to outer circumstances and the inner necessities of dynamic homeostasis and self-actualization attempts to restore the equilibrium. Dharma is also the "steady guide" for chaturvarga, the "fourfold good" (artha, kama, moksha).

eye chakra: The sixth chakra, called the Ajna or "Place of Command," governs integrity and leadership. It is located between the eyebrows. The sixth chakra looks like the third eye or a winged seed. This is the chakra where the psyche gets its inner vision, where we can see our inner, psychological world as well as the transcendent or dharmic world beyond the outer, physical reality perceived by our two eyes. No animal form is associated with the sixth chakra, since the activity here is perception of the nonmanifest dimension of reality.

God image: The archetypal perception of a higher power. There are many images of God, as many as there are spiritual traditions and religions. Many followers of religious traditions, and often the traditions themselves, typically (and unfortunately) do not distinguish between the image and what it represents. St. Paul made the clear distinction between God and God-image when he wrote: "Now we are seeing a dim reflection in a mirror; but then we shall be seeing face to face" (1 Corinthians 13:12).

heart chakra: The fourth chakra, called Anahata, the "Unattackable," governs intimacy. It is located at the heart plexus behind the sternum. The totem animal of the heart chakra is the deer or black antelope—very sensitive, always full of inspiration.

individuation: "Coming into selfhood" or self-realization. This is the powerful force in each of us that propels us to consciously actualize our unique psychological reality, including our strengths and our weaknesses. Ultimately, individuation leads to the experience of a transpersonal, regulating "authority" as the center of our individual psyches.

kama: The pleasure that gets us into relationships, fosters procreation and new life, forges our attachments, and ensures the continuation of our species. Kama addresses the experiential dimension of life: pleasure, love, and enjoyment. Earthly love, sexual love, the pleasures of the world, aesthetic and cultural fulfillment, the joys of family and friends, intellectual satisfaction—all find their place in kama. This is not true, however, in the Christian tradition. Hinduism does not make pleasure the highest good, but there is nothing wrong with pleasure and seeking pleasure so long as one obeys the basic rules of morality: don't cheat, steal, lie, or succumb to addictions. Kama also embraces the satisfactions and enjoyment of one's happiness, of one's security, creativity, usefulness, and inspiration—all "nonmaterial" and very personal.

karma: The Sanskrit word meaning "action." The law of karma implies that the universe is an eternal moral order. Behind the apparently blind mechanical forces governing the cosmos there exists a cosmic intelligence, a power that controls the operations of nature and guides the destiny of humankind. Karma emphasizes the freedom of human choice: by the choices we make today, we retire or compound the consequences of past actions and lay the foundation for the future.

karmic complexes: Psychic/somatic units into which our emotional experience is organized. Karmic complexes are, as it were, the organs that make up the body of our emotional expectations, sensitivities, and reactions. They are functional units localized in the chakras that have arisen through the interplay of maya, karma, and dharma (*see* complex). The core around which a karmic complex takes shape is a typical human situation, an inherent, archetypal pattern (*see* archetype) ready to organize our perceptions, our emotions, our imagery, and our behavior in a typically human way. Karmic complexes are archetypes in their structured, incarnated form. The archetypal patterns informing karmic complexes organize behavior, perception, representation, and emotion. These four dimensions are interrelated. Our karmic complexes can either lead us into more karmic entanglements, or serve as stepping-stones toward dharma.

labyrinth: Symbol of the process of individuation.

Laxmi: (*see* Trimurti)

maya: *Maya* is often translated as "illusion," but is actually the cosmic creative force that generates concrete worlds, as well as the captivating nature of what is created that binds souls.

moksha: Liberation in the form of "caring detachment." All individuals have the potential to achieve the state of moksha—liberation from the misery of the human condition and the repetitive cycles of maya and karma. Moksha comes through the fulfillment of artha and kama (chaturvarga) under the guidance of dharma. In other words, when we have lived life to the full and have actualized our innate potentials, then our desires for artha and kama (wealth and pleasure in their various forms) no longer drive us. Then we are no longer attached to worldly joys or sorrows. This does not mean, however, that we have become indifferent to life on this planet. Moksha is the detachment from the outcome, not from engagement in the enterprise, since to fulfill life, we must live it as duty to the spirit and to God, however we may conceive that higher power.

nadi: The channels in the chakras through which subtle energy moves. There are three nadis, two of which correspond to the sympathetic and to the parasympathetic nervous systems. Kundalini flowing primarily in one or the other nadi results in an energy imbalance that correlates with the Type A or Type B personalities. When energy moves primarily in the "hot" pingala nadi, the result is the well-known Type A personality who is always on the go. When the kundalini moves primarily in the "cool" ida nadi, the personality shows Type B characteristics, tending to be cooperative, easygoing, patient, and have a generally mellow temperament. The desirable condition is for neither nadi to dominate, but rather for energy to flow naturally as a balanced stream in the third nadi, the central channel, called the sushumna.

naval chakra: The third chakra, called Manipura, or "Plenitude of Jewels," governs autonomy. Its location corresponds to the solar plexus, between the diaphragm and the naval. The totem animal of the third chakra is the ram, the steed of Agni, the fire god.

pelvic chakra: The second chakra, called the Svadhisthna, or the "Dwelling-place of the Self," governs generativity. It is located in the area of the hypogastrum and bladder above the genitals. The totem animal of the second chakra is the crocodile (Sanskrit, *Makara*). The crocodile depicts the serpentine, sensuous nature of the person dominated by the second chakra.

persona: The term used by C. G. Jung to designate all those skills that constitute our function of adaptation to the outer world, our "outer" face. Our persona usually differs to a greater or lesser extent from our real individuality and authentic self, especially in the first life, in which maya dominates our consciousness. As we develop the persona we have chosen (or that our social environment has chosen for us), we neglect substantial aspects of our possibilities, thereby creating our shadow.

projection: Reaction that occurs when an activated complex overlays a present situation or person. Projection differs from blaming: when we blame, we do so intentionally. We do not deliberately project. Projections happen to us when someone or some situation resembles another person or experience around which a karmic complex has formed, and we do not recognize the difference between what we are seeing now and what we saw and experienced in the past.

reta dharma: The calling of the divine principle and law underlying all things. At the level of the human individual, reta dharma is that archetypal drive to relate to a higher power. We can think of reta dharma as honoring the transpersonal powers that move in us by giving appropriate expression to those powers, each of us in our unique way in accordance with our svadharma, and in the context of our ashrama dharma and our varna dharma. In other words, spirituality and caring for the soul is part and parcel of being human.

root chakra: The first chakra, called Muladhara, or the "Root Support," governs survival and security. It is situated in the perineum between the anus and the genitals. The ruler of the first chakra is Ganesha, the elephant-headed god, lord of all beginnings and remover of obstacles. The totem animal associated with Muladhara chakra is the elephant, which represents the lifelong search for food for the body, the mind, and the heart.

Sarasvati: (*see* Trimurti)

satyagraha (*satya* = truth, *agraha* = insistance): Principle of pursuit of and insistence on truth at any cost. Eventually, this became the cornerstone of contemporary Indian philosophy as *Satya Mave Jayate* (Hail the truth).

shadow: In the broadest sense, our unlived life, "good" and "bad." The shadow includes all the relatively inferior parts of our personality, which are often transparent to those who know us well, though we may not consciously be aware of them, or may wish not to be consciously aware of them. Moreover, the shadow is a real live force in the psyche with, so to speak, a mind of its own. Sometimes our shadow can take over and live through us. When that happens, we typically say, "I wasn't myself," or "I don't know what got into me." We must not forget, however, that our shadows also hold much unlived life, perhaps even our greatest gifts, that, for one reason or another, we have not cultivated.

Shiva/Shakti: Deity that presides over the creation of a spiritual attitude that can lead to a new order, a new/renewed life after the destruction of the old. The mystery of Shiva/Shakti is that destruction always holds the potential and promise to renew life and remove the obstacles that keep us from actualizing our spiritual potential. We can, for example, view the painful consequences of our choices as Shiva/Shakti trampling us underfoot. We can learn to see other people who confront us and force us to look at ourselves and our actions as Shiva/Shakti's agents. Or we may have a dream that shows something being destroyed.

symbol and symptom: Best possible expression for something otherwise unknown to us. Something whose meaning or reference is fully known—like the red octagon bearing the word "STOP"—is not a symbol, but a sign. An image becomes a symbol for us only when we find it fascinating and meaningful, even though we are at a loss to say what the unexpressed meaning is. In this sense, a person to whom we have a powerful emotional response or reaction for which we cannot account would be a symbol. In other words, the carrier of our projection (of a part of ourselves we don't recognize) is, for us, the best possible representation of that unknown aspect of ourselves.

synchronistic events: Events arranged by the Soul to draw our attention to constellations of energies, events, people, and circumstances in such a way that some aspect of our soul potential can be embodied in our life at that moment. They embody mysterious and sacred moments when cosmic forces, our soul energy, and events and people in outer life are in optimal alignment for some invisible aspect of our soul to become visible, if only we acknowledge them, attend to them, act upon them in a conscious manner. Synchronistic events are those meaningful coincidences that we notice; for example, dreaming about somebody we haven't seen or talked to in months, and getting a postcard or letter from them the same day; or the occurrence of similar or identical thoughts, ideas, or dreams, at the same time to different people in different places. Neither one can be explained by causality. Synchronistic events are evidence of a close connection between the two or more parties or things involved. They are a kind of "heads up" urging us to pay attention. (*See also* Trimurti.)

svadharma: The calling to honor and actualize our individual uniqueness. The first lesson that maya and karma teach us has to do with our innate, individual pattern that finds expression in our particular physical, mental, and emotional nature. A metaphor is helpful here: if you are an oak tree, be content to grow acorns and let the peach tree grow peaches. The fairy tale, "The Tree That Wanted Other Leaves," points to the same truth: we can realize the other three dharmas only through being what we actually are. Hence svadharma is dharma individualized. Within the limits set and the challenges posed by our svadharma, we fulfill the other three dharmas.

throat chakra: The fifth chakra, called the Vishudha or "Purification," governs initiative. It is situated in the throat at the pharyngeal plexus. The fifth chakra is the beginning of the realm of abstract ideas and psychic, rather than physical, reality. This is that aspect of our mental life where we start to see all events occurring, not only in physical reality, but in the subtle planes.

Trimurti: Hindu Trinity composed of Brahma/Saraswati, Vishnu/Laxmi, and Shiva/Shakti.

varna dharma: The calling to fulfill our responsibilities to community. Varna dharma, "the law of one's kind," defines our archetypally and socially determined interpersonal responsibilities within family, community, class, occupation, society, and nation.

Vishnu: (*see* Trimurti)

Vishnu/Laxmi: The "All Pervasive," "The Preserver," representing the cohesive force that maintains the continuity of existence and the timeless order of nature that interconnects all that exists. Laxmi is the patron goddess of wealth, prosperity, and peace, the prerequisites for maintaining the order of dharma in the world. Periodically, Vishnu reincarnates in one of his several forms *(avatars)* to reestablish the timeless order whenever necessary. Vishnu/Laxmi can work through the sage and time-tested advice our friends may give us. (*See also* Trimurti.)

yoga: To "yoke," to "join together." Kundalini Yoga aims at integrating our individual consciousness with the dharmic consciousness, the individual soul with the Great Soul. As is true for all attempts to mature and grow emotionally and spiritually, we must cultivate moral preliminaries: noninjury (ahimsa), truthfulness, self-control, the discipline to scrutinize ourselves, and the desire to reach the goal.

Bibliography

Belestgis, S., and S. Brown. "A Developmental Framework for Understanding the Adult Children of Alcoholics." *Focus: Women's Journal of Addiction and Health*, 2 (1981).

Black, C., S. F. Bucky, and S. Wilder-Padilla. "The Interpersonal and Emotional Consequences of Being an Adult Child of an Alcoholic." *International Journal of Addictions*, 21(2) (1986).

Bhagavad Gita. Antonio de Nicolàs, trans. York Beach, ME: Nicolas-Hays, 1990.

Chaudhuri, H. *The Essence of Spiritual Philosophy*. New Delhi: HarperCollins India, 1990.

Erikson, E. H. *Childhood and Society*. New York: W. W. Norton, 1950.

Grant, L. "You've Got the Stock Options, Now Get a Life," *Fortune*, 133,12. June 24, 1966.

Hamilton, E. *Mythology*. New York: New American Library, 1942.

The Jerusalem Bible. Garden City: Doubleday & Co., 1966.

Jung, C. G. *Aion: Researches in the Phenomenology of the Self*, Gerhard Adler et al, eds. R. F. C. Hull, trans. Collected Works, vol. 9, ii, Bollingen Series No. XX. Princeton: Princeton University Press, 1959.

———. "Commentary on *The Secret of the Golden Flower.*" *Alchemical Studies*, Gerhard Adler et al, eds. R. F. C. Hull, trans. Collected Works, vol. 13. Bollingen Series No. XX. Princeton: Princeton University Press, 1968.

———. *Civilization in Transition*, Gerhard Adler et al, eds. R. F. C. Hull, trans. Collected Works, vol. 1. Bollingen Series No. XX. Princeton: Princeton University Press, 1970.

———. *Experimental Researches*, Gerhard Adler et al, eds. R. F. C. Hull, trans. Collected Works, vol. 2. Bollingen Series No. XX. Princeton: Princeton University Press, 1973.

———. *Memories, Dreams, Reflections*. New York: Pantheon Books, 1961.

———. *Mysterium Coniunctionis*. Gerhard Adler et al, eds. R. F. C. Hull, trans. Collected Works, vol. 14. Bollingen Series No. XX. Princeton: Princeton University Press, 1970.

———. *Psychology and Religion—West & East*, Gerhard Adler et al, eds. R. F. C. Hull, trans. Collected Works, vol. 11. Bollingen Series No. XX. Princeton: Princeton University Press, 1969.

———. *The Structure and Dynamics of the Psyche*, Gerhard Adler et al, eds. R. F. C. Hull, trans. Collected Works, vol. 8. Bollingen Series No. XX. Princeton: Princeton University Press, 1969.

———. *The Symbolic Life*, Gerhard Adler et al, eds. R. F. C. Hull, trans. Collected Works, vol. 14. Bollingen Series No. XVIII. Princeton: Princeton University Press, 1976.

———. *The Tavistock Lectures*, Gerhard Adler et al., eds. R. F. C. Hull, trans. Collected Works, vol. 18. Bollingen Series No. XX. Princeton: Princeton University Press, 1980.

———. *Two Essays on Analytical Psychology*. Gerhard Adler et al, eds. R. F. C. Hull, trans. Collected Works, vol. 7. Bollingen Series No. XX. Princeton: Princeton University Press, 1966.

———. *The Visions Seminars*. Zürich: Spring Publications, 1976.

Larousse World Mythology. Pierre Grimal, ed. London: Paul Hamlyn, 1965.

Lessing, G. E. *Lessings Werke*, vol. 2. Stuttgart: Göschen'sche Verlagshandlung, 1877.

———. *Nathan the Wise: A Dramatic Poem in Five Acts*. Bayard Quincy Morgan, trans. New York: Ungar, 1955.

Levinson, D. *The Seasons of a Man's Life*. New York: Ballantine Books, 1978.

Mahler, M., F. Pine, and A. Bergman. *The Psychological Birth of the Human Infant*. New York: Basic Books, 1975.

Parker, D. A. and T. C. Harford. "Alcohol-Related Problems, Marital Disruption and Depressive Symptoms among Adult Children of Alcohol Abusers in the United States." *Journal of Studies on Alcohol*, 49(4) (1988): pp. 306–313.

Progoff, Ira. *At a Journal Workshop: Writing to Access the Power of the Unconscious and Evoke Creative Ability*. Los Angeles: J. P. Tarcher, 1992.

Scheffler, J. "Cherubinisher Wandersmann" in *Scheffler's Sämtliche Poetische Werke*, Rosenthal, ed. (n.d.).

Sharman-Burke, Juliet, and L. Greene. *The Mythic Tarot*. New York: Simon & Schuster, 1986; London: Random House, 1986.

Smith, Huston. *The World's Religions*, 2d ed. New York: Harper-Collins, 1991.

Subramuniyaswami, *Dancing with Siva*. Kapaa, HI: Himalayan Academy, 1993.

Wauters, Ambika. *Chakras and their Archetypes: Uniting Energy Awareness and Spiritual Growth*. Freedom, CA: Crossing Press, 1997.

Wegscheider, S. *Another Chance: Hope and Health for Alcoholic Families*. Palo Alto: Science and Behavior Books, 1981.

Whitmont, E. C. *The Symbolic Quest*. Princeton: Princeton University Press, 1969.

INDEX

BOOKS OF RELATED INTEREST

BETWEEN EAST AND WEST — *Luce Irigaray*
A leading philosopher explores ancient Eastern disciplines, meditating on what it means to learn to breathe. According to her, yogic tradition can provide a vital link between the present and eternity, allowing us to reexamine and reenvision the patriarchal traditions of the West. By returning to fundamental human experiences, she finds a way out of the endless of race, ethnicity, and globalization.

ISBN: 81-7822-215-9

BUDDHISM AND JUNGIAN PSYCHOLOGY —
J. Marvin Spiegelman and *Mokusen Miyuki*
The book speaks about Jung's views on Tibetan Buddhism, India and Yoga, Chinese Taoism, Eastern meditation and Zen Buddhism, Western rationalism and Eastern Spirituality, how to integrate East and West. It presents the findings and demonstrates the error of the Western assumption that Buddhism requires the "dissolution" of the ego.

ISBN: 81-7822-115-2

HOPE FOR A BETTER WORLD! : The Small Communities Solutions — *J. Donald Walters*
In these turbulent times when wars, religious strife, bureaucracy, and technology threaten to reduce our very "humanness" to base conditions and impersonal numbers, a fresh approach to creating a sustainable society is needed. In this book you will find viewpoints of many greatest thinkers such as Plato, Adam Smith, Darwin, Marx and Freud, among others.

ISBN: 81-7822-141-1

EASTERN SPIRITUALITY FOR MODERN LIFE—*D. Pond*
Each religion might very well see a separate aspect of truth and be blind to the others. It is clear that our shrinking world requires us to step outside of our separatist ways and seek to better understand each other. It is in this spirit that this book is written. We are all here together; there are no good religions, nor bad religions, just *different* religions—each having their own particular vantage point of the great way.

ISBN: 81-7822-199-3

BEYOND RELIGION — *Robert Powell*

Numerous meditations are possible and helpful, but there is only one of supreme importance; it is the meditation on the theme "Who am I ?" This leads eventually to the recognition that one is the Unicity, the Totality or the Consciousness Itself. It essentially consists in eternal watchfulness, the witnessing of the consciousness everlastingly falling back into seeing events as variations on the theme of body-mind identification.

ISBN: 81-7822-139-x

SOUL POWER — *Nikki de Carteret*

Juxtaposing fascinating teachings from the ancient mystics with stories of modern seekers, as well as her own extraordinary journey towards wholeness, de Carteret invites you to explore the factors that drain your spiritual energy, and what transformational forces restore it. Examining themes such as love, enlightenment, silence, compassion, synchronicity, dark night of the soul, harmony, and bliss, it serves as a friendly road map to the spiritual process.

ISBN: 81-7822-145-4

SOUL QUEST — *Anand Krishna*

This book is an honest account of the writer's journey to such an awakening... of the agony, and the ecstasy, that a soul experiences on its way to enlightenment. The writer also gives the reader numerous useful tips, including a complete program on "Self-Management", in order to help facilitatek the path for those who are desirous of undertaking their own soul's journey.

ISBN: 81-7822-234-5

HEART, SELF AND SOUL — *Robert Frager*

Western psychotherapy aims largely to help us eliminate neurotic traits formed in childhood and adapt to society. In contrast, the Sufi goal is ultimately spiritual: Yes, we need to transform our negativity and be effective in the world; but beyond that, we need to reach a state of harmony with the Divine. Full of stories, poetry, meditations, journaling exercises, and colorful everyday examples, this book will open the heart, nourish the self, and quicken the soul.

ISBN: 81-7822-231-0